Built

Canada's Intercolonial Railway

Major William Robinson, surveyor of the line that the Intercolonial Railway followed faithfully, except through Nova Scotia's Cumberland County.

(photo courtesy
Nicholas Hyde and family)

by Jay Underwood

*To my parents,
Peter and Joan Underwood
for their love and support,
and for instilling in me a love of history.*

*To my wife, Kathy,
for being my strength and inspiration.*

Railfare ✲ DC Books

Cover photo courtesy of National Archives of Canada.

Book designed and typeset in Adobe Garamond and ITC Korinna Extra Bold
by Ian Cranstone, Osgoode, Ontario.

Printed and bound in Canada by AGMV Marquis.
Distributed by Lit DistCo.

Copyright © Jay Underwood, 2005.

Legal Deposit, Bibliothèque Nationale du Québec
and the National Library of Canada, 4th trimester, 2005.

Library and Archives Canada Cataloguing in Publication

Underwood, Jay, 1958-

Built for War: Canada's Intercolonial Railway / Jay Underwood.

Includes bibliographical references.

ISBN 1-897190-00-X (pbk.)
ISBN 1-897190-01-8 (bound)

1. Intercolonial Railway (Canada)—History. 2. Railroads—
Canada, Eastern—History—19th century. 3. Canada—History—19th century. I. Title.

HE2810.I6U53 2005   385'.0971'09034   C2005-904403-9

For our publishing activities, **Railfare ❀ DC Books** gratefully
acknowledges the financial support of The Canada
Council for the Arts, of SODEC, and of the
Government of Canada through the Book Publishing
Industry Development Program (BPIDP).

**Canada Council
for the Arts**

**Conseil des Arts
du Canada**

*Société
de développement
des entreprises
culturelles*

Québec ❖❖

No part of this publication may be reproduced or stored in a retrieval system or
transmitted in any form or by any means, electronic, mechanical, recording or otherwise,
without written permission of the publisher, **Railfare ❀ DC Books**.

In the case of photocopying or other reprographic copying, a license must be obtained
from Access Copyright, Canadian Copyright Licensing Agency, 1 Yonge Street, Suite 1900,
Toronto, ON   M5E 1E5. email: info@accesscopyright.ca

Railfare ❀ DC Books

Head office:
1880 Valley Farm Road, Unit #TP-27, Pickering, ON   L1V 6B3

Business office and mailing address:
Box 662, 950 Decarie, Montreal, QC   H4L 4V9

email: railfare@videotron.ca
web: www.railfare.net

TABLE OF CONTENTS

A map of the Intercolonial published before the line took ownership of the Grand Trunk line from Quebec City to Montreal, c1898.

BUILT FOR WAR:

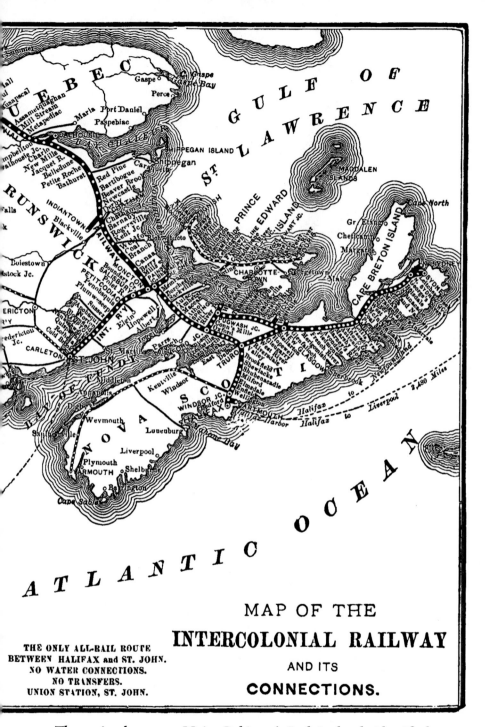

MAP OF THE

INTERCOLONIAL RAILWAY

AND ITS

CONNECTIONS.

THE ONLY ALL-RAIL ROUTE
BETWEEN HALIFAX and ST. JOHN.
NO WATER CONNECTIONS.
NO TRANSFERS.
UNION STATION, ST. JOHN.

*The section known as Major Robinson's Path is clearly identified as
the main route from Halifax through northern New Brunswick.*

(Andrew Blackburn collection)

Acknowledgements

Experience with my first two histories, *Ketchum's Folly*, and *Full Steam Ahead: the Life and Locomotives of Alexander Mitchell*, taught me that it takes more than one person to write a book. This work is no exception.

This project was my first experience with the internet as a research tool, but having said that, it must also be said that there can be no alternative for a bricks-and-mortar library, and the people on hand to help find a particular volume of reference. For all that is available on the world wide web, there is so much more that can only be found in a good, old-fashioned book. So my first acknowledgement must be to Rosalyn Morrison, Karen King and Andrew Underwood of the Elmsdale branch of the Colchester-East Hants Regional Library.

Of enormous help too were the staff of Dalhousie University's Killam Memorial Library (Microforms Department) and the staff of St. Mary's University Library. Also, Dan Conlin of the Maritime Museum of the Atlantic was helpful in the provision of photographs from the museum's wonderful display on the effects of the Halifax explosion of 1917.

I must also thank the anonymous staff of the Toronto Public Library's on-line "Answerline" service. The staff of the Nova Scotia Archives and Records Management Service (NSARMS) extended their usual courteous and efficient service, as did the staff of the Public Archives of New Brunswick, especially Allen Doiron of the cartographic section, and Burton Glendenning, director of public services.

Also from New Brunswick, via the internet, I must thank Irene Doyle of Campbellton, Ron Hoyt, and Fredericton city forester Don Murray for their help in tracking down the whereabouts of Captain John Pipon. It must seem oddly quixotic and romantic to devote so much time to one long-dead soldier, but history too often overlooks the personal sacrifices that are made by "ordinary" people, and it would be an injustice to forget that a man died building the railway that built a nation.

I owe a great debt to Art Clowes, whom I first met on the internet, and who so generously allowed me to peruse his electronic "scrapbook" of Intercolonial Railway history. He has an invaluable resource at his fingertips, and I have urged him to consider publishing it as a book of his own, because the one drawback I have found from my "e" experience is that reading from a computer screen is not nearly as comfortable as having a book or a piece of paper in my hand. Perhaps it is my years as a journalist that have made me such a hard-copy aficionado, but I make no apologies for it.

Thanks are also due to Colonel J. E. Nowers of the Royal Engineers Museum at Brompton Barracks in Chatham, Kent, England, and to Dr. Desmond Morton of McGill University's Centre for Canadian Studies, author of so many entertaining books on Canadian history. Similarly I received guidance from Cameron Pulsifer and Roger Sarty of the Canadian War Museum, and from Keith Miller and Marion Harding of the National Army Museum in England. Assistance was also received from Philip Adkins, librarian of the National Railway Museum, York, England, and Wally Dugan, curator of the Museum of Army Transport in Beverley, East Yorkshire. Thanks also to Steven Stothers, for allowing me to reprint his grandfather's letter from the frontlines of 1916.

Because of my disabilities, I owe so much to the support of my family, especially my father, Peter Underwood, and brother Simon, who assisted me in an expedition to New Brunswick and Amherst, NS, as they did when I wrote the biography of Alexander Mitchell, which required a foray into Pennsylvania.

Thanks also to Barbara Thompson of the Cumberland County Museum in Amherst for her professional responses to all my requests for help.

David Henderson deserves great praise for making the publication of this work possible. Publishers in the Maritimes appear to have developed an aversion to works combining railway and military history, which seems odd in a region where both are so ingrained in our tradition. I turned to David as the president of Railfare, which has an history of producing quality Canadian railway publications.

He saw merit where Atlantic Canada's publishing houses saw only liability, and it is for him that I now hope this work catches the public's attention and imagination.

Finally, I owe all that I am and have done to my wife Kathy, especially in the past few years of my temporary blindness. Unused to such pastimes as ensconcing herself in a library to read an old book or peer at a microfilm reader to decipher old newspaper accounts, she nonetheless stayed at my side reading what I could not, and helping me make sense of it all.

Jay Underwood
Elmsdale NS
2005

Introduction

THE VALIDITY OF A NATION'S TERRITORIAL SOVEREIGNTY IS founded upon its willingness and ability to mount a military defence whenever necessary. This tenet appears to have been lost upon early Canadians, at least until nationhood became a reasonable possibility in the 1860s, and thus the Intercolonial Railway became a viable project, at a time when railway technology was being used as a military asset by armies in Europe and North America.

While much has been written about the history of the Intercolonial—most of it either critical or condescending—the concept of the line as a military necessity has been treated as a footnote, where it has not been overlooked entirely.

In his excellent work on the Grand Crimean Central Railway, the first railway used in the conduct of a war, Brian Cooke calls the private scheme to construct a supply line in support of the British siege of Sebastopol, "the railway that won a war."

I believe the Intercolonial deserves the title, "the railway that prevented a war," because it was founded on a basic military imperative: the need to get British troops into the interior of Canada to counter possible attacks from the United States, especially in the winter months when the St. Lawrence, the great water highway into the heart of the country, was plugged with ice.

(What is surprising, and significant to both railways, is that the British army did not immediately recognize the tactical and strategic effectiveness of railways in 1854, when one of their own officers was preaching the gospel in Canada in 1849, and the report had been seen by the British prime minister!)

This imperative was first recognized in the War of 1812, long before there were any railways anywhere, and remained part of the Canadian reality until the Treaty of Washington, signed in 1871, finally restored some normalcy to Canada–US relations, setting the two countries on the long path of friendship that has been enjoyed ever since.

In order to appreciate the necessity of a railway as a military means, I have attempted to contrast the development of the railway with the military use of railways in the United States and Great Britain. Of these two, the US Civil War had a far more meaningful impact.

While that war did not force Canadians into Confederation, it did give them cause to reflect deeply upon the potential military threat that was growing to the south, and it must be noted that US talk about the annexation of Canada changed dramatically in its tone upon the cessation of the internal hostility, and the certainty that came with the construction of the Intercolonial.

What was offered instead, was the typical American approach: buy what you cannot take by force (as they had done with the Louisiana, Gadsden, and Alaska purchases.)

For that reason alone, the Intercolonial deserves to be remembered as something more than the parochial political curiosity it has been described as by historians such as G.R. Stevens and others who penned popular histories under the patronage of Canadian National, the successor to the Intercolonial Railway. Indeed, the military imperative made it crucial to the future of central Canada, whence most of the modern day criticism emanates.

Stevens' work contains a number of errors that have helped perpetuate misconceptions about the Intercolonial, which need not be enumerated here, but the most significant is that Major Robinson's choice of the Northern or Bay Chaleur route ran through a sparsely populated area with little commercial potential. This is untrue, since Newcastle, NB was at the time second only to Saint John in commerce.

This may appear to be a mere detail, but in my mind it adds to the apocryphal aspects of the Intercolonial that have prolonged the greater misunderstanding of the railway's real intent.

I have also made a deliberate effort to avoid following Sandford Fleming's own account of the building of the Intercolonial. While it remains the only authoritative account devoted solely to the project, the text—when it is not bogged down in the minutiae of sight lines, elevations and descriptions of geological formations—fairly reeks of congratulatory self-interest.

If Fleming's history of the line is so laden with engineering data, it may be wondered why so much of Major Robinson's 1849 report has been included in this work, since it too contains a great deal of that material.

Robinson's report, however, has never been widely read, and it offers an intriguing snapshot of the region that will interest more than just those fascinated by railway history. Indeed, it is intriguing that a military man charged with surveying a line for a railway should have to contemplate so many non-military aspects of the area under his scrutiny. The report, which appears in this work as Appendix One, is a partial transcript of the entire document.

Robinson's report had an effect far beyond the establishment of the line of the Intercolonial Railway. Joe Howe and the Nova Scotia government were quick to use the report as the foundation of the Nova Scotia Railway, which built the first leg of the Intercolonial at no expense to the other provinces. As well, railway promoters in both Nova Scotia and New Brunswick had access to the surveys when they planned their lines over routes approved, but not recommended, by the army engineer. It may be fair to say the report fuelled the fire of railway fever in the Maritimes, and for that reason too, it deserves not go ignored.

The research for this book involved my extensive use of the resources of the internet, my first real "e-experience." This raised the interesting question of how to credit these sources, first because so much material is published on the "world wide web" anonymously, and secondly because so much of it can be unreliable in its accuracy.

As yet there appears to be no single protocol for acknowledging electronically published material in a conventional book, but I am reluctant to let people think this kind of research represents my own work. A great deal of material, for example, was drawn from the Nova Scotia history pages published from a site in Canning, NS by Ivan C. Smith. This site contained references to newspaper accounts that I had previously gleaned from newspapers on microfiche at the Public Archives of Nova Scotia, and although I might no doubt have run across the same material given time, its existence on the internet saved me incalculable hours as well as a great deal of eye strain for a half-blind former journalist.

I have endeavoured to acknowledge these internet sources wherever possible, but I must confess that jumping from one link to another, from web page to web page, can become quite dizzying, and I may not have listed all the sources I used.

Finally, it has to be said that this is not intended to be a nostalgic remembrance of the Intercolonial Railway, for such is the grist of popular history. At some point in time the Intercolonial was destined to die, if only in name. As a nation grew around it, the concept of colonial status was quickly stripped away. Thus it is a curiosity of history, and matter for conjecture, as to why the Fathers of Confederation did not choose a name more suited to that reality; perhaps it should have been the Dominion Railway, or the Confederation Railway. It was fitting, therefore, that in 1918 it should become part of what it had been all along, a Canadian "National" railway, helping as it always had—but now no longer does—serve *all* of Canada.

Jay Underwood
Elmsdale NS
2005

CHAPTER ONE

The Impending Threat

IN HIS 1958 SERIES OF ARTICLES ON THE INTERCOLONIAL RAIL-way, published in the Canadian Railroad Historical Association's *News Report* (now *Canadian Rail*), Leonard Seton wrote:

> "The Intercolonial Railway has never been the subject of a 'best-seller' or of a 'book of the month'. It has likewise been overlooked by writers of romantic railway histories and popular novelists, and even by film producers. As the latter gentry would, in all probability, say, it has no 'box-office appeal'. A superficial examination of the facts would seem to bear out the truth of that statement: the Intercolonial Railway was not constructed in spectacular fashion, the time element was not a press-ing question and there were no financial crises, few outstanding per-sonalities, and no scandals of sufficient prominence to have made their mark upon written history. The story of the Intercolonial is obviously not, then, one of gripping romance and pulsating excitement."

While Seton makes an attempt to disprove this point, the notion has become prevalent in the popular histories of the day, and where the Intercolonial has not been regarded with a blasé eye, it has been vilified and ridiculed. Many historians have been satisfied to explain the Intercolonial simply as a mere detail of the terms of Confederation, something the united Canadas gave their impoverished brethren in New Brunswick and Nova Scotia in order to satisfy the ambitions of these provinces to become commercial equals within the new union.

But the story of the nation's first "national" railway is in fact fraught with excitement, if one considers the plight of a small population living in fear of invasion from an increasingly more powerful neighbour to the south for almost one hundred years. Its creation was intended to allay those fears, especially in the united Canadas, which would have been the principal target of any attack, and whose citizens feared the treachery of the Americans even more than did the citizens of New Brunswick and Nova Scotia.

A more rounded evaluation of the railway requires an examination of the conditions that led to its creation, viewed from outside the purely emotional trappings of Confederation. A fine distinction must be made for the Intercolonial in that it was a pragmatic railway, rather than a profitable one, and while its inception was a condition of the terms that led to the confederation of the British North American colonies, the necessity for such a railway predated that era, and would have existed for some time thereafter had Confederation not taken place.

It was not long after the War of 1812 that the British military came to the conclusion that an adequate defence of the North American colonies was impracticable. Instead of establishing permanent garrisons, as had been done in India and South Africa, the British determined that the only way to police the North American colonies would be to ship troops over the Atlantic as the situation might dictate.

This tactic would no doubt have been successful (although not timely) in the spring-summer months, but with the Gulf of St. Lawrence icebound for at least five months of the year, the only way to despatch the necessary troops to central Canada in the winter was overland from Halifax.

Historian Desmond Morton has noted that Britain viewed the defence of Canada as one of its most "intractable" problems, always regarding the apparent lack of the colonials' interest in paying for their own defence with something of a jaundiced eye. The provinces, for their part, complained they were being expected to pay for military defences made necessary by British diplomatic failures, over which the colonials had no control, and very little input.

The Intercolonial Railway appears to have been the inevitable compromise, a tacit admission from both sides that each bore some measure of responsibility if the Americans were to be held at bay every time they rattled their sabres. But while Britain entered into the project satisfied the empire was financing the construction of a military road, the colonials believed they were financing an instrument of commerce.

As time progressed and Canada/US relationships warmed, the Intercolonial became much less of a military necessity for central Canada, to the point that by the turn of the century, Ontario and Quebec politicians came to look upon it (and disparage it) as an inconvenience, an economic and political white elephant, fit only for the strategic dispersal of patronage.

The military imperative is best understood by an examination of the route the Intercolonial took through Canadian geography rather than Canadian politics, and that journey begins at the outset of the War of 1812.

Canadian winters had already left British and Canadian military leaders in no doubt that the central Canadian provinces were most vulnerable to attack during the months when the supply route, the St. Lawrence River, was plugged with ice. This had been demonstrated in the British-French Seven Years War, and the 1776 War of Independence with the emerging American nation.

This lesson was brought home in 1812, as Desmond Morton notes in *A Military History of Canada* (1985):

> "The War of 1812 was not a struggle of equals. Seven and a half million Americans were at war with half a million neighbours. Americans might be deeply divided about the war but the United States had only one war to fight. To Britain, North America was an exasperating distraction from the mortal struggle against Napoleon... In the Canadas, Prevost counted only fifty-two hundred regulars and fencibles, twelve hundred of them with Brock in Upper Canada. His strategy, inherited from Craig and Carleton, was as predictable as the American invasion plan. Surely the Americans would concentrate on Lower Canada. If they took Quebec before the ice left the St. Lawrence in 1813, no British army could ever reverse the loss of Canada."

Morton goes on to note:

> "It was a quartermaster's nightmare.... Everything, from bullets to boots, had to be lugged along a supply line strung perilously from Great Britain to Amherstburg. Most of the food supply came from the United States, smuggled by New England and New York farmers who preferred British gold to penniless patriotism. Everything else had to cross the Atlantic and came up a lake and river system that was frozen for six months and open to American attack for the rest of the year. Six companies of the 104th Regiment marched overland from Fredericton to Quebec but the experiment was not repeated."

The conditions had only slightly improved by the winter of 1813:

> "The little string of victories restored morale among Canadians and generals. At Kingston, winter allowed shipwrights to hurry completion of two powerful frigates... A few more regiments and 216 badly needed sailors and marines came overland from New Brunswick that winter and more than 1600 Royal Marines reached Quebec just before freeze up." *(Morton)*

The freeze-up was more than a matter of inconvenient navigation for ships; building a ship in the winter months was often impossible:

> "The difficulties were incredible. Every item of a ship of war, from a binnacle to a bowsprit, had to be wheedled from a British dockyard,

Arthur Wellesley, Duke of Wellington: He concluded Canada could not be defended without an improved land transport infrastructure, and oversaw capital spending on a canal system designed for defensive purposes. This portrait came from the 1906 Harmsworth Encyclopedia.

shipped across the Atlantic, and conveyed bodily up five hundred miles of river and rapids or hauled over hopeless roads." *(Morton)*

The situation was not lost upon the British commander-in-chief, the Duke of Wellington, who turned his mind to the North American conflict as soon as he had vanquished Napoleon in April of 1814:

"In such countries as America," he had written to Lord Bathurst, the Secretary for War and Colonies, "very extensive, thinly peopled, and producing but little food in proportion to their extent, military operations by large bodies are impracticable, unless the party carrying them on has the uninterrupted use of a navigable river, or very extensive means of land transport, which such a country can rarely supply." *(Morton)*

As Col. C. P. Stacey noted in *The Backbone of Canada*:

"There was an overland communication, well-known if not well travelled. It ran up the St. John valley to that river's junction with the Madawaska, up the Madawaska to Lake Temiscouata and across the lake; and thence across what was sometimes called the 'Grand Portage,' some 36 miles of rough and rocky wilderness, to reach the St. Lawrence at Notre Dame du Portage above Riviere du Loup. This portage is indicated on Mitchell's 1755 map of North America by the words 'Carriages to Canada'; but it is certain that no carriage had ever passed over it. During the last stages of the American Revolution,

Governor Haldimand used it for sending dispatches to Halifax, New York and London, and in 1783 he took steps to improve the portage road to the point where it could be used by laden horses. But this escaped the notice of British diplomatists, who in their eagerness to make peace (which the House of Commons had formally demanded) completely failed to consider the permanent military security of British North America."

In his history of Canadian National Railways, G. R. Stevens pays only cursory attention to military applications, but he makes note of the early need for improved communications between the colonies:

"In the manner of their kind, the military planners did not talk. Civilians, however, soon detected the trend, and from 1815 onwards, communications were a major subject of discussion in Canada. One of the early apostles of Canadian trunk lines was Thomas Gray, a constant correspondent of Montreal and Quebec newspapers. He saw transportation devices transforming the world; he was far ahead of his time in his appraisals of the social and economic implications of steam. He kept Canadians well informed upon the canal versus railway controversy in Great Britain and he was the first to present, in clear and forcible terms, the argument that Canada's waterways were not enough for her needs.

On December 1st 1824, the Montreal *Gazette* argued the case of railways as against canals, proposing a series of light lines to the American boundary, for trade in peace, for defence in time of war."

As far as the Imperial government was concerned, there was a financial necessity for railways, in addition to a strategic one. The transportation of troops and munitions could be as costly as it was time consuming, as the 1871 survey by J. and E. Trout noted:

"The cost of carrying goods between Montreal and Kingston, before the Rideau or St. Lawrence canals were built, seems to this generation incredible, and is worthy of belief only, because it is stated on unimpeachable authority. Sir J. Murray stated, in the House of Commons, September 6 1828, that, on a former occasion, the carriage of a twenty-four pound cannon cost between £150 and £200 sterling; that of a seventy-six cwt anchor £676..."

While the canals drastically reduced that cost, railways would do so to an even greater extent. The British were not to make use of railways as an effective military means until the Crimean War of 1853, indeed, the first use of a railway to transport troops probably took place in 1836, when Czar Alexander I opened his private railway between summer and winter palaces on the St. Petersburg–Pavlovsk line, and was forced to take a detachment of bodyguard with him to deter assassination attempts. The line was bombed once, with the loss of a locomotive, but the Czar was not on board the train at the time.

Forced then to rely on an overland trail from the main Atlantic port of Halifax (only Halifax, Canso and the Cape Breton port of Louisburg were ice-free for most of the North American winter, and suitable to Royal Navy requirements) and through New Brunswick, it was immediately obvious that an all-season route was vital to the winter reinforcement of the widely-spread fortresses that would be built in Upper and Lower Canada in the aftermath of the 1812 war.

This issue was not immediately addressed, however, even by the 1820s, as work began on the renewal of Halifax's Citadel, part of the Duke of Wellington's £1.6 million program for the defence of the Canadas. The plan called for the improvement of the major forts in Upper and Lower Canada, and the digging of several major canals, but nothing for a viable land link between them and Halifax, which the Duke himself had indicated was necessary. Such procrastination is perplexing, for the construction of a road was probably no difficult task initially.

The Duke of Wellington himself was no fan of railways in the early years. His main complaint was that railways would allow the lower classes to travel freely, and as the owner of large tracts of lands that required a stable workforce, he had a vested interest in seeing his tenants stay put. He would later warm to railways when shown how they could increase his personal fortune.

In Nova Scotia, stagecoach service between Halifax and Pictou had begun June 1st 1816, when Ezra Witter of Truro began a weekly service over albeit rough roads that were little more than blazed trails in some sections. Witter drove the Halifax–Truro section, and Jacob Lynds drove the Truro–Pictou leg. The end-to-end time was usually two to two-and-a-half days. By 1828, Witter and Lynds were operating their stage once a week from June to the middle of November.

It is obvious from such a schedule that winter still posed problems for highway travellers, although cold weather alone would not have been sufficient to stop an army on the march to the relief of central Canada, even on rudimentary roads.

In New Brunswick, as Mitch Biggar notes on his history website, stagecoaches with room enough for a dozen or more passengers, with their luggage, were making regular trips by 1836. The coaches were drawn by four and sometimes six horses, running regularly from Saint John to Fredericton, Fredericton to Woodstock, Chatham to Fredericton (the Chatham coach left Chatham every Monday morning at six o'clock and arrived at Fredericton at four o'clock on Tuesday afternoon), and from Saint John to Amherst (the Saint John–Amherst coach took three days, but the stage travelled only in the daytime.)

> "These coaches also carried the mail. British mails came overseas on the Cunard steamship to Halifax. A stagecoach carried mails and passengers from Halifax to Sackville."

Even in the relative comfort of Hiram Hyde's Royal Mail coach, the trip was physically tormenting to passengers, as Isabella Bishop described her trip from Halifax to Truro in the 1850s (*The Englishwomen in America*, 1856):

> "Do not let the word coach conjure up a vision of 'the good old times,' a dashing mail with a well-groomed team of active bays, harness all 'spick and span,' a gentlemanly-looking coachman, and a guard in military scarlet, the whole affair rattling along a road at a pace of ten miles an hour.
>
> The vehicle in which we performed a journey of 120 miles in 20 hours deserves a description. It consisted of a huge coach-body slung upon two thick leather straps; the sides were open, and the places where windows ought to have been were screened by heavy curtains of tarnished moose-deer hide. Inside were four cross-seats, intended to accommodate twelve persons, who were very imperfectly sheltered from the weather. Behind was a large rack for luggage and at the back of the driving-seat was a bench which held three persons. The stage was painted scarlet, but looked as if it had not been washed for a year. The team of six strong white horses was driven by a Yankee, remarkable only for his silence. About a ton of luggage was packed on and behind the stage, and two open portmanteaus were left behind without the slightest risk to their contents.
>
> Our road lay for many miles over a barren, rocky, undulating country, covered with var and spruce trees, with an undergrowth of raspberry, white rhododendron, and sider. We passed a chain of lakes extending for sixteen miles, their length varying from one to three miles, and their shores covered with forests of gloomy pines.
>
> A dreary stage of 18 miles brought us to Shultze's, a road-side inn by a very pretty lake, where we were told the 'coach breakfasted.' Whether Transatlantic coaches can perform this, to us, unknown feat, I cannot pretend to say, but we breakfasted. A very course repast was prepared for us, consisting of stewed salt veal, country cheese, rancid salt butter, fried eggs, and barley bread; but we were too hungry to find fault either with it, or with the charge made for it, which equalled that at a London hotel. Our Yankee coachman, a man of monosyllables, sat

next to me, and I was pleased to see that he regaled himself on tea instead of spirits.

We packed ourselves into the stage again with great difficulty, and how the forty-eight limbs fared was shown by the painful sensations experienced for several succeeding days. All the passengers, however, were in perfectly good humour, and amused each other during the eleven hours spent in this painful way. At an average speed of six miles an hour we travelled over roads of various descriptions, plank corduroy, and sand; up long heavy hills, and through swamps swarming with mosquitoes.

Every one has heard of corduroy roads, but how few have experienced their miseries! They are generally used for traversing swampy ground, and are formed of small pine-trees deprived of their branches, which are laid across the track alongside each other. The wear and tear of travelling soon separates these, leaving gaps between; and when, added to this, one trunk rots away, and another sinks down into the swamp, and another tilts up, you may imagine such jolting as only leather springs could bear. On the very worst roads, filled with deep holes, or covered with small granite boulders, the stage only swings on the straps. Ordinary springs, besides dislocating the joints of the passengers, would be wrenched and broken after a few miles travelling.

Even as we were, faces sometimes came into rather close proximity to each other and to the side railings, and heads sustained very unpleasant collisions. The amiable man who was so disappointed with the American climate suffered very much from the journey. He said he had thought a French diligence the climax of discomfort, but a 'stage was misery, oh torture!' Each time that we had rather a worse jolt than usual the poor man groaned, which always drew forth a chorus of laughter, to which he submitted most good-humouredly. Occasionally he would ask the time, when some one would point maliciously to his watch, remarking, 'Twelve hours more,' or 'Fifteen hours more,' when he would look up with an expression of despair. The bridges wore a very un-English feature. Over the small streams or brooks they consisted of three pines covered with planks, without any parapet... with sometimes a plank out, and sometimes a hole in the middle. Over large streams they were wooden erections of a most peculiar kind, with high parapets; their insecurity being evidenced by the notice, 'Walk your horses, according to law,'—a notice generally disregarded by our coachman, as he trotted his over the shaking and rattling fabric."

The hardships of the overland route through New Brunswick were not limited to winter. In the months of "good" weather, troops on the march were exposed to the dangers of disease. Evidence of this can be found in cemeteries and churches throughout the Saint John River valley. Typhus and malaria would strike regardless of age, rank or social standing, as illustrated by a tablet in St. Anne's Anglican church in Fredericton:

SACRED
To the memory of Ensign
JAMES WILLIAM HOSTE
48th Regiment Light Infantry
Second son of Lieut. Colonel
Sir George Charles Hoste, C.B. Royal Engineers
Who died at Woodstock in this Province of
Typhus fever on the 9th Day of November 1836
Aged 19 years and was buried at Fredericton.
His brother officers having caused this tablet
To be erected as a memorial of their esteem
Fro his character and of their
Regret for his loss.

These hazards were not limited to the overland trip, as the New Brunswick *Courier* of July 10th 1847 noted, quoting a report from Quebec City:

"Quebec, July 7.
H.M. troop-ship *Apollo*, from Portsmouth via Halifax, with drafts, arrived at Grosse Isle, on Sunday, where she landed her sick—having the small pox on board—and came into port this afternoon.
We are sorry to learn that Capt. Heitland, Royal Artillery, died of small pox on the 30th ult., and was interred on Hare Island."

The movement of soldiers was, and still is, not an easy task. It is not a matter of a mere parade. An infantry regiment consisted of as many as six companies of fighting men, twenty horses, six wagons and a 28-member band in the fighting unit, as many as 1,000 men in all. Following that came a baggage column consisting of 23 horses, and four heavy wagons carrying everything from food and tents to the officers' personal baggage.

An entire brigade on the march, including cavalry and artillery regiments, would involve more than 4,000 men, 100 wagons, as many as 50 heavy field guns and ammunition wagons (called limbers), and more than 300 horses. This body of men, given good weather and firm roads, was capable of travelling as much as thirty miles a day; cavalry units moved markedly faster, and artillery units predictably more slowly. That volume of traffic would take a heavy toll on otherwise fragile roads of the era.

The value of the existing roads to the military cannot be overlooked, even in the years of relative peace between the Canadas and the US after 1839. On April 6th of that year, the Nova Scotia Legislature decided on several budget allocations "for the service of roads and bridges." This appears to be the first such recorded provincial expenditure, but allowed no money for roads in Halifax, Hants, Colchester or Cumberland Counties, through which the major coach road travelled: £750 for roads and bridges in Cape Breton County, £700 for the same in Inverness County, £500 for Richmond County, £650 for Lunenburg County, £500 for Sydney County, and £500 for Guysborough County. This may be taken as an indication that the upkeep of the road from Halifax to Amherst was already being shouldered by the military, which made much use of provincial militia to help in such matters, especially as a means of peacetime training.

By 1831, as steam navigation between Halifax and Quebec (only in the non-winter months) steadily improved, the time between Halifax and Quebec had shrunk significantly. At the time of the incorporation of the Quebec & Halifax Steam Navigation Company, a courier postal service was operating between Halifax and Quebec, which usually took at least a week one way, and longer in winter.

Steam navigation, however, did not necessarily make the voyage along the St. Lawrence safer. Major William Robinson recalls details of the wrecking of a steamer, in which the perils of the river in winter were made abundantly clear to the British army:

> "About the close of navigation in 1843, a transport, having the 1st Royal Regiment on board was wrecked in the mouth of the St. Lawrence. The men got safely on shore, but there were no roads or means of getting away from that place. By the personal exertions of one of the officers, who made his way through the woods on snow shoes to the nearest settlements, and thence to Quebec, information was given of the wreck, and a steamer sent down to take them off. But for this, the consequences must have been that the regiment would have had to winter there in the best manner they could."

Seton makes note of a similar incident at Bic, Quebec, which placed the lives of 1,100 soldiers in dire jeopardy:

> "The incident at Bic, when the S.S. Persian, in danger of being caught in the freezing river, was obliged to put about 1100 men ashore, immediately demonstrated how valuable a through railway must prove, in the winter particularly."

It is not clear whether these two accounts are of the same incident, since Robinson refers specifically to a wreck, but the area is likely identical. The channel at Bic, between the mainland and Isle Bicquette, is a known shipping graveyard. There is a reference to the *SS Persian* and Bic in the *Gleaner* of November 16th 1867 which notes the hope:

> " . . . that the most advantageous route will be adopted; that it will touch the harbour of Bic, where on the 26th of December, 1861, the *Persia* embarked English troops who came bravely to our aid in order to ward off the dangers caused by the *Trent* affair."

The letters of Sir Henry Pelham-Clinton, fifth Duke of Newcastle Under Lyne (in the special collections of the University of Nottingham), contain a January 11th 1862 letter from Captain Rotton, of Quebec, Lower Canada, to Colonel Paynter, reporting on the incident, which stemmed from the captain's refusal to navigate beyond Bic. Rotton's letter noted "experienced persons" had determined that the river was navigable at the time.

Viscount Monck had transmitted the same information to the Duke in a December 27th 1861 letter. The refusal by the master of the *Persia* threw all the British plans to land troops and munitions in the region into immediate disarray, but clearly the captain was unwilling to entertain the same misery of 1843.

Certainly it was common knowledge that the coastline of Bic was dangerous from a maritime point of view, not only in winter, as the Intercolonial's 1877 *Sketches of Scenery*, a guidebook for passengers, notes:

> "A short distance to the north of L'islet du Massacre, is Bicquette Island, about half a mile long by one quarter of a mile wide. Near its centre is a light-house, exhibiting a revolving white light; a gun is fired every half-hour during fogs and snow storms."

In a touch of irony, the guidebook notes the railway's presence in the area was expected to pay a dividend for the community:

> "Bic is certain to become one of the most attractive summer resorts in the Lower St. Lawrence."

This is not to say that winter could not exercise its mastery whenever it so chose, even beyond the reaches of the St. Lawrence. On March 9th 1833, Halifax Harbour froze over completely, rendering any military use of the port or the road west impracticable.

The first agitation for an inter-colonial railway came from commercial considerations, however, as W. C. Milner notes:

> "One of the earliest efforts was made in St. Andrews, New Brunswick in 1827, two years after George Stephenson had completed the first railway England. In 1828, John Wilson convened a public meeting in St. Andrews, N.B., to discuss the question of a railway to Quebec. In 1832,

the *United Services Journal* turned the attention of the British public to Mr. Henry Fairbairn writing on the necessity of a railway system for British North America. He said: "I propose first to form a railway for wagons from Quebec to the harbour of St. Andrews, upon the Bay of Fundy—a route which will convey the trade of the St. Lawrence in a single day to Atlantic waters."

Seton goes on to note:

"Saint Andrews was a prominent trading and commercial town at the time, and public interest was immediately aroused at the prospect of making its port as great a shipping centre as advance calculations promised that it would become. An association was formed in 1835 for the promotion of the scheme, and support was obtained from the governments of New Brunswick, Nova Scotia, Canada and Great Britain, the latter advancing money for a preliminary survey. This survey was executed by one Captain Yule of the Royal Engineers, and by 1837, a satisfactory route had been located reasonably free of outstanding obstacles."

Although subsequent histories fail to identify him fully, the Royal Engineer in question was Captain Patrick Yule. Seton's history echoes the work of Milner:

"The Imperial Government made a grant of £10,000 to be expended in the exploration and survey of the proposed line of railway from Quebec to St. Andrews. This survey was placed under the control of Captain Yule, an officer of the Royal Engineers, and the work was begun on the 23rd of July, 1836. At that time, the country through which Captain Yule prosecuted the surveys was held to be wholly British territory. In 1837, the United States Government made objections to the route proposed on the ground that they claimed part of the territory. Notification of the fact was given to the Governor-General of Canada, and to the Lieutenant-Governor of New Brunswick, and orders were given by the British Government to stop the work until the boundary line was settled."

The US protest resulted in a five-year delay, as Seton notes:

"The settlement of the boundary question in 1842, by the terms of the Ashburton Treaty, gave to the State of Maine much of the territory through which Captain Yule's survey ran, and, consequently, the intercolonial scheme, as such, was indefinitely postponed."

Despite the involvement of Captain Yule, under instruction from the Secretary of State for the Colonies in London, the Saint Andrews & Quebec Railway did not appear to be based upon any military consideration. Indeed, Yule gives the work the broadest interpretation:

> "It will be the ruling principle in the execution of the proposed work to take a wider view of the undertaking than the mere general object of connecting Quebec and Saint Andrews, for although the chief advantage proposed to be derived from it may be obtained without reference to a great portion of the intervening Country its utilities ought not to be so limited; it should when completed, form such a road as will be best capable of contributing to the general benefit of the Country."

Colonization, more than national security, was foremost on the minds of the New Brunswick railway promoters, as this report from the July 10th 1847 edition of the Saint John, NB *Courier* indicates:

> "M. H. Perley, Esq. of this City, who came passenger in the last Steamer from England, resumed his duties as Emigration Agent at this Port on Tuesday last. We learn that Mr. Perley and his colleague, Captain Robinson, R.N., were so fortunate as to make very satisfactory arrangements in London for the St. Andrews and Woodstock Railway, by disposing of a large amount of stock, and forming a highly influential Board of Directors, of which the Right Honorable the Earl of Fitzwilliam is President.
>
> Before leaving London, Mr. Perley was summoned to the Bar of the House of Lords, and being there sworn, was examined for several hours on successive days, by the Special Committee of Peers on Colonization, twenty-one in number, of whom the Lord Monteagle is Chairman. The principal examiners were the Noble Chairman, Lord Ashburton, Lord Wharncliffe, Lord Stradbroke, Lord Fingall, Lord Falkland, and Lord Lyttleton, although other peers occasionally took part in the examination...
>
> ...The plan of colonizing these Provinces by the construction of Railways was strenuously advocated by Mr. Perley during his stay in England, and should the report of the officers of the Royal Engineers, now engaged on the survey of the trunk line from Halifax to Quebec, point out an eligible route for that line, a pledge has been given in a high quarter, that government will at once take measures for the construction of the line as an object of national importance."

The Americans were quick to recognize the immediate threat to their security. Quoted in Sandford Fleming's history of the Intercolonial, one New York newspaper noted:

> "It enables the British Government to send all her troops, munitions of

war, etc., with all possible speed, from that important naval position, Halifax, where the British Government is now fitting up one of the strongest fortifications in the world, to Quebec, Montreal, Toronto, the Lakes, and all along our northern and north-western territories. In five or six days, soldiers can be taken from the great military and naval depot at Halifax and put upon the St. Lawrence from Quebec to Ontario...

Military and commercial advantages prompt the British Government to expend $4,000,000, for with the harbour of Halifax, as it is near Europe, a cordon of British bayonets can be made to surround us in the shortest possible time...."

Certainly Yule did not appear at all concerned that this railway would pass so close to the frontier with the United States, a mere 2½ miles at the Houlton Road, according to the surveyors George Smith and C. R. Hatheway. In fact, Yule makes only two observations that might be construed as having military connotations:

"The Saint John River was described to be navigable, but it was scarcely so, even for canoes, from August to November 1836."

And, he notes:

"The distance between Fredericton and Quebec (which by the present Post Office Route is 350 miles) will be reduced to 274 miles by the line of the Railway."

With construction estimates varying from Yule's "One Million" (it is not clear if he meant dollars or pounds sterling), to George Wightman's "ten to twelve thousand dollars per mile," the prospects for a profitable railway did not look encouraging.

The military benefits of either a railway or a road would soon become apparent; not against American invasion, but Canadian rebellion. With William Lyon Mackenzie in Upper Canada, and Louis-Joseph Papineau in Lower Canada both calling for the creation of American-style republics, fears that the War of 1812 had been fought for nothing were quite tangible in British North America and Great Britain. Shortly after the November 16th 1837 warrant was issued for the arrest of Papineau, British troops used the rough overland route to move from New Brunswick into Lower Canada.

In the aftermath of the rebellions, in 1838, British Prime Minister Lord Melbourne turned to Lord Durham to remedy the problems within the colonies that had nurtured the uprisings. It is asserted, both by Milner and Seton, that Lord Durham (known as "Radical Jack" for his enthusiasm for reform) recommended a military railway in his landmark report to the Imperial government in 1839. While Durham does recommend a railway to unify the colonies, he does not specifically suggest a military work. Indeed, as Durham notes, the suggestion from Lord Glenelg to investigate the possibility of an inter-colonial road came too late:

"In a Dispatch which arrived in Canada after my departure, the Secretary of State informed me of the determination of Your Majesty's Government to establish a steam communication between Great Britain and Halifax; and instructed me to turn my attention to the formation of a road between that port and Quebec. It would, indeed, have given me sincere satisfaction, had I remained in the Province, to promote, by any means in my power, so highly desirable an object; and the removal of the unusual restrictions on my authority as Governor-General, having given me the means of effectually acting in concert with the various Provincial governments, I might have been able to make some progress in the work. But I cannot point out more strikingly the evils of a present want of a general Government for these Provinces, than by adverting to the difficulty which would practically occur, under the previous and present arrangements of both executive and legislative authorities in the various Provinces, in attempting to carry such a plan into effect. For the various Colonies have no means of concerting such common works with each other, than with the neighbouring States of the Union. They stand to one another in the position of foreign States, and of foreign States without diplomatic relations. The Governments may correspond with each other; the legislatures may enact laws, carrying the common purposes into effect in their respective jurisdictions; but there is no means by which the various details may speedily and satisfactorily be settled with the concurrence of the different parties. And, in this instance, it must be recollected that the communication and the final settlement would have to be made between, not two, but several of the Provinces. The road would run through three of them; and Upper Canada, into which it would not enter, would, in fact, be more interested in the completion than any even of the Provinces through which it would pass. The Colonies, indeed, have no common centre in which the arrangement could be made, except in the Colonial Office at home; and the details of such a plan would have to be discussed just where the interest of all parties would have the least means of being fairly and fully represented, and where the minute local knowledge necessary for such a matter would be least likely to be found.

The completion of any satisfactory communication between Halifax and Quebec, would, in fact, produce relations between these Provinces, that would render a general union absolutely necessary. Several surveys have proved that a railroad would be perfectly practicable the whole way. Indeed, in North America, the expense and difficulty of making a railroad, bears by no means the excessive proportion to those of a common road that it does in Europe. It appears to be a general opinion in the United States, that the severe snows and frosts of that continent very slightly impede, and do not prevent, the travelling on railroads; and if I am rightly informed, the Utica railroad, in the northern part of the State of New York, is used throughout the winter. If this opinion be correct, the formation of a railroad between Halifax and Quebec would entirely alter some of the distinguishing characteristics of the Canadas. Instead of being shutout from all direct intercourse with England during half the year, they would possess a far more certain and speedy communication throughout the winter than they now possess in the summer. The passage from Ireland to Quebec would be a matter of 10 to 12 days, and Halifax would be the greater port by which a large portion of the trade, and all of the conveyance of the passengers to the whole of British North America, would be carried on. But even supposing these brilliant prospects to be such as we could not reckon on seeing realized, I may assume that it is not intended to make this road without a well-founded belief that it will become an important channel of communication between the upper and lower Provinces. In either case, would not the maintenance of such a road and the mode in which the Government is administered in the different Provinces, be matters of common interest to all? If the great natural channel of the St. Lawrence gives all the people who dwell in any part of its basin such an interest in the Government of the whole as renders it wise to incorporate the two Canadas, the artificial work which would, in fact, supersede the lower part of the St. Lawrence, as the outlet of a great part of the Canadian trade, and would make Halifax, in a great measure, an outport to Quebec, would surely in the same way render it advisable that the incorporation should be extended to the Provinces through which such a road would pass."

The 1837-38 rebellions led to increased border tension in the Maritimes, made very real by the undeclared Aroostook "War" of 1839, when Maine lumbermen decided to re-establish the border between their state and New Brunswick. Although it came to nothing substantial—it was enough to revive Maritime mistrust of American intentions—the two crises also underscored the military imperative of an overland route, as Stacey notes:

"The rebellions in Canada in 1837, and the border troubles that followed, again underlined the absolute indispensability of the Temiscouata road to British interests. The crisis arose, as usual, after the close of navigation; but the road, which though still very bad had now been improved to the point where sleighs could be used on it, was the means of reinforcing Canada from the Maritime Provinces. Three battalions of infantry and a company of artillery came up through the New Brunswick woods; and the knowledge that they were coming enabled Sir John Colborne to send part of his small regular force to protect the menaced frontier of Upper Canada. When the second rebellion, combined with invasion by sympathizers in the United States, took place a year later, another battalion made the trip over the Temiscouata route. Colborne had already pointed the moral for the benefit of London: 'The value of the communication by the Portage to the valley of the St. Lawrence should never be forgotten in the adjustment of the boundary question.' "

The geography of the Aroostook war (see map Appendix Nine) also explains much about the route the Intercolonial eventually took, which on first analysis appears to be the wrong route for a practical railway. Logic would dictate that a railway intent on profitable operation would run from Moncton toward Saint John and up the Saint John River Valley toward the provincial capital of Fredericton, then toward Quebec near Edmundston, rather than along the lesser-populated Gulf of St. Lawrence shore.

From a military viewpoint, however, there was a danger in building too close to the New Brunswick–Maine border. The Aroostook infiltration (and those of the Fenian raiders in the post-Civil War era) was hampered by the lack of a road or railroad on which the invaders could have moved freely. From another military point of view, the river itself was an impediment. The Saint John was not navigable much beyond King's Landing north of Fredericton, and flowed in the wrong direction, eastward to the Bay of Fundy, rather than westward to Quebec. In the winter the river becomes as unusable as the St. Lawrence, and spring thaws make it dangerous to any kind of travel.

The Aroostook border dispute could very easily have led to a real war, as Stacey notes:

"In 1839 the chairman of the Foreign Affairs Committee in the United States House of Representatives wrote to the American Minister to England that he felt there could be no compromise so long as the United States admitted the right of Maine to interfere, and so long as the British were determined to have a road. 'Indeed,' he wrote, 'Mr. Fox (the British Minister) once said to me very significantly that they could not do without that road. Now when people have made up their minds all argument is idle wind.' It was to the credit of Daniel Webster, who became Secretary of State in 1841, that he drew a different conclusion

*Sir Sandford Fleming:
He surveyed fifteen routes
before accepting Robinson's
original proposal. This
portrait is taken from
Sir Frederick Young's
1906 book* Exit Party.

from the facts. He appears to have come to the view that since the British considered the road essential to the mere existence of British North America, and since they had made it amply clear that they would fight rather than give it up, the sensible thing was to let them have it. Accordingly, he approached Britain with a proposal which contained the germs of settlement—to abandon the intricate and fruitless argument over the interpretation of the treaty of 1783 and to treat for a 'conventional' or compromise line. The negotiations between himself and Lord Ashburton began with the recognition on Ashburton's side that Britain's one essential interest was the maintenance of communications between the provinces, while Webster on his acknowledged 'the general justice and propriety of this object.' And the treaty which they made did in fact secure to British North America the Temiscouata–Madawaska Road."

Only the Canadian Pacific, that most practical of all Canadian railways, would make use of the area (through northern Maine) to build from sea-to-sea. Locating the Intercolonial's path along the northern route was a deliberate military decision designed to keep the railway out of enemy hands for as long as possible, as later fears would dictate.

With the railway age quickly spreading across Great Britain, and having reached Nova Scotia with the opening of the Albion Mines Rail Road in Pictou County in 1839, it was a natural progression of military thinking to consider the logistical advantages of the new means of travel.

Renewed interest in an inter-colonial railway began with the province of Nova Scotia making the first overture. It started with an April 2nd 1846 letter from the Lieutenant Governor, Sir Colin Campbell, to William Gladstone, then Secretary of State for Colonial Affairs, calling for a survey—for which the province was prepared to pay some portion—of a railway linking Nova Scotia and New Brunswick to Quebec City and Montreal.

The letter was an address to the queen (Victoria) "to cause to be applied towards its completion the same amount of money as would have been expended on the formation of the Military Road, which it is understood Her majesty's Government had it in contemplation through Nova Scotia, New Brunswick, and Canada."

The macadamised military road had been under consideration in London since the settlement of the Maine-New Brunswick border dispute in 1842 (under the Ashburton Treaty). The road would have traversed New Brunswick from the bend of the Petitcodiac River (as Moncton was then known) to Quebec. Robinson recounts the history of the project:

> "Instead of the railway to complete the communication onwards from Halifax to Quebec, it was at first proposed to construct a great military high road across the centre of New Brunswick, which was to branch off from the existing provincial roads near the bend of the Petitcodiac River, and join about the Riviere du Loup, the road leading from thence along the River St. Lawrence to Quebec.
>
> In the year 1844 Captain Simmons, of the Royal Engineers, explored a line for this military high road."

Fleming offers a different version of history in his account of the creation of the Intercolonial:

> "This survey was made by Colonel Holloway of the Royal Engineers, aided by Sir James Alexander, then a Captain in the 14th Regiment."

This contradiction of fact is noted here for its significance to the railway, because Fleming goes on to state:

> "...Colonel Holloway, who had conducted the survey for the military road, expressed himself strongly in favour of the Railway.
>
> "4th May 1836
>
> I know that the British Government is strongly inclined for a military road, and if I see no objection on further inquiry I would gladly recommend a railway instead of the ordinary turnpike road. I believe the Government is impressed with the importance of a railway from Quebec to Halifax in a political point of view, and I am of the opinion

that it is highly desirable, if not absolutely essential for the military defence of the British American Provinces."

Tuttle picks up the narrative in his history, referring to Campbell's successor:

"A London company offered to substitute a railway, on condition that part of the money necessary to make the road should be granted to it.... The government of Lord Falkland considered it idle and visionary to expect that a vast undertaking, which held no inducement of immediate profit, could be carried through by a company."

Where Falkland was ambivalent, Sir Colin had made an attempt to make the proposal all the more attractive to London:

" The local Parliament has pledged itself to provide for the expense of the Survey, but as it would of course be desirable to diminish the amount of that charge as much as possible, I would suggest the employment of Military Engineers, the whole part of whose emolument (as may be deemed just by the Imperial Government), might be defrayed by the province..."

The matter had been under serious consideration for some time in Halifax, and was spurred on by the enthusiasm of provincial secretary Joseph Howe for all things steam driven, a direct result of his excursion to England in 1838. Howe was on board the brig *Tyrian* when it set sail from Halifax Harbour April 26th. At that time he was 33 years old, and editor and owner of the *NovaScotian*, a weekly newspaper:

"Half way across the Atlantic, *Tyrian* was overtaken by the steamship *Sirius*, which had departed from New York on 1 May 1838.

Tyrian sailed out of Halifax with six days' head start on a much shorter route, but *Sirius* was powered by steam, and could move at normal speed even when there was no wind. Lt. Commander Jennings of *Tyrian* had important mail on board which was destined for the British Government, and, when *Sirius* pulled abreast of *Tyrian*, he hailed *Sirius* and arranged a mid-ocean transfer to the faster ship.

Joseph Howe, always a journalist alert for a story, got into the boat making the mail transfer, and clambered aboard *Sirius* to have a look. Howe 'took a glass of champagne with the Captain', looked at the sumptuous quarters on *Sirius*, and decided to stay..."

Howe watched with awe as the steamer's paddles quickly took it ahead of *Tyrian*, which was left with sails flapping listlessly in a dead calm. To Howe this was a convincing demonstration that steam was the future of North Atlantic shipping.

"On 24 August 1838, a memorandum prepared by Howe, Haliburton, and several others, was presented to Lord Glenelg, Her Majesty's Secretary of State for the Colonies; the recent experience at sea was described in strong terms, and it was represented that the 1837 rebellion in Canada likely would have been avoided if there had been faster and more reliable communication between the authorities at Westminster and York (Toronto)."

[Excerpted from First Things in Acadia *by John Quinpool, published in Halifax in 1936, and internet sources.]*

The incident had repercussions on British military policy in British North America, since the proliferation of steamer service across the Atlantic made it easier for Westminster to fall back on the defence policy of shipping troops by sea as necessary. Steamers reduced the time of passage from several weeks to a matter of days. Having bridged the Atlantic, however, the British army still had not confronted the problem of an adequate overland winter route.

The most immediate effect of this episode was the move by the Admiralty Board to use steamers to deliver the mail from Falmouth (England) to Halifax and Boston, with Samuel Cunard being the first man to win a transatlantic mail contract.

As for the railway proposal, Gladstone was quick to reply (April 18th 1846). At first he was reluctant to divert funding from the proposed road to a railway venture, but quick to take up the cost-sharing scheme:

"I am happy to inform you, by this opportunity, that I have recommended to the Lords Commissioners of the Treasury to give their sanction to the employment of Officers of Engineers for the Survey in Nova Scotia, and the neighbouring British Provinces, for which the House of Assembly has pledged itself to provide, and that instructions, in accordance with my wishes on this subject, have been given to their Lordships to the Master General and Board of Ordinance, who will communicate with their officers in North America."

Gladstone was just as quick in his referral of the matter to the Board of Ordnance, his secretary writing on April 16th:

"It will not, however, be sufficient to restrict the proposed Survey only to Nova Scotia.

Mr. Gladstone does not doubt that the people of Canada and New Brunswick have been equally animated by a desire to aid in the formation of some great chain of communication, by Railway, between the several Provinces, and (although their Legislatures have not, so far as he is at present aware, adopted proceedings corresponding with those

Officers of the Royal Corps of Engineers in dress uniform c1850. When conducting surveys, the ordinary troops, known as "Sappers", and their officers, wore less formal outfits. This illustration is from Walter Richards's **Her Majesty's Army** *published in 1880 by J. S. Virtue and Co.*

of the Legislature of Nova Scotia) he considers that it will not, on account, be proper to withhold from the former Provinces the advantages of the Survey which will be afforded to Nova Scotia."

Noting that the season in which the survey could be reasonably conducted was limited, Gladstone urged the board to move quickly, with the request:

"...that the Board of Ordnance may be distinctly apprised that to render this Survey adequate to its object, it will be necessary to examine the question where the port of embarkation for England would most properly be fixed, having regard to the convenience of the Public, the purposes of despatch, and the general safety of the port and terminus in time of War."

Clearly, Gladstone intended any railway link to have a military use, and was probably incredulous at the lucky notion that Nova Scotia had volunteered to help pay for part of the survey.

The Treasury Board responded with an April 17th direction to the Board of Ordnance to order its officers in North America to make themselves available to all provinces interested in the project. On June 13th 1846, the Treasury Board was advised that Captain John Pipon and Lieutenant E. Wallcott Henderson of the Royal Engineers (a captain G. W. W. Henderson may have later joined the expedition, or the appearance of this name in the report may have been a typographical error in the printed version of the Reports of the Legislature) had been selected to survey the railway line, first by preparing an estimate of the cost:

"Mr. Gladstone considers it necessary that Her Majesty's Government should make such an advance of money as will enable Captain Pipon and Lieutenant Henderson to proceed upon their destination without loss of time, and to purchase in this country such Instruments, Camp Equipage, Stationery, and other necessities, as are indispensable for their operations."

The expense involved in this sudden move, Gladstone instructed, was to be defrayed under the cost of the officers already at work with the Northeastern Boundary Commission, settling the Aroostook dispute by surveying the Canada–U.S. boundary under the terms of the 1842 Ashburton treaty.

Pipon was equally quick to respond. On June 9th 1846 he asked for the following authority:

"…to employ twelve Non-commissioned Officers and Privates of the Royal Sappers and Miners, on duties connected with the exploration Survey for a railway from Quebec to some port in Nova Scotia."

Seven of the men were available and ready for transport from England, Pipon reported; the other five were working on the north-eastern boundary, and he recommended they be sent to Nova Scotia rather than have them return to England.

Determining, with some exactitude, that the survey to a September freeze-up would cost £1,921 and 12 shillings, Pipon warned there would be some delay upon arriving at Halifax since there was not sufficient time to get camp equipment drawn from stores in England.

By this point, matters were moving remarkably quickly in an army not known for making the best use of time. On June 18th, C. E. Trevelyan of the Board of Treasury was advising the Board of Ordnance that £700 had been made available to Pipon to meet his immediate expense in Halifax, and a further £1,300 (more than had been requested), set aside for the cost of the survey.

At this point the Lords of the Admiralty weighed in with a June 17th letter to Gladstone, in which they informed the secretary that their Captain W. F. W. Owen had already conducted a survey on behalf of the Navy:

"Having laid before my Lords Commissioners of the Admiralty your Letter of the 13th instant, representing that various propositions for the construction of a Railway between Halifax and Quebec, have been brought under the consideration of Mr. Secretary Gladstone, and requesting to be furnished with such information as my Lords may possess upon this subject, more especially with reference to the Port to be selected for the Terminus on the Sea Coast, and also with their opinion thereon, I have it in command to acquaint you, for Mr. Secretary Gladstone's information, that my Lords have received from Captain Owen certain suggestions on the subject of a Railway to Quebec, of which the following are the main points:

Captain Owen shows in his Letter, that from a Western Port of Ireland to the nearest Port of Nova Scotia, Canso Harbour, is about 2000 miles, or ten days steaming. From Cape Canso to Quebec, by direct distance, is 480 statute miles, or by a practicable Railway 540, which would be performed in twenty-two hours. He further assumes that London is twenty-six hours from a Western Irish Port, and that Quebec would therefore be twelve days from London.

The first line of Rail would, from Canso, run along the Northern Shore of Nova Scotia to the head of Petit-Coudiac, after passing the Coal Mines of New Glasgow, thus ensuring a supply of Coals. The Ports of Canso he says are good, not incommoded by drift ice, have deep water, and no outlying dangers—they were used by the French before 1760, as a winter rendezvous, and are now a rendezvous for our Merchant Vessels.

At the head of Petit-Coudiac he proposes that a branch should turn off to Halifax, from which it is distant 150 miles, or six hours. The sea route to Halifax would require fifteen hours more than to Canso, and it is a more difficult Harbour to enter. I am, however, to remark, that the tenor of Captain Owen's statement is to show the advantage which would accrue from the English Packets going direct from England to Canso, as regards communications with Quebec; and if the Rail Road were constructed from Canso to Halifax, the communication with the latter would be equally quickly preserved; but if there were to be but one Terminus in Nova Scotia, my Lords doubt whether the advantages of Canso would compensate for giving up the rapid communications with the far more important Port of Halifax as the Terminus.

My Lords, however, would strongly recommend, that the plan suggested by Captain Owen of a Railway between Halifax and Canso, and between Canso and Quebec, should be the course adopted."

In the meantime, the unpopular Lord Falkland had also been ousted by the Nova Scotia Legislative Assembly in Howe's drive to responsible government, and the new Lieutenant Governor Sir John Harvey's speech from the throne on the opening day of the legislature, January 21st 1847, made optimistic references to the railway survey:

"...The period at, and the circumstances under, which we meet, afford me the opportunity of recommending to your continued attention an undertaking second in its importance to none which has ever engaged the notice of any Colonial Legislature in any portion of the British Dominions. I allude to the projected Railroad between Halifax and Quebec, which will constitute the most important link in that great line of communication which may be destined at no remote period to connect the Atlantic with the Pacific Ocean, and to conduct to a British Sea-port, from those into which it is now forced, that vast stream of Trade, not of our own Western Possessions alone, but of the rich and extensive Wheat and Grain growing Districts of all Central America.

This view of the incalculable advantages which the completion of this great work would confer on all the British North American Colonies, and perhaps more especially upon this, its natural Atlantic terminus— this consideration alone should call forth our gratitude for the promptitude with which our appeal to the Home Government was met, on this all important topic.

With respect to the Survey which, in compliance with your request in the last Session, has been commenced, by order of Her Majesty, for ascertaining the best line through which to carry [build] the projected Railroad, although it may have unavoidably experienced some temporary interruption, from the unfortunate loss of one of the distinguished Officers to whose superintendence it was confided, I am nevertheless enabled to inform you that it is proceeding energetically, and that the operations will be renewed as soon as the season may permit."

The speech is important for two reasons. The first is that what began as a scheme to link the Maritimes to the Canadas, had by this time become the first tangible vestige of a national transcontinental railway. This too was due in no small part to the campaign waged by Joe Howe, who was also (and equally enthusiastically) using *NovaScotian* to promote the idea of a Halifax–Boston rail link, and a Halifax–Windsor, NS railway. It also set the tone for Nova Scotia's ambition for the railway as an instrument of trade rather than defence.

The second important point is the reference to the loss of the officer overseeing the survey. This was Capt. Pipon, and the details of his tragic demise were described in a terse November 7th 1846 newspaper report:

Melancholy Accident

"Private letters from Restigouche state that Captain Pypon [sic] of the Railway surveying party was unfortunately drowned in that river on Wednesday. He was crossing that river in a canoe, accompanied by a seaman and a boy, when the frail vessel in which they were voyaging unfortunately upset. The men succeeding in reaching the shore, and the boy took refuge on the bottom of the canoe from which situation he was shortly afterwards rescued.

Captain Pypon, it appears, swam after his Portmanteau, and being much exhausted, was unable to reach shore, and thus terminated his life and important labours. The body of the unfortunate gentleman was shortly afterwards recovered. Lieutenant Henderson, with the remains of his friend, passed through Newcastle on Thursday last, on his way to Fredericton where we presume they will be interred."

Pipon's successor, Major William Robinson, tells a different version in his official report:

"He was descending the Restigouche River, which falls into the Bay Chaleurs, in a canoe, with his boatman and a boy, whom he had engaged at a settler's house to act as a guide down the river.

On passing through a part called the Suction Rapids, the rickety canoe, owing to some inadvertent movement of the parties on board, upset.

Captain Pipon and the man reached the shore in safety, but the boy remained clinging on the bow of the canoe.

Moved by his cries for assistance, Captain Pipon plunged again into the stream, and endeavoured to reach him, but in vain. Encumbered with heavy boots and pea-coat, and probably numbed by the cold, he soon sank in the rapid current, and was carried down the stream. The body was found about two hours after. The boy was, very soon after the accident occurred, drifted safely to shore on the canoe."

John Hodges Pipon was born at Noirmont Manor House, on the Channel Island of Jersey, of well-to-do parents. He was 28 years old at the time of his death. He was interred in the public burial grounds at Fredericton, with military honours, on Sunday November 8th 1846. In his place, Robinson became the commanding officer of the survey. Robinson was in fact a captain, with the brevet rank of major. He had returned to Canada almost immediately after having reached England following a tour of duty with the commission working on the Ashburton boundary survey. His trail would become known as "Major Robinson's Path."

The route of the survey from Restigouche crossed the river into Quebec, and roughly followed the Kempt military trail, a partially-completed road started by Sir James Kempt, which in turn traced an old Indian trail across the Gaspe Peninsula to Metis, Quebec.

Pipon's death was not the only calamity to occur in the wilderness of New Brunswick, as Robinson relates in his report made upon his return to Exeter, in England:

"In the second season, one of the civil surveyors, Mr. Grant, of the Crown Land Office, New Brunswick, was lost for five days, being rescued in the last stage of starvation, his limbs paralysed, and extremities frost bitten."

By the winter of 1846, the survey's military purpose had taken on new impetus, as the Americans initiated their latest adventure in the fulfilment of their quest to satisfy "Manifest Destiny."

US President James K. Polk sent a force of 3,000 men under Brigadier General Zachary Taylor to defend the newly-admitted state of Texas from the Mexican army, which was equally intent upon regaining control of what the Mexicans had considered to be a rebellious province of their own:

> "Anti-American Mexicans viewed this as an act of war. Many Americans felt the same, seeing the move as a case of blatant aggression against a weaker nation, designed to satisfy the United States' lust for territory. Congressman Abraham Lincoln of Illinois was one of the most vocal critics of the war. Army Lieutenant Ulysses S. Grant, who would eventually command all Union armies in the Civil War, called the conflict in Mexico 'one of the most unjust ever waged by a stronger against a weaker nation.' " *(Waugh)*

CHAPTER TWO

Robinson's Report

IF NERVOUS BRITISH COLONIALS NEEDED ANY REMINDER OF US ambitions of continental hegemony, the Mexican War served the purpose fully. When the war ended after less than two years, the Americans had lost just 1,700 men, and won a territory that would become the states of Arizona, California, Nevada, New Mexico, Utah and a portion of Colorado.

By the time of Sir John Harvey's speech from the throne, Nova Scotia's roads were being improved at increased public expense, as the February 25th 1847 report from the Legislature made note of the resolution:

"that the sum of £30,000, granted for the service of Roads and Bridges, in the present year, be applied as follows:

For the County of Yarmouth	£1,500
For the County of Shelburne	£1,500
For the County of Digby	£1,500
For the County of Sydney	£1,500
For the County of Guysborough	£1,500
For the County of Queen's	£1,500
For the County of Richmond	£1,500
For the County of Halifax	£2,280
For the County of Hants	£2,100
For the County of Inverness	£2,070
For the County of Cape-Breton	£2,190
For the County of King's	£1,650
For the County of Pictou	£2,190
For the County of Colchester	£1,800
For the County of Cumberland	£1,800
For the County of Lunenburg	£1,860
For the County of Annapolis	£1,560"

These expenditures should be compared to the allocations made in 1839, and may provide a clue as to why Westminster would later drop the option of a military highway. Given the increased level of provincial investment in their own infrastructure, and the lessening of tensions with the United States, London was not inclined to pay from its coffers, when it appeared the provinces were able to finance such undertakings by themselves.

By this time, the military imperative for a railway may have also been less important in London. With the Ashburton treaty of 1842 having settled the boundary in the east, and the treaty of 1846 setting the 49th parallel as the boundary from the Rocky Mountains to the Pacific, the need for a railway was becoming obsolete in the minds of British politicians, who by now were pursuing a policy of fiscal frugality.

In 1849, Major Robinson offered an encouraging report on the line to the legislatures of Nova Scotia, New Brunswick and Canada, according to Tuttle:

> "It gave an enthusiastic estimate of the resources of the country, and of the importance of the railway for their development. Out of several routes explored, the preference was given to that by the cost of the gulf—the north shore—as the best for the purposes of military defence. The cost was calculated at £5,000,000 sterling. In anticipation of the immediate action of the Imperial government, Canada, Nova Scotia and New Brunswick voted aid to the extent of £6,000 a year, and ten miles of ungranted lands on each side of the railway."

Specifically, Major Robinson pointed to four observations in favour of the northerly route:

> "1st. The immediate prospect of direct, as well as the greatest amount of remuneration for the expenditure to be incurred; the opening up a large field for provincial improvements for the settlement of emigrants, and by affording the opportunity in addition to internal, of external communication, by means of the Gulf of St. Lawrence and the Bay of Chaleurs, it will tend to develop in the highest degree the commerce and the fisheries of the Province of New Brunswick.
>
> 2nd. Passing along the sea-coast for a great distance, and capable of being approached at several points by bays or navigable rivers, it possesses the greatest facilities for construction, tending to reduce the expense, and by its more favourable grades also the cost of working and subsequent maintenance.
>
> 3rd. By passing over a less elevated country, and at the least distance from the sea, there will be less interruption to be apprehended from climate, whilst the more favourable grade will increase the efficiency and rapidity of intercourse.

> 4th. Passing at the greatest possible distance from the United States, it possesses in the highest degree the advantage to be derived from that circumstance of security from attack in case of hostilities."

This fourth recommendation would become a focal point of controversy for the Intercolonial, with critics—most predominantly of the Liberal stripe—claiming it was an irrelevant consideration. As G. R. Stevens has noted, however, the same consideration pervaded political thinking when Liberal Prime Minister Sir Wilfrid Laurier was planning the route for his National Transcontinental line in 1901, more than 50 years later. Robinson's fourth reason in favour of the Chaleur route is the prime reason for his disqualification of the first route along the Saint John River through New Brunswick, which he envisaged utilizing a sea-link from Nova Scotia across the Bay of Fundy. It would become a bone of contention twenty years later:

> "The first route fails in the most essential object contemplated by the proposed railway, viz., a free and uninterrupted communication at all times and seasons of the year, from the port of arrival on the Atlantic terminus in Nova Scotia to Quebec.
>
> The intervention of the Bay of Fundy is fatal to this route.
>
> In summer the transshipment of passengers and goods to and fro would be attended with the greatest inconvenience—loss of time and additional expense; whilst in winter it would be even still more inconvenient, and liable to be interrupted by storms and the floating masses of ice which then occur in the bay.
>
> In the case of the conveyance of troops, transport of artillery and munitions of war, the crossing the bay would at any time be most objectionable, and if suddenly required in critical times might be attended with the worst consequences."

The Major does not elaborate on those consequences, whether the horrors are real or imagined he leaves to the reader, but he does make note of a further military concern:

> "Passing through New Brunswick and on the right bank of the St. John River, as it must necessarily do, to the Grand Falls, it would, for a considerable distance, both before and after the reaching that point, run along and close to the frontier of the United States.
>
> In case of war, therefore, or in times of internal commotion, when border quarrels or border sympathies are excited, this line, when most needed, would be the most sure to fail, for no measures could be taken which would at all times effectually guard it from an open enemy and from treacherous attacks.

The passage across the Bay of Fundy so close to the shores of Maine, would invite aggression, and require a large naval force for its protection,"

As he goes further into the reasons for his choice of the northern Gulf of St. Lawrence route, Robinson does a masterful selling job, drawing upon demographics and economics, immigration figures and shipping volumes that seem beyond the realm of expertise of a man used to dealing with elevations and volumes of rock and soil. The initial report is contained in Appendix One of this work, and a great deal of it is devoted to the economic benefits of a railway that are tantalizing to colonial politicians. The soldier in Major Robinson comes out, however, in this terse commentary:

"In a political and military point of view, the proposed railway must be regarded as becoming a work of necessity.

The increasing population and wealth of the United States, and the diffusion of railways over their territory, especially in the direction of the Canadian frontier, renders it absolutely necessary to counterbalance, by some corresponding means, their otherwise preponderating power.

Their railway communications will enable them to select their own time and their own points of attack, and will impose upon the British the necessity of being prepared at *all points* to meet them.

It is most essential, therefore, that the mother-country should be able to keep up her communications with the Canadas at all times and seasons. However powerful England may be at sea, no navy can save Canada from a land force.

Its conquest and annexation are freely spoken of in the United States, even on the floors of Congress.

Weakness invites aggression, and as the railway would be a lever of power by which Great Britain could bring her strength to bear in the contest, it is not improbable that its construction would be the means of preventing a war at some no distant period.

The expense of one year's war would pay for a railway two or three times over."

The Moncton *Times* of December 11th 1889 asserts that Robinson's evaluation of the route was later disparaged by a Captain Harness, who appears to have been only slightly senior to Robinson, but who had never served in North America.

At the time, Henry Drury Harness was secretary to the newly formed Railway Commission in England, and would serve in that post for four years until 1850. His expertise appears to be in road construction, since prior to joining the commission he was Inspector of Welsh Roads, but it is not clear if his objections noted by the *Times* were of a personal nature, or voiced on behalf of the Commission. There appears to be no written record of these objections extant. Harness was later knighted for his work in India, and retired with the rank of general. The newspaper's observation was not without editorial comment, as it outlined a brief history of the Intercolonial for its readers:

> "In May, 1850, Sir George Harvey, the Lieutenant Governor of Nova Scotia, made a proposition to Earl Grey, the Colonial Secretary, looking to a guarantee by the Imperial Government for the purpose of building the road. Earl Grey promptly replied that Her Majesty's Government were 'not prepared to submit to Parliament any measure for raising the funds necessary for the construction of the railway.' This was a sad blow to the hopes of Nova Scotia, and excited some astonishment. The adverse decision was generally supposed to have been due to the Report of an Engineer Officer, Captain Harness, addressed to the Colonial Secretary, hostile to the scheme of an Intercolonial Railway. It was naturally considered as singular by the people of the Colonies that the fine plan of national improvement designed by one Royal Engineer, after two years of examination and inquiry, should be so remorselessly scattered to the winds by another. They were unfamiliar then with the lively manner in which one engineer can rip up another's work and prove the absurdity of the most cherished scheme of a professional rival. Smiles' *Life of George Stephenson* did not then exist, so the colonists of 1850 may be excused for their ignorance of the ways of rival Engineers."

Robinson had more to contend with from John Wilkinson, a member of his own survey team who filed the third appendix to Robinson's report, on the exploration "of a favourable route between the valley of the Abawisquash, a branch of the Trois Pistoles, and a point on the Restigouche River." This was a portion of what would become known as the "Direct route."

Four years after the release of Robinson's report to the three legislative assemblies, Wilkinson wrote a letter to J. R. Partelowe, the Provincial Secretary of Canada (February 4th 1852) that appears to repudiate his own observations as well as the conclusions of Robinson.

The document didn't receive much attention until was published as a 38-page pamphlet by order of the House of Commons in 1868. It would seem this suited the political purpose of the opponents of the North Shore route favoured by Robinson.

In the letter, Wilkinson re-stated his claim, made in the appendix to Robinson's original document, that the country was not well explored because Robinson was determined to stay away from the US border. This appears to indicate the major went into the survey with a preconceived idea—or orders—about the route.

Wilkinson's appendix notes the difficulties presented to his team by inclement weather, and some of the terrain, but in the 1852 letter he claims his survey was shortened because Robinson withdrew half of the survey party and withheld the barometers necessary to determine the elevations and grades precisely.

He refers to this incident, albeit obliquely, in his appendix when he noted:

> "In the absence of barometers, by which to obtain an approximate section of the routes, as far as traced, the apparent difficult inclinations were occasionally tested by angles of elevation and depression; and from these checked by the approximately known height of several points in the country examined, the assumed rates of inclination have been inferred. They would in most instances, I believe, prove to exceed what in actual construction would be necessary."

As a result, Wilkinson claimed, there was a spread of terrain some seventy miles long that did not get explored properly, of which Robinson made no mention in his report, and that a pass through the Tobique range was indeed possible. He went on to insinuate that Robinson deliberately misrepresented the grades south of the Miramichi area to be more favourable for a railway line than they actually were.

Wilkinson also questions Robinson's conclusion regarding the cost of transportation between Halifax and Levis, which Robinson calculated "on good authority" as being 11 shillings per ton. He claimed Robinson's "authority" was the British commission on railway gauge, and that the comparisons were being made with specific and incomparable railways. Wilkinson produced his own table of expenditures on five US railways showing that in order to make a profit on the Halifax–Quebec line, the rate of motive power must not be doubled, as Robinson had suggested, but multiplied eight to 30 times. He set the real rate at £3, 19 shillings and four pence per ton.

For his part, Robinson called Wilkinson's claims on the gradients "absurd," and that his exploration actually took place thirty to forty miles west of the officially sanctioned "Direct Route."

The claims were made amid a rancorous exchange between the two engineers, each questioning the other's professional abilities, but strangely the Wilkinson document never got much press attention in New Brunswick, where opponents of the North Shore route might have made political hay with it.

Be that as it may, there were others willing to argue against the military merits of the Northern route, albeit some twenty years after Robinson offered his assessment.

Writing in the Woodstock *Carleton Sentinel* of May 18th 1867, a correspondent who signed himself "Carleton" noted:

> "The nearness to the frontier is only in degree for any of the projected routes, as the forces of an enemy from Fort Kent, near the Northwest angle of New Brunswick, unless strongly masked, could send raiding parties to cut our communication with the province of Quebec in winter. Recent experience has shown that a Railway, such as the Intercolonial, along a frontier is invaluable for the quick transmission of tropes to threatened points..."

Writing to the new minister of public works William MacDougall, in August of 1867, and published in the *New Brunswick Reporter*, Joseph Wilson Lawrence of Saint John offered objections to the northern route on military grounds:

> "In 1848, Major Robinson recommended the Northern route on Military grounds, since then from the revolution in naval armament, its claim has entirely disappeared. Then it would have been comparatively safe from attack from the water, now, from gunboats, steam frigates, and armour plated ships, for seven months of the year it would be exposed to the enemy.
>
> Treaties and Orders in Council since then have thrown open the waters of the gulf and bay to the world.
>
> There are no grounds for alarm from our American neighbours, their commercial and other interests are so much in common with ours, and like ours all on the side of peace, and should any disturbing element arise, it will be disposed of in the future as in the past, by the pen and not the sword.
>
> One thing is certain, should the time ever come when the American Government wished to intercept communications by destroying a portion of the Intercolonial, distance will not defeat the purpose.
>
> Better then accept the situation, and build the line on a commercial basis, knowing that as military work, should war occur, it would be in danger wherever placed. If constructed as a military road it would invite attack. While as a commercial enterprise, its peaceful mission would be its shield."

These rather weak arguments were intended to support Saint John's claim to be the natural terminus of the railway, and conveniently overlooked Saint John's vulnerability to American attack, whereas the northern route would delay, if not deter direct attack. Lawrence went on to bolster his argument:

> "Halifax, the military and naval head-quarters should prefer the Western route, as it would pass through or connect with all the military centres

of the Dominion. It would connect in one chain the military and political capitals of Toronto, Quebec, Fredericton and Halifax, as well as the military centres of Saint John and Montreal."

Lawrence then went on to propose Halifax could still be connected by way of the Annapolis Valley and a ferry across the Bay of Fundy to Saint John, ignoring the solid reasons offered by Robinson for disqualifying that option. Both opinions were shots fired in the war of words that would erupt over the choice of the railway's route after Confederation.

The Toronto *Globe* took an opposite view to the notion that a railway's commercial intent would spare it from military aggression, when it noted in October of 1868:

"In regard to the military question we are of those who believe that in case of war with the States, it is the Grand Trunk road through Maine which must be defended, not the Intercolonial. If we could not defend the one, we should speedily lose the other."

The *Globe* went on to criticize the Duke of Buckingham, then Secretary of State for the Colonies, for what it felt was an acquiescence to the wishes of the government in Ottawa.

"But we take the Duke of Buckingham on his own ground. He rejects all commercial considerations. Military ideas alone are of importance. Why does he reject the central route then? It is on the safe side of the St. John. What objection is there to it? His Grace does not give any. He makes a jump from the American frontier and lands in the mild and soothing waters of the Bay of Chaleur. Does he mean that our defenders, in the case of war, are to abandon all of New Brunswick up to the coast line, congratulating themselves that they have a real genuine military road by which they can reach their shipping and get off safe to England?"

Upon the change of government in England in 1869—and the replacement of Buckingham as colonial secretary—the *Globe* found more ammunition to fire at the railway's military considerations:

"The Colonial Minister who wrote the convenient despatch in favour of a military railway is Colonial Minister no more. With the change of Government, moreover, some military notions have gone out. Next to the disestablishment of the Irish Church, the great feature in the policy of the new English Ministry is retrenchment, and especially retrenchment in military and naval expenditure. It would be the height of absurdity for Messrs. Gladstone, Bright and Howe, and their colleagues—while cutting down Imperial appropriations for purpose of defence, and recalling the troops from the Colonies—to insist upon holding us to a needless expenditure of many millions on the false pretence that it will serve a military object."

These arguments, however, are presented ahead of history. Major Robinson's report was accepted by the Nova Scotia House of Assembly and quickly passed third reading on March 30th 1849. In the address to the Queen that followed, the Legislature noted Nova Scotians had already agreed to give the right of way to the railway:

" …a very strong feeling in favor of the work prevails among the great body of people—that in consequence of an official Circular lately issued, meetings have been held in the various Settlements situate along the Line in this Province, at which resolutions were passed as embodied in petitions, numerously and respectably signed and presented to this House, pledging the proprietors of the land thereof which the line would penetrate, to give a breadth free of expense."

The province, for its part, promised a free right of way, and an annual contribution of £20,000 toward payment of the interest on the capital cost of construction, one-fifth of which was to come from the citizens of Halifax. As a final note, the assembly pointed out:

"The projected railway will furnish a safe military road throughout the centre of British America, open a boundless track of fertile soil for colonization, facilitate the transport of your Majesty's Mails and Troops, and will create a new intercourse from Western America and the Lakes through the Saint Lawrence to Halifax, a port surpassed by none on the Continent of America."

This was not, however, a unanimous opinion. Twenty-seven members voted in favour of the address, thirteen voted against it. In spite of the offer of free land and money that would otherwise have to come from Imperial coffers if a macadamized road was to be built, it was also dawning on London that colonial railway schemes were becoming too extensive, and expensive, for the British treasury to bear. With that in mind, on July 31th 1852, a convention was held in Portland, Maine, at the behest of American financier John Poor, calling for a railway to link Halifax and Saint John with Bangor, Maine and the US railroads there. This gave rise to the European and North American Railway, which ultimately failed to come to fruition in the magnitude first envisioned by the private speculators, again because of Howe, who was opposed to the notion that a railway passing through British territory was to be controlled by Americans.

Howe instead took a letter of introduction from Harvey to Sir Edward Grey, Secretary of State for the Colonies (and father of a future Governor-General of Canada), seeking to build a railway with provincial credit guaranteed by the Imperial government. In order to demonstrate this could be done, Howe took a proposal that the province of Nova Scotia build a railway from Halifax to Windsor, with a loan of £8,000 from Westminster.

That particular venture was denied Imperial funding, but Howe was encouraged to address the proposal for the Intercolonial Railway and the potential it held for immigration. Tuttle describes the situation:

> "Mr. Howe set himself rigorously to work at his task, and by his letters to Earl Grey and his speeches in England, created so favourable an impression of the resources of Nova Scotia, that Mr. Hawes, under-secretary of state, wrote him, under date 10th March 1851, that the imperial government would guarantee the road, provided the three provinces could agree amongst themselves on a road to extend from Halifax to Quebec or Montreal, and no objection would be made to this road connecting with the European and North American so as to give access to the American railway system. A meeting of delegates from the three provinces was proposed by Earl Grey, and was held at Toronto, on 21st June 1851. After some discussion it was agreed that a line from Halifax to Quebec should be undertaken on joint account by the three provinces, they to grant five miles of crown lands on each side of the track, and the receipts to be common property until the cost of construction was paid, after which each province was to own the portion of the road running through it."

At that point, the project ran into unexpected trouble:

> "It was expressly stipulated by New Brunswick that aid should be given to the European and North American Railway, and Nova Scotia in a fit of generosity, offered to build thirty miles of the road for New Brunswick, so that it seemed as if the Intercolonial was in a fair way to be started at once. But it was not so: Earl Grey, in a despatch dated 27th November, 1851, informed the governor of New Brunswick that Mr. Howe had misinterpreted the letter of Mr. Hawes, and that it was not the intention of the British government to help the European and North American Railway at all. Still the New Brunswick men did not want the whole scheme to fall through, and offered to go on with the Intercolonial, provided the valley of the St. John route was chosen; but the Nova Scotia men refused, demanding the North Shore line or nothing." *(Tuttle)*

Howe has borne much of the blame for the misinterpretation of Hawes' letter, but it was an honest misunderstanding, as Henry Youle Hind interprets the events in his 1863 work *Eighty Years' Progress*:

> "It was stipulated that the line should pass wholly through British territory, and should be approved by the imperial government; but it was not required that it should necessarily be the one recommended by Major Robinson and Captain Henderson.
>
> In announcing this decision to the delegates, the under secretary wrote, that 'Her Majesty's Government would by no means object to its forming a part of the plan which may be determined on, that it should include a provision for establishing communication between the projected railway and the railways of the United States.' "

The blame for the ambiguity clearly rests with Hawes, but the colonial delegates all understood that the way was open for a Halifax–Boston railway in addition to a Halifax–Quebec line. It was left to Earl Grey to resolve the misunderstanding, which he did in a November 27th despatch, as Hind notes:

> "Earl Grey explained that the passage which had led the Nova Scotia delegate astray, only meant that the imperial government would sanction, not aid, the Southern, or European and North American lines, through New Brunswick—which he was quite aware, was preferred by that province to the Northern, or Quebec and Halifax line."

Meeting again in Halifax in January of 1852, the delegates were prepared to hire Jackson & Co. to build the line for a payment of £90,000 a year for twenty years and grants of 5,000,000 acres of crown land. The proposal was declined, this time by Grey's successor, as Hind notes:

> "The Canadian delegate proceeded to London in advance of his colleagues, where he found Earl Grey out of office, and Sir John Packington as his successor. Sir John, on May 20, 1852, notified him that as all previous negotiations had been based on Major Robinson's line, or something near it, the route by the valley of the St. John was out of the question; and as the delegates were authorized to treat only for the latter, he must terminate the question by declining, &c."

Compounding the problem was the lack of agreement between the provinces, upon which the Imperial government had insisted. The Intercolonial was still very much alive when a deputation to solicit Imperial aid again sallied forth to London:

> "It was soon discovered however, that the provinces were not working heartily together. The Nova Scotia delegates did not join those of

Canada and New Brunswick, and the representatives of these two provinces, Messrs. Hicks and Chandler, were left to make what arrangements they could. After an irritating delay the delegates were informed that the British government would not give any aid to a road through the valley of the St. John." *(Tuttle)*

Hind offers a harsh analysis of the otherwise farcical series of miscommunication and misunderstanding:

"Viewing the question as an imperial as well as an intercolonial one, it is evident that the first blunder committed by the colonies was in agreeing to pay the whole expense of a railway survey which was to be made solely under imperial and military control. They thereby, at the outset, assented to the position that the imperial government had no substantial interest in the question, and at the same time they failed to ascertain the facilities for other routes, if such exist, than those recommended. Without impugning the ability of the royal engineers who conducted the exploration, there is little doubt that a more satisfactory survey could have been made by civil engineers, accustomed to similar surveys in the forests of this continent; and the want of some reliable knowledge of the practicality of other lines besides that recommended by Major Robinson, has been a stumbling block in the way of every subsequent movement down to the present hour."

Hind appears to have been the only person to make the comparison between the abilities of engineers to distinguish between military and commercial objectives, and he had an equally harsh evaluation of the Imperial government's role:

"It must also be admitted that the mother country drove a hard bargain with her offspring. Her own colonial secretary, Lord Glenelg, suggested the communication to her own high commissioner, Lord Durham, not as a military road solely, but as a political measure. When the colonies took up the idea, the mother country steadily refused all aid except that which, as had been proved to her in the case of Canada, was but nominal; while she exacted for this nominal aid sacrifices from the colonies which were real and important. She would not build the road, nor aid in building it, because it would not pay; and she would not permit the colonies to build it where they believed it would pay, at least, its working expenses. She had already guaranteed a loan for the cost of the canals of Canada, which were constructed wholly on commercial principles, and with the route of which she did not interfere, though military considerations were wholly disregarded in the case of the Beauharnois Canal. She acknowledged an imperial interest to which she attached but a nominal value; she felt for the colonies, but would not feel in her pockets for them."

Hind was contradicted in his own work, however, by civilian engineer Thomas Coltrin Keefer, who noted in his essay on travel and transportation in the Canadas:

"It has long been demonstrated, that what is called the narrow or Stephenson gauge, of four feet eight and one-half inches, is wide enough for all practical purposes; and that any increased width is an unnecessary expense in first cost, and an increase of dead weight, and of resistance at curves in working.

In case of invasion, however, there would be this advantage in the Canadian gauge, that on all approaches—excepting that from Portland—the enemy must relay to his own gauge nearly the whole of our railways, before his own rolling stock could be used—unless indeed we should so blunder as to let ours fall into his hands."

New Brunswick eventually made its own disastrous deal with Jackson & Co., while Nova Scotia, again at Howe's insistence, determined to build its own railway as a public work, and with great success. Clearly, as far as the British government was concerned, there was still a military imperative to the Intercolonial and its secure route, if Westminster was expected to share in the cost.

Oddly, one of the first objections raised toward the creation of the Nova Scotia Railway came from the military establishment in Halifax, concerned that a portion of land in the city known as the Ordnance Corner, and a section closer to Sackville, which held a guard house intended to prevent deserters from leaving the area, would be lost to them.

Howe formulated a compromise in 1855, with the assistance of Lieutenant-Governor John Gaspard LeMarchant, that overcame the objections, and attempted to bolster his cause with a bold boast:

"The railroads now in course of construction will enable us to concentrate, upon either points of attack, the physical force of three or four counties in a comparatively short space of time. A forced march from Halifax to Windsor, or from Windsor to Halifax, 45 miles, could not be accomplished in less than two days. A regiment of troops, or of militia, could be taken through in either direction in an hour or two by train, and in a single day men enough could be drawn out of the county of Hants to man and guard the citadel and forts which command and protect the Dockyard and military arsenals at Halifax. When the Eastern line is completed, 30,000 men, drawn from the counties of Hants, Halifax,

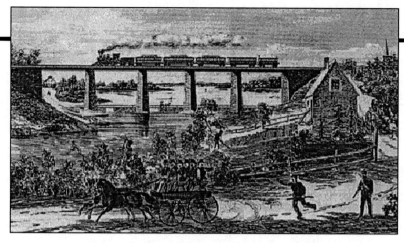

Nova Scotia militia men depart from the 8:30 am train from Halifax for the Bedford rifle range, six miles from the city, in this 1871 drawing by Russell Edward John (1832-1906) for the **Canadian Illustrated News.** *One of their members appears to have missed his ride! The range and the railway bridge are still in use.*

(*National Archives Canada #2280*)

Colchester and Pictou, could be concentrated in a week wherever their services might be most required."

This would prove to be an impossible promise. LeMarchant's successor, Constantine Henry Philips, the Earl of Mulgrave, writing in January of 1859, the year after the railway officially opened, notified Westminster that Nova Scotia's militia force was a shambles. He made no bones about his view of the cause:

" The difficulty… which exists in a country like this, where labour is scarce and wages are high, is so to arrange the Militia as to ensure its efficient training without rendering the service obnoxious to the people, or interfering to an injurious extent with the commercial and agricultural pursuits of the province, which could not fail to be the case were the Militia called out even for three days' training in the year, under the old system."

There was another problem, however, one that led Philips to suggest creating a volunteer force:

"The finances of this province are unfortunately so heavily taxed at the present moment, on account of the railway operations now in progress, that it would be utterly impossible for the Government to bring forward any measure that would require large expenditure."

Philips' concern was for the security of the Pictou County and Cape Breton coal mines, which supplied the Royal Navy's steamers in the north Atlantic with coal. Writing again to Downing Street in June of the same year, he noted:

"In the event of any hostile movement in this neighbourhood, there is little doubt that these mines would be the first object of attack, on account of the injury which their destruction would inflict upon the British navy, and I am therefore anxious to secure as large a local force in those districts as possible."

Philips was successful. The General Mining Association, operators of both mines, responded by supplying uniforms for 170 men at Sydney, and 120 at the Albion Mines in Pictou County. These men needed weapons, however, and Philips practically begged the new colonial secretary, the Duke of Newcastle, for arms, even if they were out of date.

Newcastle responded by providing 3,000 Enfield rifles that were in storage at Montreal and Quebec, but even this bounty would have left one rifle to every ten of the men promised by Howe in 1855.

Several factors now combined to put the Intercolonial Railway on a political backburner. Each of the three provinces were more immediately concerned with their own railway ventures; The Grand Trunk in Canada, the European & North American in New Brunswick, and the Nova Scotia Railway in that province. On June 5th 1854, Canada's Governor-General Lord Elgin signed the Reciprocity Treaty with American Secretary of State W. L Marcy:

"This treaty was to continue in force ten years, after which it could be terminated by either party on giving one year's notice. Under the provisions the produce of the sea, the soil and the forest could be exchanged between the United States and the British possessions duty free; the Americans were allowed to fish in the waters of Nova Scotia and New Brunswick, and to use the Canadian canals on the same terms as Canadian vessels. The treaty was very acceptable to Upper Canada, but caused considerable excitement in Nova Scotia, where it was denounced as unjust to the province, the imperial parliament having given away her right in the fisheries without consulting the wishes of the people or securing them any adequate equivalent." (Tuttle)

A week later, on June 13th 1854, Nova Scotia's new Lieutenant Governor (Harvey having died suddenly) LeMarchant turned the first sod at Governor's Farm in the Halifax district of Richmond to commence construction of Howe's Nova Scotia Railway. Howe had resigned as provincial secretary in order to become chairman of the bi-partisan board of railway commissioners overseeing the construction. The Nova Scotia government's intention was made clear by Howe's successor, William Young:

> "Mr. Young, in a letter to his constituents of Inverness, laid down the railway policy of the new government to be, a trunk line from Halifax to Pictou, one westward to Windsor and through the eastern countries to Digby, connecting Halifax with the Basin of Minas, and a line from Truro to the New Brunswick frontier, to connect with any Inter-colonial line which might be built." *(Tuttle)*

The creation of the Nova Scotia Railway was an important step forward in policy, in that it ran contrary to the US and British practice of encouraging private capital to undertake such enormous costs. Howe had never left any doubt about the role his railway would play:

> "We may be told that the railroads are not matters in which government should interfere. I differ entirely with those who entertain such an opinion, and I do not hesitate to propound it as one of the guiding principles of policy which shall run through the whole course of my after life, that I shall, while in any government, press them to take the initiative in such works as this. It is the first duty of a government to take the front rank in every noble enterprise; to be in advance of the social, political, and industrial energies, which they have undertaken to lead. There are things they should not touch or attempt to control; but the great highways—the channels of intercommunication between large and wealthy sections of the country—should claim their especial consideration...."
> *(March 25th 1850 resolution pledging provincial money for construction of the Halifax–Windsor railway.)*

As if to recognize the military importance of a railway, the Nova Scotia Railway carried militia members free of charge, usually in the summer training months when the province's citizen-soldiers attended camps that involved a few weeks of drill, weapons training and some manual labour fixing roads and building earthworks.

Still, the military aspects of the road were not held in great regard by some politicians, as Martin Wilkins indicated in his February 28th 1859 address to the Legislature of Nova Scotia, calling for the extension of the provincial railway from Truro to his constituents in Pictou:

> "I think it must be plain to every man of reflection that there is only one way in which it is possible that the intercolonial railway can be constructed, and that is as a great national work at the expense and cost of the British exchequer. But, sir, before the British Government would

venture on a work that will cost four or five millions, it must be made to appear to be of really national importance that it should be constructed—her Majesty's ministers have too much good sense not to perceive that its advantages, in a national point of view, are insignificant in the extreme. The road could be of no real service in time of war, for a few Yankees and Indians could cross over the line and burn and destroy as much of the road in one night, as could be repaired in one year. All the munitions of war can be carried through Pictou by the Gulf to Quebec in summer. If the Americans were foolish enough to attempt an invasion, which would at any time blow up the flames of a civil war among the States of the Union, they would not make the attempt in winter, unless they wanted their army to freeze to death like that which invaded Moscow, and left their bones bleaching on the inhospitable plains of Russia.

England well knows that she need have no apprehension of a loss of these colonies, at the hands of foreign invaders. So long as she retains the warm affections of her colonial subjects, no enemy can wrest us from her dominion. The armed stranger may try the experiment of invasion, but his army, if not repulsed, as it assuredly would be, by the strong arms of the militia, would but occupy the ground on which it stood."

One of the first major movements of troops over a British North American railway occurred on the Nova Scotia Railway in August of 1860, when the Prince of Wales (the future King Edward VII) travelled from Halifax to Windsor, and from Windsor to Truro on a return trip. Provincial militiamen provided the trappings of pageantry for the affair, reported by the *NovaScotian*:

"On Thursday morning at 4 o'clock, a special train with 132 men of the Volunteer Rifles, and 60 men and 6 guns of the Volunteer Artillery, left Richmond for Windsor. At half-past 6 a.m., a pilot engine, with Inspector Marshall, left Richmond, calling at the principal stations, and leaving the time of her departure.

At a little before 7 a.m., a Guard of Honor, composed of the Mayflower and Chebucto Greys, under the command of Captain Chearnley, formed at the south end of the Station, lining the approach to the Prince's Car which was tastefully decorated. On the front of the engine was a shield with the Prince's Coat of Arms, beautifully painted by Mr. Jones, and on each of the cars a Prince's Feather tastefully ornamented with artificial flowers."

This grand occasion was not without its controversy, especially when Howe's political rivals began using their newspapers to criticize the accommodation of the soldiers, who did not enjoy first class carriage. The *NovaScotian* retorted:

"We shall not stoop to combat these untruthful charges. That many of the Volunteers were of necessity compelled to travel in the second class cars, every person knows; and nobody more certainly than the Volunteers themselves, are aware that, if they traveled by rail at such a time, this was absolutely unavoidable. There are but ten first class carriages on both lines. One of these was fitted up, as we all know, for the Prince and suite, and could be used for no other purpose. Nine first class divided up, make three for Windsor, three for Truro, and three for Richmond—their utmost capacity being accommodation for sixty passengers each—one hundred and eighty for the three. Over two hundred Volunteers were detailed for Windsor, besides rifles, sidearms, and field pieces. Over three hundred, some how or other, got there, and got back, all in one train. Upwards of two hundred were sent to Truro. A first class [car] in every case was provided for the officers, the men occupying the remainder of it. The Volunteers passed up and down at public expense, and during one whole week, from the time the Prince came till after his departure, the lines, as everybody knows, were traveled and crowded with people of rank and fashion—females and children constituting a large proportion of the passengers.

Now, would it have been right or seemly to have given up the three first class cars to the Volunteers, which, as we have shown, had it been done, would not have sufficed, and to have thrust men, women and children promiscuously—parties traveling at private expense—not to speak of the Legislature, the Executive Government, Executive Committee, and heads of departments—into the second class cars? We know the Volunteers better than to believe that they desired or expected anything of the kind. Besides, it is very well known that, here and elsewhere, when the regulars travel by rail, they invariably travel second class."

Even though political circumstances kept Howe on the sidelines for most of the ensuing campaign leading to Confederation, the Intercolonial Railway was conceived—if not operated—on the same lofty principles as his provincial line. It may well also have been intended to run on the frugal guidelines laid out for the Nova Scotia Railway, where expenditure was limited by statute, and the contract tendering policy was conducted in full public view. The concept was reported by J. and E. Trout in 1871:

"In the Province of Nova Scotia the construction of railways was first authorized by an Act of the Legislature, passed 31st March, 1854. During the same year another Act of that body authorized the issue of Provincial six per cent debentures, having twenty years to run, in order to raise the necessary capital to proceed with the work of construction determined upon. These bonds were mostly sold in London, through Messrs. Baring Bros. & Co.; the Hon. Joseph Howe having been sent thither as a delegate with that object in view; a small amount found purchasers in the Province. It was provided that the proposed railway should be constructed under the supervision of one or more Commissioners, who were empowered to draw on the Receiver-General for the monies disbursed to the contractors. They were restricted to the expenditure of £800,000 in any one year, beyond which amount they could not incur any liabilities.....

The total cost of the Railway, with equipment to 30th June 1868, was $6,699,647.69; and the total amount expended on construction account alone up to the 30th June, 1869, was $6,781,254.50."

This expenditure would greatly reduce the eventual actual cost of the Intercolonial. Much of this was lost, however, amid the public's attention to the Crimean War, which threatened a military disaster for Great Britain, until a railway's true military value became apparent.

The war (1854-56) had its roots in the decision by Czar Nicholas I to proclaim himself the protector of Christians living under the Ottoman Emperor, the Sultan of Turkey (then about three-fifths the population of European Turkey), albeit a ruse to take control of the port of Constantinople, which controlled the passage from Russian waters in the Black Sea to the Mediterranean.

The Turks repulsed Russian attacks at Varna (in what is now Bulgaria) and the French and English immediately committed troops in support of the Sultan. The decision was made to carry the fight to Russian soil, and attack the Czar's Black Sea naval port at Sebastopol. So it was that Britain's Lord Raglan and the French commander General Canrobert landed in the late summer of 1854.

Raglan has since earned himself the title of being one of Britain's greatest military buffoons, for under his command—despite winning the famous battles of Inkerman, Alma and Balaklava—a series of logistical disasters and dithering took place that decimated his forces at the hands of disease and a relentless Russian winter, and provoked horror in England as the events were duly reported by an almost unrestricted press.

It was on the basis of the dismal reports to London that MP Samuel Morton Peto (a partner in the firm of Peto, Jackson, Brassey & Betts, which had offered to build the Intercolonial, and which was building the Grand Trunk Railway) went to the government and broached the idea of a railway to support Raglan's siege of Sevastopol.

Brian Cooke, in *The Grand Crimean Central Railway: The railway that won a war*, suggests this was not entirely a patriotic undertaking:

"One cannot help feeling that the predominant factor in making his suggestion was nothing more than the sheer, almost gleeful, self-confidence shared by many railwaymen at the time, that almost any problem could be solved by the building of a suitable railway in the right place at the right time."

Whatever his motive, Peto's method saved British honour, if not its army, from certain disaster, as Cooke has so brilliantly documented. Military men were quick to learn the lesson:

"No relief that could be named will be equal to the relief afforded by a railway. Without a railway I do not see how we can bring up guns and ammunition in sufficient quantities to silence the guns of the enemy."
—Col. Gordon before Sebastopol, January 1855.

It should be noted, however, that the success of the Crimean railway was not due to the military involvement, but to an army of patriotic and pugnacious navvies, recruited by Peto's partner, the dynamic Edward Betts, as Terry Coleman notes:

"On 30 November (1854) Edward Betts... wrote to (Secretary of State for War) Newcastle saying they proposed to send 200-250 platelayers, navvies, and miners, ten gangers, twenty rough masons or bricklayers, eighty carpenters with three foremen, twenty blacksmiths and foremen, ten enginemen and fitters, four timekeepers, one chief clerk, one draftsman, two practical assistant engineers, and one chief engineer. He also stipulated that this force must come under the direct superintendence of the contractors' engineer. The men were civilians; they were not to be subject to military law, and were to be known as the Civil Engineer Corps.... Many of those engaged had already served for a while in Canada, on the Grand Trunk, as had Beattie, who was to be chief engineer of the Crimea Railway."

Beattie was James Beatty, Peto's right-hand man on the survey for the European and North American line in Nova Scotia and New Brunswick, and the Grand Trunk in Upper Canada. While he was not a military man by nature or training, Beatty was well aware of the military implications of the Crimean line. Joe Howe and his Nova Scotia colleagues were certainly aware of the early military importance of railways. The rabidly pro-British *NovaScotian* rarely let any development from the Crimea go unnoticed, as evidenced by this report in the edition of May 28th 1855:

The camp railway

"The line commences from both sides of the harbour and proceeds direct up the valley to Kadikoi, where it turns sharp to the west round the foot of the hill on which is placed the sailor's—or four gun— battery, and through the French camp, thence along the side of the hill to the top of the plateau and about half a mile from headquarters, the line then diverges to the north, and proceeds direct to the Woronzoff Road; this is about seven miles from Balaklava. There is also a branch about one mile long, to accomodate the Third and Fourth divisions and last seige train. The railway daily takes up about 12 tons supply of provisions, consisting of biscuit, salt, meat, groceries, corn, hay and food to the front. To the 23rd ult. it had taken up as nearly as can be determined, 1,000 tons of shell and shot, 300 tons of small arms, 3,600 tons of commisariat stores (fuel and forage), besides 1,000 tons of miscellaneous—vz. guns, platforms, Quartermaster general's stores etc. The railway was commenced on the 8th of February by the navvies; it conveyed commissariat stores to Kadikoi on the 23rd and on the 26th of March; it conveyed shot and shell to the summit of headquarters, 4 1/2 miles from Balaklava; which with the Diamond wharf branch and the double line from Balaklava to Kadikoi, means upward of seven miles of railway was laid down in less than seven weeks."

Ironically, as the *Synoptical History of Canadian National Railways* (published in 1962) recounts, it was the Crimean War, and the depression in its wake, that brought the European and North American line from Shediac to Saint John into the Intercolonial fold:

"On September 29, 1852, a contract was entered into between the Province of New Brunswick, the European and North American Railway Company and the firm of Peto, Betts, Jackson and Brassey for the construction of a railway from the boundary of the State of Maine to the Boundary of the Province of Nova Scotia. The Government of Nova Scotia organized surveys from Halifax to the New Brunswick Boundary.

Construction was started in 1853 but owing to financial difficulties the contractors had to suspend operations in 1854, and construction work was held up until July 6, 1856, when the New Brunswick Government purchased the railway from the contractors and renewed construction."

Those financial difficulties stemmed from Peto, Betts, Jackson and Brassey's deep involvement in the construction of the Crimean railway, but the war's influence did not end there:

General George Brinton McClellan. An observer in the Crimea, and a railroad executive in civilian life, he advocated early use of railroads to speed troop deployment.
(Library of Congress)

"In 1856 the European and North American Railway Company in New Brunswick was dissolved because of financial difficulties owing to money stringency which occurred as a repercussion of the Crimean War. The Government of New Brunswick purchased from the contractors such portions of the railway as had been completed and went ahead with the completion of the railway between Rothesay and Moncton. The last link of this section, Sussex to Moncton, was finished on August 1, 1860, and the line from Saint John to the harbour of Shediac was finally opened for traffic on that date."

The military lessons of the Crimean War were not lost on the Americans. The British use of a railway in logistical support of combat arms was keenly observed by a young West Point-trained engineer, a US army staff officer despatched by Washington, George B. McClellan. Finding himself in charge of the Union army early in the American Civil War, he made immediate use of the railway infrastructure available.

Amid the backdrop of the Crimean War, which brought an economic depression with it, the North American colonies nurtured the prospect of a railway to unify them. Perhaps as result of the success of the Crimean railway, the Intercolonial's military application took on a new meaning that was quite apparent to Nova Scotia's delegation to London in 1858.

Attorney General James W. Johnston and Adams G. Archibald represented Nova Scotia as the colonies again attempted to secure Imperial financial backing. In their letter to the Secretary of State for the Colonies, the two men noted:

"In case of hostilities with the United States, the facility which such a Railroad from Halifax through British Territory would afford for the transport of troops and munitions of war would be of incalculable advantage; and, in a mere financial point of view, would probably, in a few months, repay all that the Government might have contributed. In connection with large steamers on the ocean, enabling the Government to transport in a few weeks, on any threatened emergency, an Army to any point of Her Majesty's North American possessions, it would render unnecessary the constant maintenance of a large military force within them."

This was certainly what the powers in Westminster had wanted to hear from colonies that had for so long appeared to have taken the cost of their protection for granted. Indeed, Johnston and Archibald held the hope that the mere existence of a railway would dissuade the Americans from venturing north at all:

"Nor is it the least of the advantages that would result from the facility, that the knowledge of its existence would tend to avert hostilities that otherwise might grow out of a sense of comparative impunity, attendant on aggressive movements. Not less than seventeen lines of American Railroads lead through the United States to the borders of Canada, and give the means of rapid hostile approach—not a single line of British Railroad connects the Provinces together, or affords communication from the Atlantic shore through national territory. Of the three routes by which Canada is reached, viz., by the St. Lawrence, by lines of Railroad that traverse the United States, and through the wilderness, the latter would alone be available for the transportation of troops or munitions of war, in the case of hostilities or threatened at the beginning of winter.

On such an event, the spectacle might be presented, of a large and prominent Colonial possession of the Empire, assailed by a superior force and cut off—except at great exposure, expense and delay,—from effectual aid, not only from the Parent State, but from the adjoining Colonies.

None more than the inhabitants of Nova Scotia, appreciate the advantages of peaceful relations with the United States. They, however, who are placed in close proximity, are less credulous than others may be, as to the impossibility of hostilities between the two Powers. And yet it is apparent to all, that the foreign relations of no government are so subject, as those of the United States, to the influence of popular impulse or of party interests. This consideration, illustrated as it recently was by the enlistment dispute, sufficiently indicates that a policy founded on an assumed impossibility, or high improbability, of hostilities with that people, must be deficient in the forecast that seeks, by timely and suitable preparation, to prevent aggression, or successfully repel it."

Yet the Nova Scotians saw the dual possibility of the railway:

"The great work we advocate is as necessary to enable Her Majesty's North American Colonies to promote their mutual progress in peace, as it is requisite for their common defence in war."

The report won the approval of Nova Scotia Lieutenant Governor Sir John Gaspard LeMarchant, himself a military man, who wrote to the Secretary of State for the Colonies that he was:

"Deeply impressed with the importance of inter-communication by Railroad between the Colonies of Canada, New Brunswick, and Nova Scotia, both to the Imperial Government and these Colonies, calculated to draw more closely the bonds of union between the latter and the Parent State, and to afford security to the Colonial Possessions in the event of war..."

The governments of Canada and New Brunswick sent supporting delegations, but it should be noted, in fairness to New Brunswick, the concept of a railway as a military necessity was not raised. This may have been the attitude that spurred the comments by Johnston and Archibald about those who doubted the possibility of war with the United States, but it may also explain New Brunswick's position when the topic of the route to be taken by the railway became public debate fifteen years later.

What New Brunswick subscribed to at the time, according to the delegates' address to Lieutenant Governor J. Manners Sutton, was:

"To the three Provinces such a Railway would be of highest importance as a means of developing their resources, promoting their material interests, and strengthening that mutual sympathy and unity of interest and feeling so essential to secure for them that commercial and political position to which they are entitled from their situation and resources."

The New Brunswick delegation continued to promote the line through Saint John, the centre of the colony's commerce, and any notion of a military undertaking appears to have been studiously avoided.

The folly of such deliberate ignorance was made clear to both the British North Americans and the US during the French Emperor Napoleon III's Italian Campaign of 1859, when the lethal potential of railways as a military tool was made apparent. The radical effect of railways on military command and control has been described by Richard Brooks:

> "Strategically, the French victory owed much to their efficient use of the railway network in the south of France and northern Italy. This allowed them to concentrate their forces rapidly, and then to steal a march on their Austrian opponents with the first operational manoeuvre to depend for its success not on soldiers' legs but on machine power. Tactically the French found a distinctive solution to the problem of increasingly lethal 'arms of precision.' Exploiting the mobility and aggression of their infantry, the French gave the rifle and spade no chance to establish the tactical stranglehold that would characterize such battles as Fredericksburg or Cold Harbour."

The architect of the French success was Marshal Francois de Certain-Canrobert, commander of the French III Corps, and a veteran of the Crimean campaign. He also demonstrated the defensive effectiveness of rail-borne troops, as Brooks describes:

> "Canrobert objected to the Piedmontese plans to defend their capital of Turin directly, along the Dora Baltea line. Instead, he proposed an indirect defense, moving four of the five Piedmontese divisions south, by rail, to the fortification around Alessandria and the Po bridgehead at Casale. There, they threatened (the Austrian general) Gyulai's lines of communication if he persisted with his advance on Turin and could expect to hold out until joined by French troops from Genoa."

Brooks suggests this war was significant in that both sides made use of railways for the first time (contrary to claims by US historians that this occurred during their Civil War.) While the Austrians did use railways to move soldiers, their command structure was still locked in a pre-Crimean mentality, and had much more limited access to railways.

CHAPTER THREE
Of Unions and War

Secession first
he would put down
Wholly and forever,
And afterwards
from Britain's crown
He Canada would sever.

Yankee marching song
sung to the tune of "Yankee Doodle"
1861

Writing in *Railway Economics*, his landmark examination of the financial operation of railways in Europe and America in 1850, Dionysius Lardner held on to lofty ideals for the future:

> "After having for ages approached each other only for war, peoples will henceforward visit each other for purposes of amity and intelligence, and old antipathies, national and political, which have so long divided and ruined neighboring states, will speedily vanish.
>
> But if, in spite of this general tendency toward pacific progress and peace, war should occasionally break out, the improved means of intercommunication will aid in bringing it to a prompt close. A single battle will decide the fate of a country, and the longest war will be probably circumscribed within a few months."

Future events would show how false that hope was.

The American Civil War brought home to British North America just how costly years of delay and procrastination in defence matters could be. Despite the intervening years of relative peace between the two sides, the rapid secession of states following South Carolina in December of 1860 showed how fragile

---

international relationships can become when domestic peace is shattered on one side or the other, as Robinson had warned in his report. G. R. Stevens recounts:

> "...in the wake of President Lincoln's call to arms, there was a good deal of loose talk in northern newspapers about the attitude of Great Britain and the vulnerability of her North American provinces. Many of the London banks and merchant houses had old soldiers on their boards who pricked up their ears, sniffing battle from afar. During the summer of 1861 there was much coming and going across the North Atlantic. By autumn the situation had developed sufficiently to warrant yet another conference on North American communication.
>
> On September 30th fifteen delegates from the three provinces assembled at Quebec. There it was decided to re-submit the Galt-Tupper offer of the previous year (a guarantee of one half the interest) to the Imperial government, which would be allowed to choose the route of the railway.
>
> For the first time, therefore, the provinces had reached the degree of unanimity postulated in the Imperial offer of 1851."

Joseph Howe led a three-man delegation to London to restate their case, and did so with great force, according to Sandford Fleming, noting:

> "Their frontier was unprotected and exposed to the concentration of hostile troops at the termini of seven railways of the United States. A hundred thousand men, they said, could be sent across the frontier with more ease than a single battery of artillery could be transported from England or a single barrel of flour carried to the seaboard."

In his memorandum of the visit, written in February of 1863, Howe makes note of the Treasury Board minutes of the agreement, which state categorically:

> "The money to be applied to the completion of a railway connecting Halifax with Quebec, on a line to be approved by the Imperial Government."

This point appears to have been lost upon the Canadian and New Brunswick delegates in the squabble that erupted later. In the meantime, what may have most alarmed the Canadian colonies was how the Union states could have construed Britain's May 13th 1861 declaration of neutrality in the war as an act of aggression against the North.

That one act appears to have set the tone for Anglo–US relations throughout the war, exacerbated by a series of events beyond the control of the British colonies, compelling them to pursue a union based as much on long-neglected defence issues as it was on politically-desirable economic terms.

John Slidell, seized from the British mail steamer Trent, *steered Alexander Keith's guns to his compatriots in the Confederacy.*
(Library of Congress)

The first of these incidents was the November 8th 1861 *Trent* affair, when British neutrality was thrown into question by the arrest of Confederate diplomats James M. Mason and John Slidell, by Captain Charles Wilkes of the *USS San Jacinto*. The two men were bound for England and France when Wilkes learned of the voyage while in a Cuban port, and he acted without consulting his government. Wilkes was determined to intercept the British mail packet *Trent* on the high seas and remove the two men.

Shots were fired across *Trent's* bow and the ship was boarded. After a bit of a scuffle, the two men were forcibly removed. *Trent* sailed on to Southampton to report the incident to the British government, while Wilkes made for Boston with his prisoners. In light of the declaration of neutrality six months before, the captain of the *San Jacinto* had openly committed an act of war, but he naturally found sympathy in the Union.

While northerners saw it as a bold slap in the face to an old rival, the South saw it as an indication they might have allies on the other side of the Atlantic, and that position was reinforced December 3rd 1861, when Britain sent 10,500 reinforcements to Canada in a deployment that matched the mobilization of the Crimean War in its urgency. The greater portion of the contingent was obliged to use New Brunswick's overland route, as C. P. Stacey describes:

> "A desperate attempt was made to get those destined for Canada up the St. Lawrence before the ice closed it; but this failed, and in the early weeks of 1862 the largest military force ever to use the old overland route was passing over it in sleighs. Nearly 7,000 men with 18 guns were thus sent into Canada at this time."

US Secretary of State William Seward, who arranged the purchase of Alaska from the Russians, was quite prepared to use force against Canada. He believed that war with Britain would unite the divided union. (Library of Congress)

Certainly there was no inclination on the British side to take the matter lightly:

> " 'I don't know whether you are going to stand for them,' (British Prime Minister) Palmerston shouted as he hurled his hat on the table, 'but I'll be damned if I do.' On both sides of the Atlantic, war fever surged. Canada would be the battlefield." *(Morton)*

Britain demanded the release of the two men December 23rd 1861, and the demand was promptly met December 26th.

> "In Washington, (Secretary of State) Seward made a grudging apology for the *Trent* affair and ostentatiously invited the British troops to land at Portland Maine, to take the British-owned Grand Trunk Railway to Canada. The British, equally stubborn, insisted on despatching over seven thousand men by the winter trail through New Brunswick." *(Morton)*

Seward's hubris was widely reported, as Andrew Wellard notes in his April 2000 article in the magazine *Crossfire*:

> "William Russell (the famous war correspondent) attended a ball in Washington on December 16 1861. He recorded in his diary, 'I met Mr. Seward at the ball... and as he was in very good humour, and was inclined to talk. He pointed out to... all who were inclined to listen, and myself, how terrible the effects of a war would be... 'We will wrap the whole world in flames!' he exclaimed. 'No power so remote that she will

not feel the fire of our battle and be burned by our conflagration.' It is inferred that Mr. Seward means to show fight. One of the guests, however, said to me, 'That's all bugaboo talk. When Seward talks that way, he means to break down.' "

There was no war, thanks to the calming efforts of Abraham Lincoln on Seward, and Queen Victoria's consort, Prince Albert, on Palmerstone, but that did not stop the British military from evaluating their options for the defence of Canada, a situation that was considered expensive (£2 million for defence works), labour intensive (150,000 regular troops) and all but impossible given the legislature of Canada's rejection of a bill to raise and equip its own militia force. (Nova Scotia responded to the threat by enrolling 59,379 militiamen, and training 45,600 of them for immediate service.)

Nevertheless, the British took the threats seriously, as Wellard has noted:

"As of 1st December 1861 there were four battalions of British regular infantry, three batteries of artillery and just six Royal Engineers in Canada. There was also the thousand-odd men of the Royal Canadian Rifle Corps (including a hundred who garrisoned Fort Garry in the far west) and approximately two thousand regulars in New Brunswick and Newfoundland. Although these may not have seemed much to oppose the might of the Army of the Potomac (or rather that part of it General McClellan could have been persuaded to spare) they represented a bigger garrison than Canada normally boasted.

As a self governing colony, Canada had assumed the main responsibility for its own defence, but the outbreak of the American Civil War had persuaded Britain to more than double the metropolitan troops there during the summer of 1861. Backing up these regulars was a rather greater number of militia of variable fighting value. The 'Active' militia had been limited to 5000 men in 1855 out of deference to Canadian taxpayers. These were reasonably trained and equipped with Enfield rifles. There were also a number of enthusiastic but very inexperienced volunteers such as the Civil Service Rifle Corps formed in October just before the crisis. Finally there was the Sedentary Militia of whom 38,000 were eventually called out, of whom perhaps double that number might have been available if an invasion had actually taken place. The following may show something of their quality. They 'showed up in all manner of dress, with belts of basswood and sprigs of green balsam in their hats, carrying an assortment of shotguns, rifles and scythes.' "

The reinforcement of these troops did not proceed without incident other than the weather:

"In total 16 batteries of artillery (mostly equipped with breach-loading Armstrong guns), 11 battalions of infantry (including two of Guards) and 4 companies of Royal Engineers were sent out. With those from the Maritimes over 17,000 regulars were added to the garrison of Canada in a space of less than three months. Despite the general efficiency of the operation there were some semi-farcical incidents such as elements of the commissariat corps having to disembark at Boston and travel north in civilian clothes." *(Wellard)*

The man sent to command the British troops was Major General Charles Hastings Doyle. Born in London, he studied in Sandhurst and saw army service in the East and West Indies, rising to eventually become the Inspector-General of the militia in Ireland. He was well aware of, and had no doubts about, the military importance of the railway.

In an October 16th 1862 letter to the Duke of Newcastle, Doyle noted:

"So much has already been written and said upon the subject of the very great importance of this line of Railroad, and being fully aware of the favorable opinion entertained by Your Grace with reference to it, I feel I should only intrude upon your time if I was to enter generally upon the whole question; but I trust I may be excused in bringing to your notice the very essential benefit in a military point of view, which would be derived from its construction.

I would take leave to bring to Your Grace's recollection the very great difficulty and enormous expense which was incurred in December last, when I was called upon to pass a force, consisting of upwards of ten thousand men, through the Province of New Brunswick, along the frontier of the State of Maine, into Canada, which, owing to a combination of favorable circumstances, but which in time of war, could scarcely be accomplished at all, and certainly not without great loss of life.

Although, in the event of any rupture between Great Britain and the United States, the Metis Road is being prepared for the purpose of enabling troops to proceed to Canada during the winter, out of the reach of any hostile force, it must be borne in mind that the risk of passing large bodies of men over it during an inclement season, would, as in the former case, be considerable, the delay unavoidably great, and the expense enormous; whereas if railway communications were once established, both troops and munitions of war could at all times be rapidly and safely transported to Canada, and mutual military operations would thereby be vastly facilitated.

Under all these circumstance, the great advantages which would be derived from a Railway such as is in contemplation (provided the site be judiciously selected), cannot, in my opinion, be overestimated."

Later knighted for his services, Hastings Doyle would go on to serve as the Lieutenant Governor of Nova Scotia from 1867 to 1873.

Among the measures taken by the British was the appointment of railway engineer Alexander Luders Light, as George Rose's *Cyclopedia of Canadian Biography* notes:

"During the affair of the *Trent*, Mr. Light was chosen by the Horse Guards and War Office to accompany the Imperial troops; and in the event of war he was designated for other service in North America."

Light was a British-born, Canadian-educated engineer (a classmate of Prime Minister Sir John A. Macdonald at the Royal Grammar School in Kingston), who was no stranger to military life. His father was Colonel Alexander Whalley Light, a former commander of the 25th Regiment, the King's Own Borderers, and who had served with Sir Ralph Abercrombie, Sir Eyre Coote, the Duke of York and the Duke of Wellington.

It was to have been Light's task to assist the British troops in any movement to meet the invading Americans, and evidently to oversee the construction of any necessary transportation routes, most likely by way of the Grand Trunk Railway in Upper Canada. A veteran of railway construction in Canada and Brazil (he had been chief engineer of the European and North American Railway), Light would be appointed in 1869 to oversee the construction of the Intercolonial's Miramichi district, perhaps the most difficult section of the line.

Lincoln may well have set the tone for his foreign policy during the *Trent* Affair with his wry observation to Seward that the US could afford only "one war at a time." He expressed the sentiment more definitively when he met with a group of concerned Canadians, as recorded on the National Library of Canada's web site:

"When Newton Wolverton, born at Wolverton, Ontario, was 15 years old and working as a teamster in Washington, he presented a petition for peace to President Lincoln from a committee of Canadians at the time of the Trent affair. President Lincoln said to him: "Mr. Wolverton, I want you to go back to your boys and tell them that... as long as Abraham Lincoln is President, the United States of America will not declare war on Great Britain."

During Lincoln's second inaugural address of March 4th 1865, he pledged the nation to pursue a policy:

Ontario-born Newton Wolverton sought peace from Abraham Lincoln, then joined Lincoln's army to fight the South. An accomplished marksman who returned to Ontario to fight the Fenians, he became a prominent church leader.

(Lois Darroch Fonds #F 4354-4-0-26
Archives of Ontario)

"with malice toward none; with charity for all... let us strive on to finish the work we are in... to do all which may achieve and cherish a just, and lasting peace, among ourselves, and with all nations."

Within weeks of that speech, Abraham Lincoln was dead.

The Union, however, would have cause of its own to doubt British neutrality, when it protested the July 1862 launching of the Confederate raider *CSS Alabama* from a Liverpool shipyard, armed and ready for action intercepting merchant ships in the waters around Britain.

Canada was in turn left in doubt about any friendly Union intentions when notice was served March 17th 1863, that the Reciprocity Treaty (so reviled by Nova Scotia) would be abrogated. Canada's new government quickly enacted a new militia bill, but the crisis would pass before that force became any semblance of an effective defence against Union aggression.

The Union had reason to be suspicious of North American colonials. While Canadian colonials grumbled that their defence was predicated upon squabbles initiated by the failure of British diplomacy, they were more than capable of creating their own causes for war. Union army code breakers were all too aware of the activities of Southern sympathizers like Halifax's Alexander Keith, who routinely smuggled firearms to the South, and hosted visits from "Crimps," Southern recruiters who bribed, kidnapped or otherwise lured colonial soldiers to their cause.

In December of 1863, for example, the Union's top code breakers worked on a letter intercepted by postal censors and addressed to Keith in Halifax. Michael Antonucci describes the message thus:

Alexander Keith, the Nova Scotia beer baron, supplied weapons to the Confederates, and in doing so, risked dragging the British North American colonies into a war with the Union.

(Nova Scotia Archives and Records Management Services)

"Willis is here. The two steamers will leave here about Christmas. Lamar and Bowers left here via Bermuda two weeks ago. 12,000 rifled muskets came duly to hand and were shipped to Halifax as instructed. We will be able to seize the other two steamers as per programme. Trowbridge has followed the President's orders. We will have Briggs under arrest before this reaches you; cost $2,000. We want some money; how shall we draw? Bills are forwarded to Slidell and rec'ts rec'd. Write as before."

The name of Slidell, mentioned in connection with the *Trent* affair, is particularly interesting. Clearly Keith, known to the Union as a Confederate sympathizer, was deeply involved in an activity that was, for a British colonist, illegal in his own country, and dangerously close to giving the Union reason to widen the scope of their hostilities.

It has generally been supposed this Alexander Keith was the beer baron of Nova Scotia, a man who was no social lightweight. He had migrated to Halifax from his native Scotland in 1817, to become sole brewer and business manager for Charles Boggs. By 1820, he owned the brewery.

In 1843 he was elected as Halifax's third mayor, a position to which he would succeed more than once, as the result of his personal popularity, and that of his beer. He became a widely respected philanthropist, involved in several charitable and cultural societies. In 1869, he was unanimously elected Grand Master of the Masonic Lodge of Nova Scotia.

Lately there has been an attempt to rehabilitate Keith's reputation, with claims that the Keith in question was his nephew, and that there were no fewer than six Alexander Keiths living in Halifax at the time! (See *Alexander Keith*, by Peter L. McCreath, Four East Publications, Tantallon, Nova Scotia 2001). The *MacAlpine's Directory for the City of Halifax* dated 1869, however, lists only one Alexander Keith; beer baron.

The man in question, however, had to be one of substantial wealth in order to afford the ships and capital to supply weapons in such quantity.

Keith's contribution cannot be understated, or lightly dismissed. The rifled musket was state-of-the art weaponry at the time, and its importance has been described by Lance Herdegen of Carroll College's Institute of Civil War Studies:

> "The technology did not increase the rate of fire by individual soldiers (about two or three shots per minute) and, in fact, there was a drawback. If a soldier under ideal conditions was able to hit a man-sized target at 500 yards, the lobbing arc of the "Minnie-ball" (as it was called by the soldiers) was about 12 feet above the point of aim at mid-range. That made it easy to over or under shoot a target at the longer distances. Even clear-eyed marksmen would find it difficult to consistently strike a moving line of infantry at distances of more than 300 yards.
>
> The tragic significance of the rifle-musket came at ranges under 200 yards—it was there the massed fire knocked apart battle lines with brutal efficiency. The point-blank killing range became 150 yards (not 50 yards) and all the previous experiences of officers and the training of soldiers was based on the shorter distances of the smoothbores.
>
> This was especially critical to a regiment or brigade making an assault on earthworks where the defenders could simply shoot them down at longer distances while taking limited casualties. It also meant a smaller number of soldiers could hold an entrenched position against a larger force.
>
> It was a technical advantage Confederate Robert E. Lee would use with telling ability in the closing months of the war."

In the same year that Keith was aiding the Confederates, and in the midst of the wariness of a spreading conflagration, Henry Youle Hind was raising his own doubts about the military efficacy of the Intercolonial Railway:

> "The provinces will, doubtless, build the road, at their own expense, on whatever route the mother country wishes it built, if solicited to do so by her—the loans being guaranteed, so that the money can be raised on terms not oppressive—because there will then be an implied pledge on the part of the empire, that if built as a military work, it will be used as such whenever occasion may require. In other respects its value to Canada will be more political and commercial than military, because, unless extended, with the same avoidance of the frontier, far beyond

Quebec, it will be of little value in the defence of the province at large. Though it might bring men and munitions of war without interruption (except from snow) to Quebec, a fortress which does not require this protection, these could not reach Montreal or Western Canada by rail, unless the Grand Trunk Railway were maintained for a distance of nearly 400 miles between St. Hyacinthe and Toronto, every portion of which, except, perhaps a mile on the Island of Montreal, would be exposed to a sudden raid of a superior force."

By the time of the Union victory at Gettysburg, July 1st to 3rd 1863, both sides in the Civil War had demonstrated the effectiveness and vulnerability of railroads as a means of conducting war. Although the Union held a distinct advantage in the amount of mileage and number of locomotives and rolling stock available to move troops quickly from battlefield to battlefield, both sides proved equally adept at destroying railway connections.

One of the first of the Union's military planners to realize the strategic importance of railways was General George B. McClellan, a witness to events in the Crimean campaign (with Philip St. George Cooke, also later a Union general):

" ...himself a former railroad man... McClellan proposed in November 1861 a combined Army-Navy campaign to capture key Southern seaports and to drive inland, wrecking enemy rail systems. McClellan rightly termed the Southern railroads 'the nervous subsystem of the Confederate armies' and held that the Southern armies would be severely curtailed if not completely starved through the loss of their railroads." *(Rogge)*

McClellan was abetted by the Union's true railroad general, D.C. McCallum, whose contribution was recorded by the Chicago *Tribune* of Tuesday, October 9th 1866:

"On the 11th of February, 1862, the Secretary of War appointed D.C. McCallum, 'Military Director and Superintendent of Railroads in the United States, with authority to enter upon, take possession of, hold and use all locomotives, equipments, appendages and appurtenances that may be required for the transport of troops, arms, ammunition, and military supplies of the United States.'

Government was at that time running a railroad seven miles long from Washington to Alexandria. Commencing with this light duty, General McCallum organized the largest railroad system in the world, and held it till the war was over, purchasing, or capturing four hundred and nineteen locomotives, and six thousand three hundred and thirty cars."

General William Sooy Smith.
His soldiers became masters at
wrecking enemy railroad lines.
(Library of Congress)

As soon as the railroad became an acknowledged military asset, its use by the enemy became an equally important military threat, and both sides were quick to respond. Union General William Sherman later took up McClellan's doctrine as he marched through the south, and the extent of the devastation his men would wreak can be seen in this description of Major General William Sooy Smith's heavy cavalry operation in Mississippi in 1864:

> "Sherman had thoroughly discussed with Smith his role in the upcoming campaign, and on January 27, he had left Smith detailed written instructions. Sherman believed Smith's cavalry to be 'superior and better in all respects than the combined cavalry which the enemy had in all the State of Mississippi.' The union cavalry did, in fact, outnumber and outgun its opponents. What it lacked was the bold, aggressive tactics of (Nathan Bedford) Forrest, who had recently been given command of the defence of northern Mississippi." *(Rogge)*

Forrest had 2,000 horsemen under his command, and was to engage Smith's 7,000 well-equipped and better-trained, heavily-armed riders.

> "Smith's troopers tore up tracks for miles along the M&O line before being set upon by Forrest's yelling cavalry at West Point, Miss., 100 miles north of Meridian... Smith's losses were slight, 188 dead, wounded or missing, but his defeat was total. Sherman never forgave him, although Smith claimed credit for the destruction of 2 million bushels of corn ('corn' included all types of grain), 2,000 bales of cotton and 30 miles of M&O track and bridges." *(Rogge)*

A typical method of firing enemy rails: heating them on burning ties, then later bending the soft iron around tree trunks.
(Library of Congress)

Smith was undoubtedly the right man for the job. A graduate of West Point in 1853, he left the army in 1854 to pursue a career as a railroad engineer. Perhaps it was his experience in destroying Southern railway bridges that led him into his post-war career as an expert in bridge construction.

The common methods employed for railway sabotage were to burn bridges and their wooden abutments, and to rip up track in large sections, separating the rail to be heated over burning ties and bent against trees, making them useless for replacement by enemy engineering battalions.

This kind of work was undertaken by fast-moving cavalry in advance of the infantry, or by the infantrymen themselves, who seized upon railroad track and bridges as targets of opportunity.

Once a territory was firmly under Union control, the army's railway service set to work repairing the damage done by its own soldiers, and putting troop trains into service to support the Union advance deeper into the South.

Such would have been the American strategy in Canada had war indeed broken out after 1866. This practice alone made sense of Major Robinson's recommendation to keep the Intercolonial Railway as far from the border of any potential enemy as was possible.

Moreover, the Americans would prove to be willing students, learning from the errors made by the British, who had been slow to adapt railway technology in the Crimea, as Aaron Klein notes:

Union soldiers tear out a section of enemy track in typical fashion. The speed with which these troops could move made railways vulnerable to numerous attacks.

(*Library of Congress*)

"When Union General William Rosecrans was put under siege at Chattanooga, he appealed for reinforcements. The closest available troops, some 16,000 men, were near Washington, more than 1000 miles away. According to military thinking of the time, at least three months would be required to move the troops. The chief of the Army Telegraph Corps, who had railroad experience, suggested that the men could be moved by railroad in about two weeks. Disbelieving generals were opposed to even trying, even though Rosecrans had been attacked by troops deployed quickly by rail. The doubting generals were overruled by Secretary of War Stanton, and President Lincoln, who ordered the movement. By the time the deployment started, the troops had increased to 25,000 men. The troops and their equipment, including several batteries of artillery, were transported from Virginia to Tennessee in less than 11 days."

While the railways' logistical capability was of prime importance to both sides, it was not limited to the role of merely moving troops and munitions, as Alan Koenig notes in his article on the *Historynet* web site maintained by Cowles Magazines:

General Herman Haupt, the organizational genius behind the Union's military railroad policy. He was as adept at rebuilding railway lines as Smith was at destroying them.
(Library of Congress)

"While armies campaigned, locomotives and rolling stock provided logistical support, and some also performed tactical missions. These missions included close combat, especially when the situation was fluid or when the railroad provided a convenient avenue of approach to an opponent.

In such situations, commanders sometimes sent locomotives to reconnoiter the terrain and gain information on enemy troop dispositions. While this may seem like a risky venture, gathering information was often worth the risk, a lone locomotives could quickly reverse direction and move as fast as 60 mph, far faster than pursuing cavalry. With such great mobility, locomotives were also useful as courier vehicles when commanders had to rush vital intelligence to headquarters. This communications service was an important advantage in a war where raiders frequently cut or tapped telegraph lines."

Of equal importance was the Union army's ability to repair a wrecked railway and use it to strategic advantage, spearheaded by the ingenuity of US Military Railroad administrator General Herman Haupt, another railway engineer seconded into wartime service:

"Of General Herman Haupt, who was put in charge of military railroad construction and repair in the eastern war theatre, President Lincoln commented, '...That man Haupt has built a bridge across Potomac Creek about 400 feet long and nearly 100 feet high, over which loaded trains are running every hour, and... there is nothing in it but beanpoles and cornstalks.' The bridge had been constructed in less than two weeks with inexperienced labor. When it had to be destroyed because of Union setbacks, it was rebuilt—three times." *(Klein)*

Haupt did not work alone. The coordination of civilian railway operations and telegraph services was overseen by US Assistant Secretary of War, Thomas Scott. The operational differences between the combatants in the Civil War has been concisely evaluated by Martyn Witt on his internet page:

"Perhaps the greatest single lesson to be drawn from the role of military railways in the Civil War was the need to establish a clear and authoritative command structure at the appropriate level. First, rail tends to become a strategic asset and so needs to be managed at the highest level of command. Secondly, it has its own operational requirements, which are both technical in nature and not necessarily always in synchronization with the military imperative. It is more than coincidence that the outcome of the Civil War paralleled the way in which the two sides reconciled the command and control issue.

The Confederate philosophy enshrined freedom from Government direction and so ironically it prevented the South from establishing firm and effective control of rail: there were constant conflicts of interest between railway operators and local military commanders, and only in the last days of the War did the Southern Congress grant real powers to the government. On numerous occasions, army officers refused to release motive power or rolling stock; railroad operators frequently put profit before patriotism. Thus despite being the innovators—with the first genuine military railway on the continent (Manassas–Centreville 1861-62), the first to deploy ambulance cars and rail-mounted artillery—the South was never able fully to make use of its vast railway resources.

The Federal side, on the other hand, passed an Act of Congress in 1862, and appointed a Director of Military Railroads, Daniel C. McCallum. The USMR operated its own purpose-built military railways out of Alexandria (near Washington) and lines captured from the enemy. The US Secretary of War came down hard on military officers who failed to release stock or whose local decisions had a detrimental effect on overall railway efficiency, and to a great extent, the acceptance by the Federal military of the primacy of the railway management in operating matters was a lesson carefully noted by the Prussian government."

From a Canadian perspective then, the decision to build the Intercolonial as a military project under government control made eminent sense. What British colonials lacked, however, was the expertise to run a military railway. It should

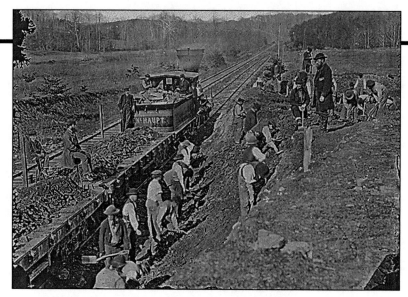

Union Army corps of engineers repair damage to a railroad cutting. General Herman Haupt, Chief of Construction and Transportation, US Military Railroads, is standing on the bank supervising the work. The "General Haupt," the locomotive pulling the train in the photograph, was named in Haupt's honour. Photographed by Captain Andrew J. Russell.

(Library of Congress)

be borne in mind that throughout the course of the Civil War, US President Abraham Lincoln had no fewer than 35 generals on whom he could count for first-hand expertise in railway matters. This staff included generals with pre-war experience in civilian railroad management, surveying and construction; three veterans (two French, one Russian) of the Crimean War; an American who had served with the French Emperor in his Italian campaign; and six former soldiers of the Prussian Army who were quite familiar with the art of moving troops by train.

In contrast, Confederate President Jefferson Davis could count on only twelve generals with such experience (two Crimean veterans among them).

The British army was certainly as keenly aware of the tactical importance of the railway. As Edwin Pratt notes in his 1915 work, *The Rise of Rail Power*, these issues had been addressed as early as December of 1859:

> "While it was evident that the railways could be efficiently worked only by their own officers, it was no less obvious that plans for the movement of large bodies of men, and especially of troops, with horses,

guns, ammunition and stores, should be well considered and prepared long beforehand, and not left for the occasion or the emergency when the need for them would arise.

In the next place it was suggested that the engineering talent of the country should be made available for the purpose of supplementing the services of the Royal Engineers in carrying out various defensive works, such as the destruction of railway lines, bridges and roads, the throwing up of earthworks, or the flooding of the lowland districts, with a view to resisting the advance of a possible invader."

In order to carry out these tasks, the Royal Engineers established the Engineer and Railway Staff Corps. By 1867, the corps of volunteer engineers numbered 6,580. This expertise would have been made available to Canada if necessary.

A few Canadian railways quickly mirrored American practices. The Grand Trunk Railway had its own Brigade Engineer Company, and a Railway Regiment listed on the militia roll in 1866 (the regiment would be listed again in 1881), while the Ottawa and Prescott Railway listed a rifle company. Even Nova Scotia's six-mile Albion Mines Rail Road had, in 1860, mustered its own infantry and band, which welcomed the Prince of Wales when he visited Pictou in that year.

As with military units established in the US by various railroads, the main purpose of these units was to protect the track from sabotage, quickly repair damage to the right of way, or install new track where it might be necessary for logistical support.

Adding to the alarm of the colonials was the strength of the US army after the war; General Ulysses S. Grant took command of a million-strong army on March 9th 1864. But that million-man complement, though it rolled off the tongues and pens of scaremongers, served only to feed Canadian paranoia, as Paul T. Scheips explains in *Daylight and Darkness*:

"The military might of the Union was put on display late in May 1865 when Meade's and Sherman's armies participated in a grand review in Washington, Sherman's army alone taking six and one-half hours to pass the reviewing stand on Pennsylvania Avenue. It was a spectacle well calculated to impress on Confederate and foreign leaders alike that only a strong government could field such a powerful force."

This display, however, was only so much "smoke and mirrors":

"The military might in being in May 1865 was ephemeral, for the volunteers wanted to go home and Congress wanted to decrease the size of the Army. Because of the needs of occupation in the South and the French threat in Mexico, demobilization was spread over a period of eighteen months instead of the three in which it could have been accomplished. Nevertheless, it was rapid. On May 1, 1865, there were 1,034,064 volunteers in the Army, but by November 15, 800,963 of them had been paid, mustered out, and transported to their home states by the Quartermaster Corps. A year later there were only 11,043 volunteers left in the service, most of whom were United States Colored Troops. These were almost all mustered out by late October 1867."

There is no doubt though that, even drastically scaled down after the Civil War, the US forces far out-numbered Canadian strength:

"General Grant, the General in Chief, wanted to increase the Regular Army, kept small during the Civil War, to 80,000 men, but neither Secretary Stanton nor Congress would agree. Congress, on July 28, 1866, voted an establishment of 54,302 officers and enlisted men. Actual strength reached about 57,000 on September 30, 1867, a peak for the whole period down to 1898.

In 1869 Congress cut the number of infantry regiments to 25 and the authorized strength to 45,000; in 1876 the regimental tables of organization were reduced so as to limit the total authorized force to 27,442, an authorization that remained virtually stationary until the Spanish-American War."

If the notion of a growing Union army was not alarming enough to Canadians, the report of Lieutenant-Colonel William Jervois must surely have been. The military engineer's assessment was considered at the September 1st 1864 closed-door sessions of the Charlottetown Conference.

"As befitted an engineer, Jervois' report called for massive fortifications and the abandonment of hopeless outworks. In the tradition of Carleton, Prevost and Carmichael Smyth, Jervois appealed for earth-work defences at Montreal, but it was Quebec, the ultimate citadel for a British army that needed the most massive works. Whatever its military realism, Jervois' analysis destroyed any basis for Confederation. It demanded too much from Britain, already more preoccupied with Prussia than with the United States." *(Morton)*

Specifically, Jervois' report addressed twenty-six questions posed by William McDougall, the provincial secretary for Canada, regarding action to be taken should war between Great Britain and the United States become a serious threat to the interior colonies. He predicated his plan of defence on the assumption that the US would attack in overwhelming force, making use of their railways to speedily advance:

"The enemy's principal base of operations would no doubt be at Albany, a central point where there is an arsenal from whence his expeditions may be supplied, and to which there is access by the Hudson River for large steamers from New York, and by road and railway from all quarters....

In connexion [sic] with the main direct operation from Lake Champlain against Lower Canada, he would almost probably send a large corps by railway either from Albany or Rouse's Point, or from both of these places..."

Jervois' system of stone fortresses and temporary earthworks would provide points to which the Canadians could fall back and, if the seasons were favourable, wait out the winter:

"It should be borne in mind that a large force can only move and keep the field for about five months in the year, viz., from about the middle of May to the middle of October; during the latter part of October to the middle of December, the communications would be more or less difficult, according to the amount of rain or snow which falls; between the middle of December and the end of March, the intense cold forbids an army encamping, and the deep snows prevent the movement of troops except on beaten tracks, on which they could show no front, and numbers would consequently be of no use; from the beginning of April to about the middle of May the state of the road owing to the thaw of the winter snows, is such that many are impassable for an army."

This logic echoed the Russian strategy that had worked so well in defeating Napoleon as he advanced on Moscow in 1812; Russians were confident "General Winter" would come to their aid. Jervois avoids, or ignores, the fact that railways, by their very construction, changed the dynamics of winter travel, especially for large groups, be they armies of soldiers or civilian passengers.

Jervois noted, however, that there was a need to keep a "moveable" force of soldiers in reserve, but oddly, he discounts the value of the railways for military purposes, even though he began his report by acknowledging the American alacrity to use their railways:

"With respect to land communication above Montreal, the Grand Trunk Railway, after leaving Vaudreuil, passes along the left bank of the St. Lawrence, close to the river, and subsequently close along the northern shore of Lake Ontario; consequently no sure reliance could be placed on it as a means of communication in times of war."

He then focuses upon the use of the military roads through New Brunswick:

"As regards the power of communication between Great Britain and Canada in time of war during the winter season, when the St. Lawrence is closed, the route from St. John, New Brunswick, through Fredericton, and thence by Grand Falls &c., usually called the Temiscouata route, runs for the most part so close to the boundary of the States, that after the commencement of hostilities it is exposed to be cut off; but the route from Halifax through Nova Scotia, and along the eastern shore of New Brunswick, commonly called the Metapediac route, which is 75 miles shorter, would afford access to Canada during that period, and, except the part where it runs along the southern shore of the St. Lawrence (where owing to the nature and position of the country in the adjacent part of the States it is scarcely liable to attack) at such a distance from the frontier that it would not be liable to interruption by the enemy— unless he had previously obtained possession of the harbour of St. John. Troops would however, take about three weeks to proceed by it from Halifax to Quebec; and it would be of advantage, in a military point of view, to have a more rapid means of sending reinforcements by land than this road would afford."

Having apparently set the ground for the vindication of Robinson's argument for the Intercolonial's route, Jervois goes on to say:

"The Intercolonial Railway from Halifax to Quebec, which has been proposed to follow nearly the line of the Metapediac road, would supply such rapid communication. But, if the works of defence recommended in this paper were constructed, the necessity for such rapidity of communication by land would be greatly diminished, for the enemy would be forced to accomplish a successful siege before he could gain any advantage of moment; and in a short time the St. Lawrence would be open for the passage of reinforcements to Quebec."

This apparent contradiction may underscore a schism that existed within the Corps of Royal Engineers long after the Crimean campaign had proved the efficacy of railway logistics. Cooke illustrates one aspect of the opposing attitudes:

"After the building of the railway had actually begun, Col. Henry Clifford VC was to write: 'For my part, I wish they would make us a good road, for I have little faith in the railway.' Though this was a personal view it is probably typical of the whole Army, both the fighting members and Sir John Burgoyne's Corps of Engineers. They had little faith in railways because they knew nothing about them."

As Robinson and Yule demonstrated, however, this was untrue. The views of Clifford and Jervois may be more representative of the old-style senior officers whose intractability created many of the problems that dogged the Crimean campaign, while the new generation of young officers was represented by engineers, like Major William Robinson, who surveyed railways in British North America and India.

The British military was indeed aware of the important potential of railway transportation, as Pratt noted in *The Rise of Rail Power*:

> "In the Railway Regulation Act, 1842 (5 and 6 Vict., c.55,) entitled 'An Act for the better Regulation of Railways and for the Conveyance of Troops,' it was provided by section 20:
>
> Whenever it shall be necessary to move any of the officers or soldiers of her Majesty's forces of the line... by any railway, the directors shall permit them, with baggage, stores, cars, ammunition and other necessaries and things, to be conveyed at the usual hours starting at such prices or upon such conditions as may be contracted for between the Secretary at War and such railway companies on the production of a route or order signed by the proper authorities.
>
> This was the first provision made in the United Kingdom in respect to the conveyance of troops by rail. It was succeeded in 1844 by another Act (7 and 8 Vict., c.85,) by which (sec. 12) railway companies were required to provide conveyance for the transport of troops at fares not exceeding a scale given in the Act, and maximum fares were prescribed in regard to public baggage, stores, ammunition, (with certain exceptions, applying to gunpowder and explosives) and other military necessaries. In 1867 these provisions were extended to the Army reserve."

Indeed, Sir John Burgoyne (perhaps by then a late convert to the railway cause) presented a paper entitled *"Railways at War"* to the British Association in 1865, and the government continued to refine its policy toward military use of the railways right up to the outbreak of the First World War. There is no doubt most of these policies, where they affected military operations, would have been put to use in Canada. What made the Intercolonial so attractive to Westminster was the unsolicited offer by the colonies to waive any fares for the conveyance of troops in British North America.

Whether the topic of a military railway took precedence at the Charlottetown conference, the first of the gatherings to lay the groundwork of Confederation in 1864, is a matter for pure speculation. Even George Brown's accounts (the most extensive from a sitting delegate) are light on the substance of the talks. What is certain, however, is that Jervois was present at the October 10th Quebec Conference, armed with a revised analysis, and that, although it appeared as Resolution No. 68 on a list of 72, the Intercolonial Railway was back on the negotiating table.

Interestingly, Resolution 67 proclaimed:

> "All engagements that may before the Union, be entered into with the Imperial Government for the defence of the Country, shall be assumed by the General Government."

The Intercolonial took the very next breath:

> "The General Government shall secure, without delay, the completion of the Intercolonial Railway from Riviere-de-Loup, through New Brunswick, to Truro in Nova Scotia."

Was this a tacit acknowledgement that the military imperative for the railway had been re-established? If it needed further reinforcement, it was found just nine days later, with the October 19th 1864 St. Albans Raid, as described in this account by John Hedley:

> "A profound sensation was created all over the United States and Canada on the morning of October 20, 1864. The papers published the particulars of a raid upon St. Albans, Vermont, by a band of Confederate soldiers. It appeared that the attack was made by a party under the command of Lieut. Bennet H. Young of Kentucky. The town had been fired upon, several citizens had been shot in the melee, and a large sum of money taken from three of the banks. The guerrillas had been chased by the citizens. Young and his comrades preferred to await their fate in the courts of Canada, since their extradition had been demanded by the Government of the United States."

The take was $200,000 and, after killing one American pursuer on the way, the raiders fled across the border to Montreal on stolen horses. The Canadian government arrested the men and returned the money but a judge set them free, noting he had no jurisdiction in the case. This did not reduce the anger of many Northerners who saw it as hostile to their cause. American troops were ordered to pursue the raiders into Canada and wipe them out. Had this occurred it would have violated Canadian neutrality in the same manner as the *Trent* Affair had threatened, and war could once again have been the result. Lincoln revoked the order, fearing a Canadian–American conflict would only serve to divert resources from what seemed to be the imminent defeat of the South.

The raid also served to illustrate how porous the border was to attack from either direction, a lesson made clear just two years later with the Fenian Raids. Nova Scotia's Joseph Howe well understood the predicament faced by the provinces of the interior. Speaking in 1866 he noted:

> "The Province of Canada is as large as Great Britain, France, and Prussia put together, and will, if ever peopled, sustain a population of

50,000,000. If her territories were compact, and her frontiers defensible, she might develop into an empire large enough to tax the administrative talents of a Bismarck or a Louis Napoleon. On such a territory one would naturally suppose that there was work enough to exhaust the energies of statesmen for the next two centuries, without their coveting more land, or desiring to interfere with neighbouring communities developing their industry in a peaceful and legal manner on either side."

Such might came with drawbacks, however, as Howe observed, making specific mention of the military impossibilities the vast region faced:

"But Canada is not compact. She has yet only 3,000,000 inhabitants, or about 8 to every square mile of territory. She has an exposed frontier of 1000 miles, with no natural defences for 800 miles above Quebec. Along the whole of this frontier line she is menaced or overlapped by the great republic, with 34,000,000 inhabitants and 1,000,000 trained soldiers who have been under fire. These troops, accustomed to obey officers of great ability, familiar with the art of war, could, by means of twenty railroads, pointing to the Canadian frontier, be massed in a week, and thrown into the Province. Whether, when they got there, the Canadians could drive them out, with their comparatively small force of volunteers and militia, even when assisted by the troops this country could spare, is a military question which I will not undertake to decide. Distinguished members of Parliament declare they could not; and that if Canada, thus overrun, is ever recovered to the British Crown, it must be after campaigns in other directions, and a successful naval war, in which it is evident that that Province, being frozen up for five months of the year, and having no ships or sailors to spare, can render no assistance."

The end of the US Civil War did little to calm colonial fears that they would be the next target. George Brown, one of the leading proponents of Canadian entry into Confederation, was still hinting at the strategic necessity of the Intercolonial in an 1865 debate:

"I have not belief that the Americans have the slightest thought of attacking us. I cannot believe that the first use of their new-found liberty will be the invasion, totally unprovoked, of a peaceful province. I fancy that they have had quite enough of war for a good many years to come—and that such a war as one with England would certainly be, is the last they are likely to provoke. But, Mr. Speaker, there is no better mode of warding off war when it is threatened, than to be prepared for it if it comes. The Americans are now a warlike people. They have large armies, a powerful navy, an unlimited supply of warlike munitions, and the carnage of war has to them been stript [sic] of its horrors. The American side of our lines already bristles with works of defence, and unless we are willing to live at the mercy of our neighbours, we, too, must put our country in a state of efficient preparation. War or no war— the necessity of placing these provinces in a thorough state of defence can no longer be postponed."

This from a man who had earlier crowed with delight when it appeared the Intercolonial agreement struck in 1861 had been scuttled by the actions of Canada's emissaries to London, as Stevens explains:

"L. V. Sicotte (Attorney General) and W. P. Howland (Finance Minister) had come to London with restricted terms of reference. They set out to haggle rather than to negotiate. They took particular exception to the proposals... for a sinking fund for the repayment of the principal of the railway loan. They stated that such a fund was a burden that Canada could not bear; they saw no need for it: Canada's pledged word provided all necessary protection to the lenders.... W. E. Gladstone, Chancellor of the Exchequer, modified the British proposals to meet the Canadian objections in both major particulars. He agreed to forgo sinking fund allocations for the first ten years and he authorized investment of such moneys thereafter in six-per-cent colonial bonds.

To everyone except Sicotte and Howland these concessions were eminently satisfactory. The Canadian representatives, however, who expected either everything or nothing, stated their views anew in a long letter which described the sinking fund proposals as 'illiberal' and 'obstructive' and as derogatory to Canadian dignity. In one paragraph... the intercolonial railway was described as an Imperial responsibility of little or no interest to Canadians. Having done as much damage as possible, Sicotte and Howland packed up and went home. On arrival in Canada they announced that negotiations for a railway loan had been abandoned."

Stevens suggests the two Canadian delegates were simply echoing the sentiment of their government, that the railway, less of a military necessity, was regarded by many as an act of charity meted out by Canada to its poor cousins in the Maritimes.

"George Brown had declared that the fifty thousand pounds that it would cost the Province of Canada annually was more than Confederation was worth; when news of the Sicotte–Howland double-cross came through, the editor of the Globe indulged in one of his ferocious gloatings. He declared that it was a fitting end to the inter-colonial project, which was no more than a ramp by which Edward Watkin hoped to help the Grand Trunk; he added that it meant less than nothing to Upper Canada...

Fortunately, prominent Canadians were equally alert and recognized the magnitude of the Sicotte–Howland blunder. Galt enlisted the support of the Governor-General, Viscount Monck, and in February 1863 an attempt to repair the damage took form in a Canadian statement which laid the blame for the breakdown of negotiations on that convenient whipping-boy, the British Cabinet."

The American abrogation of the Reciprocity Treaty of 1854 was also cause for immediate concern, especially for the Province of Canada. Glazebrook summarizes the events:

"In 1849 an influential body of Canadians professed to be in favour of annexation by the United States. In so far as this was the expression of an economic grievance, it was met by the Reciprocity Treaty of 1854, which established free trade in agricultural and forest products, minerals, and fish in the waters of Canada, Nova Scotia, New Brunswick and Prince Edward Island, and to navigate the St. Lawrence. On the whole the treaty seems to have been advantageous to both parties, but especially to the British provinces, whose exports to the United States rose steeply, especially when the Civil War created an abnormal demand in the States. Before the treaty had been in force for many years, however, it began to be attacked in the United States as a one-sided bargain, the particular complaint being that it did not cover manufactured articles. Such objections were felt more strongly when Canada began to adopt a protective tariff; and the whole arrangement was further compromised by the irritation arising out of the war. Throughout 1862 and 1863 the treaty was discussed in congress, its critics dwelling chiefly on the iniquity of the Galt tariff. At the end of 1864 it was sent to the senate's committee on foreign relations, which reported in favour of abrogation. In spite of the efforts of the friends of the treaty, the senate voted against it, and in 1865 official notification was given to the British government that it was no longer in the interests of the United States to continue the arrangement."

Given the role played by the Galt tariffs in the failure of the treaty, there is clear evidence here that an American invasion, or simply the fear of such, could be provoked by more than just faulty British foreign policy. Stevens notes, however, that the military necessity of the railway was by now making itself clear even to the most smug Canadians:

"The Civil War was drawing to a close and the northern states, with victory in their grasp, were eyeing the British North American colonies belligerently. Bonding privileges upon Canadian goods in transit through the United States had been rescinded; the reciprocity agreement was about to be dropped. Along the international boundary Confederate sympathizers in Canada and the Fenian Brotherhood in the United States were intent on making trouble. More British troops might be needed in a hurry; if for a third time they were compelled to march across the New Brunswick forest in mid-winter they might arrive too late."

By this time, and in need of expanding its markets to make up for the loss of those in the United States, Canadian interest in the Intercolonial took on new impetus, as Glazebrook goes on to note:

"The situation was threshed out again and again in both branches of the Canadian legislature when the Quebec resolutions were brought down in February 1865. The view of the government was ably put to the legislative council by Sir Etienne Tache on the first day of the debate. 'If the opportunity which now presented itself were allowed to pass by unimproved,' he told the council, 'whether we would or would not, we would be forced into the American union by violence, and if not by violence, would be placed upon an inclined plane which would carry us there insensibly.' "

Nor could the Canadians be certain that the threat would come from the United States. The Fenian raids of 1866 were launched by Irishmen intent upon striking a blow against the British Empire, as Mitch Biggar succinctly notes:

"Ancient Irish warriors were called Fianna and in the spring of 1866 discharged Irish soldiers were recruited into an Irish national movement called the Fenians. The Fenians were formed in New York under the leadership of Bernard Killan. The purpose of the Fenians was to overthrow the British rule of Ireland. One of their goals was the invasion of British North America.

In April of 1866 over 1000 of the Irish brotherhood gathered along the New Brunswick border from Machias to Calais. Three British men of war from Halifax sailed up the St. Croix River while several regiments of the New Brunswick militia marched to Charlotte County. There were minor border crossings but no full-scale invasion occurred. The American authorities feared that the Fenians would attempt to take over Eastern Maine. So General Meade was dispatched to keep the Fenians out of trouble.

Although the Fenians caused little trouble, the impact of their threats had a lasting effect. The leader of the Fenians had declared in Calais that preventing the union of British North America would strike a blow for Ireland. What New Brunswickers took this statement to mean was that if they voted for Confederation it would be a blow for Britain and against the Fenian threat."

Contrary to Canadian fears, however, the Fenians were not intending to occupy Canadian soil, merely secure the military attention of the Imperial government, as P. G. Smith notes in his article available on the *Historynet* web site of Cowles Magazines:

"More realistic members of the Fenian Brotherhood understood the farfetched nature of the plan. They focused instead on the more likely possibility that the attack could precipitate war between the United States and Great Britain, or at least cause enough of a disturbance to force the British Empire to reinforce Canada with large numbers of Regular troops. Either of those circumstances would create a favourable climate for an armed uprising in Ireland itself."

Morton notes, however, that the greatest threat from the Fenians came in an area far removed from the territory of any possible Intercolonial Railway:

"Repeatedly in 1865 and 1866, thousands of militia turned out to face an imminent invasion. For St. Patrick's Day, 1866, more than fourteen thousand Canadians volunteered for duty. Two and a half months later, on the night of May 31, the attack finally came. Instead of the promised thousands, "General" John O'Neill led a mere six hundred Fenians across from Buffalo to Fort Erie. At Dawn on June 2, near Ridgeway, the Fenians ran into two thirsty, sweaty battalions of militia, marching across country to join a British column. The Canadians turned, advanced like regulars, and on the verge of victory, were tumbled into confusion by contradictory orders. Moments later, a flood of panic-stricken volunteers poured down the sunken road to Ridgeway. The shaken Fenians soon retraced their steps to Fort Erie. After scattering a few militia who had arrived in their absence, most of O'Neill's men crossed to Buffalo to be interned. The Canadians tried their prisoners and sent most of them to the penitentiary."

The railway played a significant part in the Canadian "victory", as Stevens notes:

"F. W. Cumberland, General Manager of the Northern Railway, received orders to concentrate the militia to meet the enemy; within twenty-four hours he had delivered 1,240 men at the threatened point, and

Fenian soldiers wait for the train at Malone, NY prior to their "invasion" of Canada. Although they were experienced officers of the Civil War, the Fenian leaders showed a terrible grasp of how to use the railway as a military asset. This picture was published in the June 18th 1870 edition of Canadian Illustrated News.

(National Archives Canada #1126)

twice that number were on their way. The invasion was over before it had begun; the iron horse had been worth a division of the Queen's cavalry."

In his *Short History of Canada*, Morton also notes:

"At Pigeon Hill, just over the Vermont border, another eighteen hundred Fenians camped for a day before American authorities seized their leaders and supplies. The most fatuous but also the most significant incursion had ended a month before when Fenians clustered on the Maine border had tried to raid Campobello Island."

That the Fenians did not cause more trouble may have been due to the fact that once across the border, like the Aroostook invaders two decades before them, their transportation options had been limited. Although O'Neill (a former Union cavalry officer) and his followers were veterans of the Civil War from both Union and Confederate ranks, they failed to make use of railway facilities to speed their mobilization. It was not as though they did not try, as Smith notes in his history of the attack from Buffalo. O'Neill led his men to a railway yard near Ridgeway, Ontario:

> "O'Neill's force reached the rail yard shortly after a locomotive had chugged away with the last of the rolling stock. A small party set off on a handcar but could not catch up to the train."

Similarly, the attack at Pigeon Hill apparently failed because of an inability to get control of the Grand Trunk's facilities, as the Cariboo *Sentinel* of June 1st 1870 reported, quoting the pro-Fenian Boston press:

> "Boston, May 25—Reports at headquarters state that the advanced guard occupied Pigeon Hill, the Sixth Rifles falling back with out firing a shot. The Grand Trunk Railroad is torn up for quite a distance to capture a cattle train."

It was during the Fenian scare that the necessity for a separate military priority on the railways became apparent, when on June 19th 1866, a Grand Trunk train from Quebec City stopped at Danville, on its way to Montreal. The web site of the Royal Green Jackets Association notes:

> "Locked in converted boxcars were 800 German immigrants. In another boxcar was 2000 pounds of ammunition for use against the Fenian raiders."

Accompanying the car, tasked with guarding the ammunition, was twenty-year-old Timothy O'Hea, and four other members of the 1st Battalion, Rifle Brigade (Prince Consort's Own):

> "Late in the afternoon, O'Hea noticed that the boxcar containing the ammunition was on fire and after shouting an alarm, discovered the railwaymen and other soldiers had fled. O'Hea grabbed the keys to the boxcar from a dithering Sergeant and climbed aboard. He ripped burning covers off ammunition cases and tossed them outside, then for almost an hour, making 19 trips to a creek for buckets of water, he fought the flames, the immigrants cheering him on unaware of their peril.
>
> By evening, the ammunition had been loaded into another car and the train—immigrant coaches still attached—was on its way again. O'Hea not only displayed great courage and total disregard for his own life in putting out the fire in the boxcar, but also saved 800 immigrants from certain death had the ammunition exploded. His was the only Victoria Cross ever won in Canada."

The medal is usually awarded for actions "in the face of the enemy." From 1858 to 1881 an amendment allowed for it to be awarded under "circumstances of extreme danger" and it was under this provision that O'Hea received his commendation.

The threat of Fenian invasion had barely passed when the British North American colonies found themselves once again the focus of American interest, this time in the form of a July 2nd 1866 bill placed before the US Congress. Entitled "A Bill for the admission of the States of Nova Scotia, New Brunswick, Canada East and Canada West, and for the organization of the Territories of Selkirk, Saskatchewan, and Columbia", the bill was given inauspicious recognition in the *Congressional Globe*:

> "Mr. Banks, by unanimous consent, submitted a bill (H. R. 754) establishing conditions for the admission of the States of Nova Scotia, New Brunswick, Canada East and Canada West, and for the organization of territorial governments; which was read a first and second time, ordered to be printed, and referred to the Committee on Foreign Affairs."

The bill was sponsored by Massachusetts representative Nathaniel Prentiss Banks, and read more like an invitation (however unwelcome) to join the repaired union by the method most favoured in the US—a purchase offer in the same manner as the Louisiana, Gadsden and Alaska territories were acquired:

> "ARTICLE II
>
> In consideration of the public lands, works, and property vested as aforesaid in the United States, the United States will assume and discharge the funded debt and contingent liabilities of the late provinces at rates of interest not exceeding five per centum, to the amount of eighty-five million seven hundred thousand dollars, apportioned as follows: To Canada West, thirty-six million five hundred thousand dollars; to Canada East, twenty-nine million dollars; to Nova Scotia, eight million dollars; to New Brunswick, seven million dollars; to Newfoundland, three million two hundred thousand dollars; and to Prince Edward Island, two million dollars; and in further consideration of the transfer by said provinces to the United States of the power to levy import and export duties, the United States will make an annual grant of one million six hundred and forty-six thousand dollars in aid of local expenditures, to be apportioned as follows; To Canada West, seven hundred thousand dollars; to Canada East, five hundred and fifty thousand dollars; to Nova Scotia, one hundred and sixty-five thousand dollars; to New Brunswick, one hundred and twenty-six thousand dollars; to Newfoundland, sixty-five thousand dollars; to Prince Edward Island, forty thousand dollars."

Of particular importance to the history of the Intercolonial Railway, however, are the provisions of Articles VIII and IX:

"ARTICLE VIII

The United States will appropriate and pay to 'European and North American Railway Company of Maine' the sum of two millions of dollars upon the construction of a continuous line of railroad from Bangor, in Maine, to Saint John's, in New Brunswick: Provided, That said 'The European and North American Railway Company of Maine' shall release the government of the United States from all claims held by it as assignee of the States of Maine and Massachusetts.

ARTICLE IX

To aid the construction of a railway from Truro, in Nova Scotia, to Riviere du Loup, in Canada East, and a railway from the city of Ottawa, by way of Sault Ste. Marie, Bayfield, and Superior, in Wisconsin, Pembina, and Fort Garry, on the Red River of the North, and the valley of the North Saskatchewan River to some point on the Pacific Ocean north of latitude forty-nine degrees, the United States will grant lands along the lines of said roads to the amount of twenty sections, or twelve thousand eight hundred acres, per mile, to be selected and sold in the manner prescribed in the act to aid the construction of the Northern Pacific railroad, approved July 2, eighteen hundred and sixty-two, and acts amendatory thereof; and in addition to said grants of lands, the United States will further guarantee dividends of five per centum upon the stock of the company or companies which may be authorized by Congress to undertake the construction of said railways: Provided, That such guarantee of stock shall not exceed the sum of thirty thousand dollars per mile, and Congress shall regulate the securities for advances on account thereof."

This offer would make the construction of any intercolonial railway attractive to any number of railroad contractors in the United States, but it was an all-or-nothing-at-all deal:

"ARTICLE XII

SECTION 3. And be it further enacted, That if Prince Edward Island and Newfoundland, or either of those provinces, shall decline union with the United States, and the remaining provinces, with the consent of Great Britain, shall accept the proposition of the United States, the foregoing stipulations in favor of Prince Edward Island and Newfoundland, or either of them, will be omitted; but in all other respects the United States will give full effect to the plan of union.

> If Prince Edward Island, Newfoundland, Nova Scotia, and New Brunswick shall decline the proposition, but Canada, British Columbia, and Vancouver Island shall, with the consent of Great Britain, accept the same, the construction of a railway from Truro to Riviere du Loup, with all stipulations relating to the maritime provinces, will form no part of the proposed plan of union, but the same will be consummated in all other respects."

The same stipulations were attached to the Ottawa and western railways guaranteed in Article IX. The bill attracted little attention or debate in Congress, although it did proceed to the committee level, but it was sufficient to reinforce the suspicion in British North America that the United States once again had designs upon their territory. The bill added new urgency to the tempo of the Confederation negotiations, which proceeded apace despite the domestic political hiccups that led to New Brunswick at first, then Prince Edward Island, backing away from the talks. This in turn gave new urgency to the construction of an intercolonial railway, as evidenced by the wording in the British North America Act (commonly referred to as the Union Act) of 1867, by which a nation was born:

> "X INTERCOLONIAL RAILWAY
>
> 145. Inasmuch as the Provinces of Canada, Nova Scotia, and New Brunswick have joined in a Declaration that the Construction of the Intercolonial Railway is essential to the Consolidation of the Union of British North America, and to the Assent thereto of Nova Scotia and New Brunswick, and have consequently agreed that Provision should be made for its immediate Construction by the Government of Canada: Therefore, in order to give effect to that Agreement, it shall be the Duty of the Government and Parliament of Canada to provide for the Commencement within Six Months after the Union of a Railway connecting the River St. Lawrence with the City of Halifax in Nova Scotia, and for the Construction thereof without Intermission, and the Completion thereof with all practicable Speed."

Thus it was that the Intercolonial, built as a strategic railway on a military imperative, rather than as a commercial line with a profit motive, came to have 55 years of history behind it even before the first spike was ever driven.

CHAPTER 4

Battle of the Routes

EVEN AS CONFEDERATION WAS TAKING PLACE WITH LITTLE more than the promise of a railway, the British were realizing the military importance of railways, this time in the Abyssinian Campaign of 1867-68, and once again it was the Royal Engineers who took the lead. Martyn Witt describes the events on his web site:

> "The Abyssinian Campaign of 1867-68 included the building of a railway under Royal Engineers supervision, from Zula to Magdala, to supply Lord Napier's forces.
>
> This was undertaken by 10 Pontoon Company RE, which was later to be reincarnated as one of the Sappers' long-standing railway units. Their achievements were outstanding, given the problems they faced— a mixed workforce of Indians and Chinese, and 'used' equipment bought cheaply from India, with rotten sleepers, rails of different lengths, unserviceable spikes, non-fitting wheels etc.
>
> Emperor Theodore II (Tewodros II) of Abyssinia, a Coptic Christian, had hoped to enlist British support in his ruthless campaign against the Muslims and desire to become the dominant regional monarch, but the British declined. He was a competent military leader, and established a professional army, but his political judgement failed him and was to be his downfall. In 1864, he imprisoned the local British representative, and about 50 other Western diplomats.
>
> General Robert Napier (a trained engineer) commanded part of the Indian Army in Bombay, and was tasked to mount a rescue expedition. This was somewhat daunting, as the Emperor had established his headquarters in Magdala, a fortified town 7000 feet up in the highlands, separated from the coast by some 320 miles of hot, arid desert. Napier's plan hinged around the building of a railway from the port of

embarkation right up to Magdala, along which he could assemble and supply an assault force of 5000, with 8000+ support troops and 30000 animals."

Napier fought off pre-emptive raids by the emperor's soldiers, and it was decided that the self-proclaimed "King of Kings" had to be removed. This was done when Napier attacked the mountain fortress on April 12th 1868, at which time Theodore II, sensing his end was near, committed suicide. Because the railway had been completed by that time, it served another purpose, in speeding the removal of the British forces back to the coast before the rainy season would have made it impossible.

Canadian confederation having taken place, and a commitment to the Intercolonial Railway having been made constitutionally, the "war" that was immediately to follow included a battle over which route the line was to take. This was the last aspect of the railway to be settled, and it effectively pitted New Brunswick against Canada and Nova Scotia, and split the first federal cabinet evenly.

The first step after Confederation, however, was to secure the financing of the project, and the Imperial government in London left no doubts as to its intentions for the line.

"On 12th April, 1867, an Act was passed by the Imperial Parliament authorizing the Commissioners of Her Majesty's Treasury to guarantee a loan not exceeding Three Millions Pounds Sterling, at a rate not exceeding four per centum per annum, to assist in the construction of the Railway, and providing that the guarantee should not be given unless and until the Parliament of Canada should, within two years of Confederation, pass an Act providing to the satisfaction of one of Her Majesty's principal Secretaries of State, as follows, viz,:-

I. For the construction of the Railway.

II. For the use of the Railway at all times for Her Majesty's military and other service.

III. Nor unless and until the line on which the Railway is to be constructed, has been approved by one of Her Majesty's principal Secretaries of State.

On 21st. December, 1867, an Act was passed by the Parliament of Canada for the construction of the Intercolonial Railway. The Minister of Finance then placed a loan of Two Million Pounds Sterling upon the London market, seventy-five per cent thereof having the Imperial guarantee, and twenty-five per cent being without it; and the whole was taken up at once on favourable terms." *(Trout)*

The routing decision was ultimately left to the first Canadian Parliament, and although the British North America Act determined that work should begin on the railway within six months of union, it did not necessarily fix the date on which the first spike would be driven. In fact, it took almost a full year to determine what route would be taken.

In this matter, the chief engineer Sandford Fleming was not helpful. Whereas Major Robinson had identified five possible routes, Fleming muddied the waters and exacerbated the debate by identifying fifteen. Here the opinion of history diverges. The New Brunswick press reported that Fleming had proclaimed his preference to be the line through central New Brunswick that Robinson had disqualified.

This news created a storm of argument that was at times parochial, partisan and petty, with New Brunswick as its crucible. The leading newspapers of that province, which were at that time located in communities along the valley from Saint John to Fredericton, immediately called out in favour of the central route.

This is certainly borne out by a report in the Fredericton *New Brunswick Reporter* of March 13th 1868:

> "WHO IS HARTLEY?—Well, Hartley is a gentleman who has received a telegram from Ottawa somewhat to this effect:
>
> 'Are you prepared immediately to take charge of a line of survey for the Intercolonial Railroad north of Fredericton under my instruction?
>
> S. Fleming'
>
> Hartley is a gentleman who has set a ball rolling, which, increasing in size as it rolls along, is destined to obscure the vain pretension of the North Shore as the great Intercolonial Highway. Hartley has shown by the result of his Railway resolutions in New Brunswick, that two-thirds of this Province favour a more Central route, and he has shown to merchants and capitalists of Montreal the advantages of this route, that they have brought such a pressure to bear upon Mr. Cartier as he will find it difficult to resist.
>
> The fact the tide has turned, and is now setting with resistless force towards the Keswick Valley route."

Hartley was Charles R. Hartley, a respected New Brunswick surveyor, who delighted the opponents of the Robinson route with his announcement that a suitable route through the centre of the province was possible, supporting the claim made by Wilkinson almost twenty tears before.

The Fredericton *Reporter* crowed with triumph in its May 8th 1868 edition:

> "It stated, on Mr. Hartley's authority, that he had been successful in finding a practicable and economical route across the height of land

forming the water-shed between the Tobique and the Miramichi. This ridge has supplied the chief argument against the several short routes proposed for the Railway. It has been one grand excuse for advocating the North Shore route, that by going round over the route surveyed by Major Robinson, the 'ridge' in North-Western New Brunswick could be avoided. Major Robinson himself, in his report, was careful to bring out this argument, and every advocate of the long route since has rung the changes upon the story. Mr. Hartley's report, however, shows that the difficulties of grade in the way of a short route have been wonderfully exaggerated. He has surveyed about fifteen miles of the most difficult section of the whole survey, and finds the average grade per mile only 43 feet. On three miles of the fifteen the maximum grade is 65 feet per mile, with the probability of this being materially decreased in the final location. This is much more favourable than the result of Mr. Fleming's hurried survey, and much more favourable than Major Robinson's estimate of the grades in that locality. It was to be expected, however, that a more careful survey by a man thoroughly conversant with that region of country, should develop an easier route that hurried examination by strangers would do. Mr. Hartley's survey, even if he should be unable to reduce these grades further, proves the route which he was employed to explore to be quite practicable. Even the maximum grade of 65 feet for the short distance of three miles is not worse than some of the grades on existing railways in this country. The Grand Trunk has, we believe, some quite as difficult. The grades reported by Mr. Hartley, as the result of his survey, are very little heavier than those admitted in Major Robinson's report as the result of a survey of the North Shore route. That report concedes grades of from 40 to 50 feet, and of from 50 to 60 feet per mile for several miles upon that route. For no less than 12 miles—though four of that, it is said may be avoided by a change in the route—a grade of from 50 to 60 feet is admitted. Surely 12 miles of such grades, and a greater distance of a grade from 40 to 50 feet, is quite as bad as the grade reported by Mr. Hartley on the worst fraction of his survey."

The *Reporter*'s editor drove home his point, proclaiming a final nail in the coffin of the North Shore route:

"It may be fairly claimed that Mr. Hartley has succeeded in disposing of the bugbear of 'the height of land.' He has shown that it presents no greater difficulties than any other railways frequently encountered. He has shewn that it can be crossed at grades which are not by any means unusual. As compared with the bridging and difficulties of the North Shore road, Mr. Hartley has proved the obstacles in the way of a shorter route to be almost insignificant. The argument from 'engineering difficulties' has disappeared like that of 'military necessity,' and it is difficult to see what the advocates of the North Shore route have to fall back upon."

The *Reporter* pressed its point even further in the May 15th edition, noting Fleming had been leaning toward an acceptance of the Central Route:

"There is no doubt that every means has been adopted to prejudice the public mind against the shorter Central routes, and various interests have conspired to place the advantages of those routes in a false position. We know that at one time Mr. Sandford Fleming was decidedly proposed in favour of a Keswick Valley route, that he thus expressed himself to some of our leading politicians; but now, *mirabile dictu*, he is all North, and glories in the smile of the honourable Minister of Marine."

Milner, Seton and Stevens, however, are all adamant that Fleming had always supported Robinson's route:

"Fleming favoured a line by the Bay of Chaleur, not only as providing the best military advantages, but as making it possible to establish an ocean port on the Bay, which was bound to possess many advantages for travel between Montreal and Liverpool, as much time would be saved by the longer rail and shorter steamship journey." *(Seton)*

Stevens adds a new dimension to the history, when he claims Fleming dismissed the eligibility of all his surveyed routes, with one exception:

"That exception was the north shore. Fleming went on to declare that except in unusual circumstances the Intercolonial could not expect to handle any great bulk of Canadian traffic from Halifax. On the other hand, 'the adoption of an available harbour on Baie des Chaleurs as a shipping port for through passenger and mail traffic, would for the reasons referred to constitute the Intercolonial railway as an important channel of traffic.' It was, therefore, with the full knowledge of his chief that he examined a number of possible transatlantic terminals and considered the creation of a new port. He eventually settled on Shippegan Harbour, forty-five miles east of Bathurst, on the tip of the Tracadie Peninsula to the south of the Baie de Chaleur."

Whether this is a matter of Fleming merely musing, or a figment of Stevens' fancy, is irrelevant. The idea fails on several points, the first being that Shippegan would not have provided an all-season harbour, since the Gulf of St. Lawrence–Northumberland Strait area was ice-bound for the winter. Thus, for military purposes it would be useless in winter. Secondly, being further westward, Shippegan was several days' additional sailing than Halifax. Finally, it was highly unlikely that Nova Scotia would have supported the creation of a rival to Halifax, either from a military or commercial point of view. Fleming may have been a man of myriad ideas, but not all of them were sound.

There are also clues to suggest Fleming did indeed initially favour the direct, or Central, route. In his history of the Intercolonial, published in 1876, he devotes one map to the sum total of routes surveyed, and another for the Central route alone. Fleming also devotes more than a chapter to the consequences of the Ashburton treaty on the Central route, and criticizes Ashburton for giving away too much territory to the Americans. All this while at the same time proclaiming that he had been specifically told not to promote any one route over another. The engineer goes on to note:

> "The settlement of the boundary question did not lessen the necessity for a military road; indeed some line of communication for military purposes was the more necessary, as the new Boundary interposed a wedge of foreign territory which threatened to sever all connection between the Maritime Provinces and Quebec."

The Hartley report may well have been the invention of a newspaper with an axe to grind. On the other hand, Fleming may well have been converted to the cause of the north shore route by a discreet reminder that the British government would not consider any other course.

If the military application of the railway was intended to be a secret, it was one of the worst-kept in any of the colonies, where newspapers discussed it openly, largely from the viewpoint of editors who formed a curious mix of small-town chamber of commerce jingoists, armchair generals and amateur railway engineers.

The Fredericton *Head Quarters* of September 19th 1866, quoted the Montreal *Commercial Review*:

> "The objection that the road to Saint John would run too near the frontier is, we believe, overstated. Whichever way the road runs, whether by the Northern route or via Woodstock, it will still be impossible to get over the difficulty of having to pass along the neck of land between the St. Lawrence and Maine, beginning in a line with St. Joseph, extending down to Granville. If the Americans wished to break Canada's connection with the seaboard, that would be the point attacked; and if a strictly military road, secure from attack, be a sine qua non, engineers must locate the railroad by some other route than by the neck of land which joins Canada to New Brunswick."

The Halifax *Morning Chronicle* of April 16th 1867 observed:

> "It was pretty plainly intimated by the principal speakers in the debate that the railway loan, guaranteed by successive Secretaries of State, without condition, is now the price of Confederation—the assumption by the New Dominion of the charge of defending these Provinces, which had previously been borne on the Imperial Exchequer. In other words, three millions of pounds, sterling, have been loaned towards the construction of a railway through the wilderness of New Brunswick, with the understanding that the Queen's troops are to be ultimately withdrawn from British America, and these Provinces left to defend themselves from the Fenians or the Americans, as the case may be, as best they can. That is the price. And a pretty bargain it is; the withdrawal of from 12,000 to 14,000 troops from these Provinces, who expend from four to five millions of dollars a year among us, in exchange for a profitless railway, which, in interest and sinking fund, (to say nothing of working expenses,) will extract over a million of dollars per annum from the tax-payers of the New Dominion."

This observation, however, conveniently ignores the fact that, had the Imperial government wished to withdraw troops at any time for the sake of mere cost-cutting, it could have done so, even without a railway, and that the mobilization of troops from Britain by way of the railway would be that much faster.

In a July 20th 1867 letter to William McDougall, the new federal minister of Public Works, published in the Woodstock, New Brunswick *Carleton Sentinel*, J. W. Lawrence wrote:

> "The Honourable John A. McDonald [sic], now Premier of Canada, and the Honourable John Rose, then President of the Grand Trunk Railway, wrote the Colonial Secretary in 1858, 'That the North Shore route was considered by the Colonies and especially by New Brunswick as being comparatively of little value, except in a military point of view. It was long and circuitous; it would pass through a country but little settled, and could not be expected to make any returns on the cost of construction for years. The line by the city of Saint John and its Valley promises great commercial advantages and a fair pecuniary, return, and it is understood in Canada that competent military men do not now consider it objectionable as a military road; nay there are strong reasons for its selection as such, at all events there is no difficulty in finding a line combining the requisites of a military and commercial one.' For the past 60 years, summer and winter, troops of the line and Horse Artillery with their munitions of war have always followed its course."

This letter was roundly applauded in the *Reporter*, but it must be remembered these two newspapers were published in communities that would not be connected to the Intercolonial, and which constantly lobbied for the Saint John valley route or the direct route through central New Brunswick.

Lawrence went on to cast aspersions on the military integrity of the Robinson line in a similar letter, August 30th:

> "In 1848, Major Robinson recommended the Northern route on Military grounds, since then from the revolution in Naval Armament, its claim has entirely disappeared. Then it would have been comparatively safe from attack from the water, now, from gunboats, steam frigates, and armour plated ships, for seven months of the year it would be exposed to the enemy."

In November of that year, another engineer, Walter Buck, entered the fray with a ten-page pamphlet supporting the Central Route, and advocating its use on military grounds.

Buck dismissed the Frontier route as being unacceptable for military purposes, then argued the same was true for the Robinson route:

> "Recent events in strategic movements of war, as illustrated abroad and at home, have shown the fallacy of the former notion; that, as a means of defence, the most suitable location for a railroad is along the line of defence, and not at an inaccessible distance to the rear."

This philosophy only held true, however, if the defence of New Brunswick was the railway's only intent, and overlooked the necessity of supplying troops to a more remote front line in the Canadas.

Buck's reasoning drew some unreasonable responses that went reported, but not uncriticized, by the *Reporter* in its November 29th edition of 1867. The letters came under pseudonym from "Cannuck" and "Dion," and were of such a tone that the editor felt compelled to note:

> "It is unnecessary to follow up the arguments of these worthies by further contradiction. The style of the writing, which is positively insulting to Mr. Lawrence and Mr. Buck, will rob them of every importance. Witness the following reference to Mr. Buck:
>
> 'Is the man stupid himself, or does he merely presume upon the supposed stupidity of his readers? This question I confess I am at a loss to answer. Sometimes I think he is more knave than fool, at others I am in doubt.'
>
> This is the gentleman who proposes a compromise."

It is to Fleming's credit that none of this criticism deterred him from hiring his detractors when construction of the line finally got underway. Buck, Hartley, John O'Hanley and Robert Shanly all saw service in some capacity.

It was no coincidence that most of these arguments were made by New Brunswick engineers. It was claimed that since Nova Scotia was well-pleased with the route (the province had built its own rail line from Halifax to Truro along Robinson's original survey, and was obliged by its 1854 legislation to carry it on to Amherst and the New Brunswick border), and Quebec was happy with the Robinson line through the well-populated east bank of the St. Lawrence, New Brunswickers should therefore be allowed to choose the route through their own province.

For any other railway this might have made sense, but there was the inescapable condition laid out by the colonial office in London, the same criteria that had led to the British government refusing to finance the line in the 1850s: the military imperative of security against interdiction, and, according to the loan act, the choice made by the Canadian Parliament had to meet with the approval of the Secretary of State for the Colonies.

At this point it should be noted that Fleming's own words apparently catch him in a lie. In his history of the Intercolonial (the passages no doubt relied upon by Seton, Milner and Stevens for their argument), the chief engineer insists that he offered no opinion on the preferred route until requested to do so by the Imperial Government in 1868. Yet, in 1867, he had published a pamphlet that prominently advocated the Northern route for its military merits, and as he noted in his history:

> "The Imperial authorities never lost sight of the military element which the railway should retain. On several occasions they clearly intimated that a northern or Bay Chaleur route was the one which they preferred, not only Major Robinson, but other military authorities pointed out the northern route as the proper location. The commissioners appointed to consider the defence of the Province of Canada reported in 1862 that no time should be lost in opening a road by the valley of the Metapedia to Metis on the St. Lawrence, and that, for military purposes the preference should be given to the line of Railway by the Bay Chaleur."

Even had Fleming not written the pamphlet, it certainly echoes the views he offered to Henry Youle Hind, who wrote *A sketch of an overland route to British Columbia* in 1862, and sought the surveyor's input into the practicability of a transcontinental railway. Indeed, although Hind's work was focused upon a Pacific railway, Fleming left no doubt he considered the route of the Intercolonial equally important:

> "...although a railway between the two oceans on British territory, cannot be considered perfect without the completion of the road between

Halifax and the most easterly extension of the Grand Trunk in Lower Canada, yet as there is some prospect of this section being made independently, it does not appear necessary to embrace its length in the present consideration."

His dissertation then took on tones similar to that of Robinson in 1848:

"The railway would throughout the year be open to transport 'through' as well as 'local' merchandise and passengers, and would, taken with the telegraph, in a military aspect be available at all times and seasons, and would undoubtedly prove an important as well as permanent measure of defence to the country."

The then-recent confrontation with the Americans over the ownership of western territory was still fresh in the minds of many, including the engineer of the Northern Railway of Canada:

"In times of peace we are apt to overlook the importance of being able to concentrate troops and munitions of war at any given point on our extended frontier, but the recent difficulties betwen [sic] the British and American governments, could not fail to illustrate the military value of the several Canadian railways as well as the isolated and defenceless condition of the far interior. Had war not fortunately been avoided it is difficult to see how that vast and prospectively most valuable territory between the Lake District and the Rocky Mountains could have been protected from invasion and permanent occupation, and we are forced to the conclusion that until a highway is formed the interior of our country is indefensible."

And Fleming saw a greater purpose in a great railway, in a statement that had a prophetic ring that would not become apparent until the turn of the century:

"True, we are again at peace with our neighbours to the south, and perhaps likely to remain in that happy state for a considerable time, but possibly not always; some good authority has laid down as a maxim, that to maintain peace, a nation must be well prepared for an opposite condition of things, and therefore we must see the value of the railway route to bind the several North American Colonies of Britain together. But it is not alone as a work of defense that the British Pacific Railway would be serviceable in a military sense; it cannot be forgotten that within a very few years back the British troops had to be transported with the greatest possible rapidity to India and again to China. Such exigencies may at any time occur again, either in the same lands or at other points in the same hemisphere, and it must be of the utmost importance to the Imperial Government to possess the means of carrying military forces more rapidly by a route over entirely British soil than by any other route along which they may come in contact with antagonistic nations."

In the same year, George Thomas Cary, Sir James Le Moine and Nicholas Woods published their travelogue *The Lower St. Lawrence, or, Quebec to Halifax via Gaspé and Pictou, to which is appended Mr. Wood's description of the River Saguenay, also Legends of the St. Lawrence and all about fishing,* and even the sportsman could not ignore the military necessity of the railway. On arriving at Shediac, New Brunswick, the trio noted:

"Shediac is the only point at which the Quebec and Halifax Railway will touch this coast, after which it will take an inland curve leading west, and then northwards towards Trois Pistoles, on the St. Lawrence. A well-constructed branch of the great inter-provincial railroad is running here, and the actual existence of so important a link for military purposes should be an inducement to the home government to carry out the long talked of Railway, and secure to Quebec a winter communication with the sea board through British territory. The present aspect of American affairs makes this subject of paramount importance."

Curiously, even British sportsmen were predicting the route the line would take!

The military imperative was in all likelihood made clear to Fleming when he received his appointment as chief engineer of the Intercolonial Railway from Lord Newcastle, whom Fleming had cultivated as a personal friend after Newcastle attended the opening of the Toronto-headquartered Northern Railway when Fleming was chief engineer of that line. As an avowed imperialist (as his promotion of the All-Red Route attests) Fleming was quite finely attuned to the desires of the Imperial Government. It would be wrong to assume that he entered into his task without preconceived notions of which route to take.

Fleming himself appears to have understood that he was building a railway with military applications, but this is by no means certain, judging by the content of his 1867 pamphlet, *The Intercolonial Railway; A National Military Work.* Indeed, in his opening statements, the engineer admits to only two criteria for the line:

"The grand object of the Intercolonial Railway, it is admitted, is to secure the cohesion and integrity of the New DOMINION; its secondary object, to promote the development of the resources and industry of the country. The route which will best combine these objects is the one which should be chosen."

From that point onward, while paying lip service to military considerations, the pamphlet becomes less the observations of a railway engineer, and more a piece of political propaganda aimed at denigrating the compromise proposed by New Brunswick's Peter Mitchell, the Minister of Fisheries and Marine, for a line that would combine the Chaleur route with a link to Apohaqui and then to Saint John.

It is a curious document, one in which Fleming admits he is not of a military mind, but one in which he succinctly reflects much of the popular feeing of the day.

> "In considering the dangers which may beset the onward progress of the Dominion, only one from without presents itself—the disposition of our republican neighbours. It cannot be disguised that with the mass of people of the United States there is a strong aversion to the perpetuity of British institutions on the American Continent—an almost unaccountable insane hatred of everything British. The 'Munroe Doctrine' is the first article in their political creed, and they impatiently await an opportunity to gratify at once their national vanity and lust of territory, by extending their flag and institutions over 'this vast and unbounded continent.' He must be blind, indeed, who does not see how little commercial or social intercourse tends to allay this spirit which is being constantly augmented by Fenianism and jealousy. There was a time when the people of the United States expected that, in the isolated condition of the provinces, they would fall an easy prey into the arms of the Great Republic; but the last few years—of civil war on their part, and the development of national spirit in the colonies—has dispelled this delusion, and no hope now remains to our avaricious cousins but to wrest by force what they cannot obtain by stealth."

Decrying the sentiment within Canada that a nation of four million could not hope to resist the ambition of a neighbour with 30 million citizens, Fleming warms to his subject:

> "That there are weak and assailable points in the Dominion may not be denied. What country has not such? But there are strong places and impregnable defences; and the Dominion is not to be left alone to face thirty millions in a death struggle for the maintenance of its rich and undeniable inheritance."

The first, strong defence, Fleming insists, is the attachment to Britain. He paints a portrait of the United States as a demoralized and despotic power.

> "On no other terms than perfect freedom and equality can commercial relationships with the United States, however desirable, tend to any-

thing else than the absorption of the weaker into the stronger power. In pursuing such a national policy, the Dominion must, in the second place, make the most of its defensive position.

HALIFAX AND QUEBEC, the Gulf and River St. Lawrence, and the Great Lakes, the ice of winter and the iron-clads and wooden walls of Old England! These need only to be named to suggest a power of which the maddest annexationists must stand in awe.

But Halifax and Quebec must be in safe communication at all seasons of the year: the safety of the coalfields of Pictou and Cape Breton, the integrity of the Gulf and Gulf-ports, the navigation of the St. Lawrence, and access to the Great Lakes and the populous cities of Ontario, but be secured; and all this cannot be accomplished without the INTERCOLONIAL AS A MILITARY WORK.

In considering the route, it must be admitted the North Shore line—surveyed and recommended by Major Robinson—is the safest and best, as a military line, which can be adopted.

If a chain can only be as strong as its weakest link, it is manifestly worth while to test the link before risking the ship to a fate which a little forethought might have averted."

In statements certain to arouse sectional passions, Fleming goes on to illustrate how the port at Saint John was the weak link in that chain:

"What could prevent an ironclad fleet leaving New York, Boston, and Portland without observation, and appearing off St. John in twenty-four hours—capturing that city, and giving its civilians the first intimation that a state of war existed? What preparations could be made to oppose a simultaneous movement of troops from the frontier upon Woodstock, Fredericton, St. Stephen, St. Andrews and St. John?

Long before succour could be dispatched to their aid, the city of St. John and the river St. John, with all the western portion of New Brunswick (including the towns named) would be in the hands of an enemy, unheralded by any of the warning notes which usually precede the thunderbolt of war among civilized nations."

The engineer goes on to note that Saint John's trade with American cities, while being a strong point in favour of the Dominion, is a double-edged sword from a military point of view:

"St. John may be said to be par excellence the American city of the Dominion. Much of her business, her steamboat communications, her telegraph lines, her railway extension westward, are in the hands of American companies. The latter work openly, and avowedly undertaken as a United States military line, and approved as such by a Committee of Congress!"

From that point onward, Fleming launches into his diatribe discrediting Mitchell's alternative Apohaqui route, noting:

"Without professing to be a strategist, we have endeavoured to take a common sense view of the military aspect of the question; and if we are correct in the position that the city and river St. John are the weak points of the Dominion, then the location of the Intercolonial Railway by Apohaqui would be the worst possible. An enemy's gunboats in summer, and artillery on sleds in winter, could ascend the Washdamoak and Grand Lakes with the greatest facility, and completely command the greatest portion of the line through New Brunswick, entirely destroying its value as a military work, if not turning it to account against us. We trust, however, this point will not be lost sight of by the British Government."

Fleming does not repeat much of his argument in his 1876 history of the railway, saying only:

"The safety of the railway from attack in time of war continued to occupy a prominent place.... It was asserted that the Northern route, recommended by Major Robinson because 'passing at the greatest distance from the United States, and possessing in the highest degree the advantage of security from attack in case of hostilities,' was, in reality, greatly exposed to attack as, at several points, it was close to the sea, and that operations could be more successfully carried on against it than against the Central route, which at all points was at least 30 miles distant from the American frontier. It was held that this distance was sufficient to make the Railway safe, or at least as safe as a considerable portion of the Grand Trunk Railway westwards from River du Loup, and that it would be so regarded by the British Government.

On the other side, it was denied that the Northern route was open to attack, as only vessels of light draught could enter the waters which it touched; and that an enemy's fleet could not enter the Gulf of St. Lawrence, except at the risk of being cut off from support and supplies, whereas, an attack could be much more readily made on the Central route, Saint John city and river being comparatively near American harbours. Besides, the long vulnerable portion of the Central line would not be so defensible as the portion of the Grand Trunk Railway lying nearest the American frontier, because, in the latter case, there was an intervening range of mountains impracticable for the passage of troops and heavy artillery; while in the former, the line passing into the valley of the St. John, the river would afford ready means of attack."

Fleming goes on to make a strong argument against a privately-owned railway with military applications, a position that was missed amid the rhetoric of the newspaper pundits:

> "As in the case of the Frontier route, an argument was advanced in favour of the Central route on account of the less length of railway required. But to maintain this argument it was stated that no railway on the route would have to be purchased, because the companies owning them would willingly grant running powers over such as were constructed. On the other side it was shown that the project was not in accordance with the designs of the British Government, as evidenced by their proposed guarantee being for £3,000,000, with the condition that the Dominion Government would raise a further £1,000,000, whilst the estimate for the cost of the Central route was less than the £3,000,000. It was accordingly argued that a continuous line of railway was contemplated, and not a connection with railways in operation. A forcible objection was made to the Central route that one of the railways proposed as a connection was owned or controlled by citizens of the United States. Offers to carry troops in case of need were made to meet this argument. But it was evident such offers could not be enforced, [since] on the declaration of war the railway companies could readily withdraw all their rolling stock within the United States frontier, and leave the railway useless to the Dominion though available to the enemy."

It is clear that a commercial railway was not a high priority with Fleming. Indeed, in the year prior to his appointment as the chief engineer of the Intercolonial, he was advocating that it be built as quickly and as cheaply as possible without any thought to its commercial potential. In his *Memorial of the people of Red River to the governments of Canada and Great Britain* in 1863, he wrote:

> "Rather than indefinitely postpone the advantages of a steam connection between Canada and the Atlantic Provinces by attempting to secure as heretofore the precipitate construction of nothing less than a fully appointed Railway, would it not be more prudent to satisfy ourselves with a scheme which proposes at first a road of a less perfect character, and leaves the Railway and its sources of traffic to be built up by a gradual process? This policy not only appears to be that most likely to secure the desired object within a a reasonably short period,

but it seems most in harmony with the gradual development of a country from a wild an unoccupied condition, and equally in keeping with the state of the Public Finances."

If the British government was well aware of the military dangers outlined by Fleming, the Canadian government apparently was not, and there was by no means unanimous agreement within either parliament or Prime Minister Macdonald's cabinet. Indeed, cabinet was evenly divided, and the route of the Intercolonial posed the first real threat to the stability of the nation's first government. On March 28th 1868, the *Reporter* noted:

"With reference to dissentions in the Cabinet on this question, doubtless such do exist, but not sufficiently developed as yet to indicate a crisis. It is a question more over, whether, in the event of the North Shore route being adopted, Mr. Tilley's constituents would gain anything by his resignation. 'The minority must yield, and it is generally wisest to accept the situation. The division in the Cabinet is thus given:
    'For Robinson's line: Messrs. Cartier, Langevin, Kenny, Chapre?, Mitchell and Archibald. Against it: Messrs. J. A. MacDonald [sic], Macdougall, Howland, Tilley, Campbell and Russ?.' "

The "Chapre" referred to was J. A. Chapleau, one of Macdonald's Quebec lieutenants, while "Russ" was David Russell, a Saint John promoter.

This accounting indicates the deep division that existed in New Brunswick, for the Mitchell named as being in support of Robinson's path was Peter Mitchell, one of New Brunswick's Fathers of Confederation, while the Tilley in opposition to the route was Sir Samuel Leonard Tilley, another New Brunswick Father of Confederation who had gone so far as to threaten to resign from cabinet if the Bay of Chaleur Route was adopted.

It should be noted that Mitchell was from Newcastle, which was on the Bay of Chaleur route, while Tilley was from Gagetown, outside Fredericton, and thereby on the proposed Central route. Other New Brunswick parliamentarians took a more strident view. The Halifax *Chronicle* reported from Ottawa on March 27th 1868:

"The New Brunswick members of the Senate and House of Commons opposed to the North Shore route for the Intercolonial Railway, held a caucus yesterday, and resolved that if that route was adopted they would advocate a Repeal of the Union Act."

This antagonism carried on into June of 1868, until the news broke that the contractor retained by Fleming to survey the Central route (presumably Hartley, as reported a few months earlier by the *Reporter*,) had been told to suspend his work. Perhaps by this point Fleming's enthusiasm for any Central route had been tempered by a timely reminder from Lord Newcastle. In any event, by early July the Montreal *Gazette* was reporting:

> "Rumour has it that the Intercolonial Railway is one of the subjects now engaging the serious consideration of the Privy Council, and for our part we should not be surprised if the question of route were finally agreed upon at a very early day."

Indeed, the day the decision was made may well have marked the first Canadian use of the telegraph to transmit a news "scoop" by wire, as the *Reporter* reported on August 21st:

> "We have received the following important intelligence by telegraph. It is not all new, but it is entirely reliable:
>
> 'Intelligence reached Dalhousie on Saturday by telegraph, but was not generally believed until this morning, when the Newcastle *Union Advocate Extra* was received, giving an authoritative announcement that the Major Robinson route for the Intercolonial Railway has been chosen, the formal consent of the British Government given, and the money partly borrowed already.
>
> 'The work commences at the Nova Scotia boundary. Matapedia and Riviere du Loup immediately. Large party now locating the track at Matapedia. Commissioners to be appointed first meeting of Ottawa Cabinet—probably in three weeks.' "

The *Reporter* would later note, with some acrimony, that the *Advocate* was published in the constituency controlled by Peter Mitchell, but in fact, as Trout notes in his 1871 work, the cabinet had made its decision almost a month earlier:

> "The Duke of Buckingham's despatch, dated 22nd. July, 1868, is as follows: 'I have received your Lordship's telegraphic message that the route by the Bay of Chaleur has been selected by the Canadian Government, as the one to connect Truro with Riviere du Loup, and thus complete the Intercolonial Railway. I understand three routes to have been under the consideration of the Government of Canada, namely: one crossing the St. John River, either at Woodstock or Fredericton; the second in a more central direction through New Brunswick, and the third following the line selected by Major Robinson in 1848. The route crossing the St. John River, either at Woodstock or Fredericton, is one to which the assent of Her Majesty's Government could not have been given; the objections on military grounds to any line on the south side of the St. John River are insuperable. One of the main advantages, sought in granting an Imperial guarantee for constructing the railway, would have been defeated if that line had been selected. The remaining lines

were the central line, and that following the general course of the route surveyed by Major Robinson; and Her Majesty's Government have learned with much satisfaction, that the latter has been selected by the Canadian Government. The communication which this line affords with the Gulf of St. Lawrence at various points, and its remoteness from the American frontier, are conclusive considerations in its favour, and there can be no doubt that it is the only one which provides for the national objects involved in the undertaking."

By September 16th 1868, Fleming was issuing a notice that tenders for work on the various divisions of the railway would soon be issued, and all but confirmed that the line was following Robinson's route:

INTERCOLONIAL RAILWAY
To Contractors.

The undersigned is instructed by the Governor-General of Canada to inform intending contractors that, at an early day, tenders will be invited for the execution of certain portions of the Intercolonial Railway between Riviere du Loup and Rimouski, in the Province of Quebec; between Truro and Amherst, in the Province of Nova Scotia, and between Dalhousie and Bathurst in the Province of New Brunswick. It is intended to let the work in sections, or divisions, varying from fifteen to thirty-five miles, according to the situation and local circumstances. The surveys are now in progress and part completed, and the object of this notice is to afford intending contractors ample opportunity of examining the ground at once. The plans, profiles, specifications, conditions of contract, forms of tender and other documents required for the information and guidance of contractors, are now being prepared, and when ready, of which due notice will be given, may be seen at the Railway Engineer's offices in Halifax, Saint John, Dalhousie, Rimouski, Riviere du Loup, and at Ottawa.

SANDFORD FLEMING,
Chief Engineer.

Intercolonial Railway Office,
Ottawa, September 12, 1868.

Even when the route was acknowledged as being that of the North Shore, its opponents were unwilling to drop their criticism of the choice. The *Reporter* of August 20th 1869, took advantage of rumour to throw one last barb at the proponents of the Frontier Route, most of them based in Saint John:

"There is trouble about the Intercolonial Railway route through New Brunswick even among those who were delighted at the choice of the

Robinson line. The alarm is sounded that the Commissioners are about to adopt a route that will not accommodate the North Shore people at all. According to a Saint John paper friendly to the Government, a dreadful blunder is about to be made. We are told that 'the line will cross the Miramichi many miles above Chatham, pass into the interior of the country, and cross the Richibucto from ten to fifteen miles above the head of navigation; thus, with the exception of Campbellton and Bathurst, avoiding almost every settlement on the North Shore.'

So serious a matter is this thought to be, that an attempt is being made, it is said, to get up an agitation in Saint John in the hope that the Commissioners may yet be induced to change their decision. The idea is, of course, that Saint John, though preferring the St. John Valley route to any North Shore line, is still interested in having the latter, since it is to be built, pass as near as possible to the "settlements" and sea-ports of the North Shore. If the railway does that, it may bring some local traffic from the northern counties to the city; if it passes through the wilderness, it will bring very little.

The *Repeal* paper in Saint John suggests with a fine sneer that the 'military' argument may have induced the Commissioners to carry the road away from the settlements.

It was decided, argues one contemporary, that it would never do to take the railway through the valley of the St. John, in proximity to the American frontier, where Yankee soldiers could come and tear it up. In the same way, if it touches the harbours on the North Shore, Yankee gunboats can come and destroy it—so that it is wisdom on the part of the Commissioners to avoid the sea as much as possible, and cross the rivers in most cases ten to fifteen miles 'above the head of navigation,' there it will give the Yankee sailors some trouble to blow up the bridges or tear up the rails. This is very well as a turning of the 'military' arguments at which the North Shore advocates made so much, and which were so thoroughly devoid of real force. We have heard before, however, that engineering difficulties stood in the way of the accommodation of the people of the North Shore, and that to carry the line around by the seaports would involve, besides very heavy bridg-ing, a great deal of rock cutting and other difficulties. Considerations of economy did not prevent the selection of the North Shore route in the first place, and the North Shore people will think it strange that even the most formidable engineering difficulties should have much weight against the political influence they can bring to bear. What has become of Mr. Peter Mitchell, Minister of Marine and Fisheries—the great champion of the North Shore? Where is his boasted influence, of which we heard so much in the contest over the location of the railway? But the case is different. In the fight for the Robinson line Mr. Mitchell was simply assisting Sir George Cartier, the great dictator, in the business. Having got the line in the Province of Quebec located to suit him, Sir George is possibly somewhat indifferent to the interests of Mr. Mitchell and his neighbours of the New Brunswick North Shore. —Toronto *Globe*.

Briefly commenting on the above from the Toronto *Globe*, we may state that any hope of the Saint John merchants bestirring themselves to alter or amend the route of the Intercolonial is simply forlorn. While matter were in such a position as to give opportunity to Saint John to exert its influence in affecting the course of the road, we all know how idly that city looked on until the chance was lost. Presuming upon her favourable position on the seaboard, and the fact that much of the intercolonial trade in any case must pass through her ports, Saint John has never yet concerned herself as she might have done to encourage either local or general railway enterprise. In the only case where the Saint John men apparently displayed any vigour, we know that after beguiling others into the venture by first appearing to take stock themselves, they suddenly turned about and repudiated the whole affair. Witness the Western Extension scandal."

This report repeated the conviction that it was George Etienne Cartier who determined the final route of the line, threatening to resign from the cabinet in Canada and thus throw that colony into political chaos if he took the French vote from the St. Lawrence shore with him. In truth, even if he had not made such a threat, the Imperial government's preference would not have changed.

Even in the aftermath of Confederation and the period of reconstruction in the United States, when relations between the new-born and re-born nations appeared to be warming, the threat of war was never far away, as evidenced by Prime Minister Sir John A. Macdonald's experience at the Washington convention of 1871.

The scene is best set and explained by Lloyd Duhaime, in *Hear! Hear! 125 Years of Debate in Canada's House of Commons*:

"For Macdonald's Liberal–Conservative government of the first Parliament of Canada, continental trade was problematic. In the very year before Confederation, a bi-lateral trading agreement with the United States had expired. The Reciprocity Treaty had been of great benefit to Canadian industry but the United States steadfastly refused to renew it.

Prime Minister John A. Macdonald bided time during his first administration, administering a moderate policy of customs enforcement.

American fishing vessels were required to obtain licenses when fishing in Canadian waters. But when, in 1868, the fees were substantially increased American fishermen balked and responded by fishing without license. On January 8th 1870, the Canadian government suspended the licensing system and set afloat police cruisers. Seizures were made and the stage was set for a showdown.

In the American capital, President Grant, in his 1870 opening address to Congress, threatened retaliation. Macdonald could skirt the issue no longer. On February 1st 1871, events fell into place, offering him both a politically acceptable solution, negotiated and fully endorsed by the Imperial government. During the months of March and April 1871, the Prime Minister of Canada was stationed in Washington, DC, acting as a member of a Joint High Commission to discuss issues of concern between England and the United States. Ten commissioners convened in the American capital, and included Earl de Grey and Ripon, President of the Imperial Privy Council and Hamilton Fish, the American Secretary of State.

The Canadian Parliament was not sitting when the Treaty of Washington was signed on May 8th 1871. From the apposition of his signature on the parchment until the day he scheduled House time to table the Treaty, Macdonald refrained from public comment on the Treaty. The interim was not a quiet one. In September 1871, an American schooner *E. H. Horton* was seized for fishing in Canadian waters without license. A month later, left unguarded, the ship's moorings were quietly cut. The vessel escaped to Gloucester, Massachusetts and became the subject of much embarrassment to Canada.

May 3rd 1872 was the day for Macdonald's statement. Canada's first Prime Minister usually compressed speech notes on the back of a used envelope. Rare were the times when he would speak with any great degree of preparedness. But the speech he offered in the House of Commons, introducing the Washington Treaty, was different, and was the object of meticulous preparation. His biographers refer to it as one of his greatest speeches.

Right Hon. Sir John A. Macdonald—Prime Minister (Kingston): Mr. Speaker, on proceeding to Washington, an American statesman said to me, 'the rejection of the treaty now means war.' Not war tomorrow or at any given period, but war whenever England happened to be attacked from other sources. You may therefore imagine, Mr. Speaker, the solemn considerations pressing upon my mind if by any unwise course or from any rigid or pre-conceived opinions, we should risk the destruction for ever of all hope of a peaceable solution of the difficulties between the two kindred nations."

Sir John goes on to outline his reasons for signing the treaty, even though he realized it might have earned him the title of Judas or Benedict Arnold at home (especially from Maritime fishermen who felt their fishing rights had once again been sacrificed to the Americans by Upper Canadians, as they had under the old Reciprocity treaty.)

> "Reject the treaty, and you will find that the bad feeling which formally and until lately existed in the United States against England will be transferred to Canada. The United States will say, and say justly, 'here, when two nations like England and the United States have settled all their differences and all their quarrels upon a perpetual basis, these happy results are to be frustrated and endangered by the Canadian people, because they have not got the value of their fish for ten years.' "

Duhaime goes on to note the speech was a triumph for Macdonald:

> "The House ratified the Washington Treaty by a large majority of 121 to 55. For Macdonald, the Treaty was the last piece of his electoral plat-form for the 1872 federal election, an election which would return his Conservative party to power, but with a small majority of six over Blake and Mackenzie's Liberal party. The subject of free trade with the United States remained a pivotal issue for Canadian lawmakers for years to come, culminating in the North American Free Trade Agreement signed in the early 1990s."

There was some basis for Macdonald's trepidation about the United States' ability to attack, as Scheips explains:

> "In April 1877, as a result of the compromise by which Rutherford B. Hayes became President after the disputed election of 1876, the last of the troops on reconstruction duty in the South were transferred to other duty and the federal military occupation of the South came to an end."

Nor had the Union's army been allowed to stagnate in peacetime:

> "The record of the Army's technical development in the years down to the end of the century was not one of marked and continuous progress in every field, for it was hampered by military conservatism, insufficient funds, and the nation's slowness in adapting inventive genius to the art of war. Yet there was considerable progress. In transportation, with the extension of the trans-Mississippi railroads, it became possible to move whole wagon trains by lashing the wagons to flatcars and trans-porting the mules in closed cars."

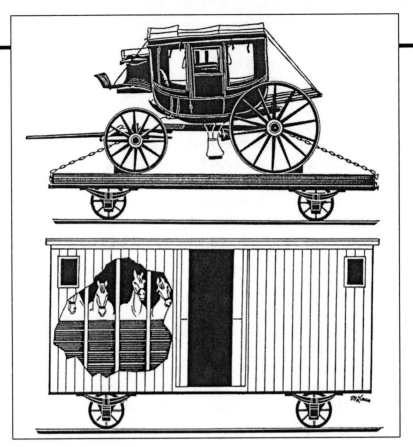

*Piggy-back service offered by the Nova Scotia Railway in 1856
was quickly adapted for military transportation.*
(*Canadian National Railways/Author's collection*)

As Stevens notes, however, this was not an American innovation:

"The 'piggy-back' idea was not new even a century ago; in 1801 James Anderson of Edinburgh was experimenting with wagons which would be swung on and off rail trucks. Howe is usually credited with bringing the idea from Auld to Nova Scotia... There were separate charges for horse, vehicle and load; the carter rode free. A flat car carried the vehicle, a box car the animals... in 1857 the railway carried 786 coaches and 2,900 coach horses. At one time 'piggy-back' freights earned one quarter of all freight revenues... The service, however, remained in operation during the lifetime of the Nova Scotia Railway, being discontinued soon after that line was taken over by the Intercolonial Railway."

It should not be accepted, however, that the Americans had perfected the movement of troops by train. As the events of the mobilization for the invasion of Cuba during the Spanish-American War illustrated, the success of the operation depended largely upon the ability of the military commanders, and General William Shafter and his officers put in a poor showing. This note is from the Spanish American War centennial website:

> "The Fifth Corps consisted mainly of US regulars, though there were some volunteers, such as the 71st New York, and the 'Rough Riders.' By this time, Shafter, at age 63, was a corpulent three hundred pounds in weight and suffering from the gout. He was in no condition to command troops in either Florida or in the jungles of Cuba. Visitors to his Fifth Corps camp commented that there seemed to be no discipline, though Shafter had the reputation of being a disciplinarian.
>
> Though it was not the original intention to use the Fifth Corps in this manner, the corps was soon being hastily ferried to Cuba to begin an all-out assault on the island. The entire process of embarking, transporting and landing troops and supplies was disorganized, and generally occurred in spite of itself. The general was not provided with a proper staff, and was not able to handle all the necessary arrangements with the officers who served under him."

Also vital to the success of the railroad mobilization was the degree of synchronization of military and civilian trains, which also did not go smoothly, as the Diary of Aubrey L. Whetton. of the First Missouri Volunteer Infantry shows. The unit was moved from St. Louis to Camp Thomas at Chickamauga in Georgia. It was intended to transport them to Shafter's headquarters and embarkation centre at Jacksonville, Florida, but the unit never saw action in Cuba:

> "May 21, 1898: Three or four miles out of Chattanooga our train stopped and all kinds of rumors spread from coach to coach as to the cause. After waiting about one hour we were allowed to get off our coach and take exercise. The boys strolled off in directions of farm houses near the track.
>
> Whetton, Cody, Frankel got some eggs and pie and heard organ played by one of our boys at one of these houses and then started back for train.
>
> Frankel wandered on to a house where some of the company were singing and playing and went in. After balance of boys went he made love to youngest daughter and as a result had a good dinner of cold meat, potatoes, salad, strawberries, cake & milk.
>
> After getting back to train learned there had been a rear-end collision between first section of our regiment and passenger train.

It was first stated that 6 men and a number of horses had been killed but we learned that 1 man Gen. Walker of Co. H. was the only man killed. H. Brolaski of Co. H and another man of same Co. were seriously injured but would recover."

One of the problems that plagued the US mobilization was the logjam of railroad traffic that delayed men, munitions and materiel around Atlanta, Georgia until well after the invasion of Cuba began.

CHAPTER FIVE

Coming of Age

GIVEN THAT IN 1871 THE INTERCOLONIAL WAS STILL FIVE YEARS from completion, and that even with the railway in service, Canada might find itself without the Empire's ability to fully co-operate in the relief from an American attack, Macdonald had little choice but to sign the contentious trade treaty. He was in all likelihood influenced by events in Europe where, in 1870, the Prussian army had invaded France in what might at first appear to have been—from a British and Canadian point of view—an unimportant squabble over the succession to the Spanish throne.

The Germans ultimately triumphed in a war that would lay the foundations for the Great War of 1914-18, but it sparked British concern that a total victory by the Prussians would result in a significant shift in the balance of power internationally. In the tangled web of European alliances, the French were important to Great Britain in that they provided a significant territorial barrier to the Atlantic. Only the construction of the Kiel Canal (1895) allowed the German navy to escape the confines of the Baltic, and challenge Britain for mastery of the waves.

That the Germans did not gain such an advantage was more a matter of good luck for Britain than it was an illustration of the ability of the French military. Indeed, the Franco-Prussian war of 1870-71 was the fourth great test of the railway as a military asset, as John Westwood notes:

> "When the Franco-Prussian War broke out in 1870 the German railways were well prepared and had some success in the first few weeks. However, later, when the battles moved onto French territory, supplies were slow in coming up, with transit times so long that meat was often foul-smelling by the time it was delivered. German locomotives and rolling stock were used inside occupied France, but as French bridges were lower than German, a number of locomotive chimneys were

knocked off; from then on Prussian locomotives were designed with 2-piece chimneys, the cap being detachable.

Where the German railways excelled was in the mobilization period, troop movements and schedules having been planned meticulously in advance. The Prussian conscription system, which entailed army service for all young men and the creation of a 'citizens' army' of ex-conscript reservists, depended on the railways to carry reservists to their army depots and then, with their regiments, to the front. Other continental European governments soon followed the Prussian example, thereby taking a long step toward total war, a concept that would not have been possible before the Railway Age."

Total war, whereby the resources of the civilian home front were directed toward the support of military operations, had already been achieved in North America by the Union army of the US Civil War. Obviously the Prussians had been as quick to learn from that conflict, as the Americans had been to learn from the Crimea.

What the Franco-Prussian War did from a defensive point of view, however, was place the French in the unenviable position of having to destroy their own railway infrastructure situated too close to enemy lines of advance, and thereby deny them, albeit temporarily, to the Germans. The string of German victories—Saarbrucken, Metz, Sedan—were all predicated on use and control of the extensive French railway system against a defending army that was ill-equipped to deal with the tactic.

Indeed, the French had planned to use their railways in support of a quick first strike against the Prussians, but their failure to do so could have served as a lesson to Canadian military planners, as Paul B. Hatley notes in *Military History* magazine:

"A concomitant weakness that also hampered mobilization was the lack of a clear understanding as to how French soldiers were to reach their respective zones of concentration along the German frontier. The French generally assumed that transport would be handled by rail, but when mobilization began there was no one with the primary responsibility of overseeing and coordinating rail transportation—that vital ingredient in the emperor's surprise offensive simply had been overlooked. It would not be until August 11 (almost a month after war had been declared) that the Ministry of Public Works appointed the Count of Bonville 'to oversee to the greatest extent possible the military transport required by the present war.' "

Had Canada been obliged to use the Intercolonial, or any of its other railways, in support of the defence of an American invasion, the new nation's military

Damage to a German troop train during the Franco-Prussian war of 1870-71. Not even iron bridges were safe from sabotage, although repairs to the damaged spans were easier to effect than repairs to the damaged stone abutments.

would have found itself similarly lacking such a key ingredient. The Royal Military College at Kingston would not open until 1874 to provide such training, meaning Canada would have had to call upon British expertise, and, in doing so, reduce itself in status from sovereign power back to supplicant colony.

In any event, had Britain been drawn into the Franco-Prussian war, or any escalation resulting from it, the Americans might have found their opportunity to expand northward, with the empire otherwise too engaged to send troops across the Atlantic.

In the meantime, the American leadership emphasized the importance it placed upon the railways by the unprecedented use of federal troops to break up strikes and keep materiel moving, as Scheips explains in *Darkness and Light*:

"In the summer of 1877 the Hayes administration used troops in the wave of railway strikes that marked the country's first great national labor dispute. These strikes spread to a dozen or more states and led to a number of requests for federal help. Thereupon, the Hayes administration pursued a policy of moving troops only to protect federal property or upon the request of a governor or federal judge. The Army stripped every post in Maj. Gen. Winfield Scott Hancock's Military Division of the Atlantic of its available men and also obtained troops from other posts. Additionally, President Hayes used some marines."

It is one of the great ironies of Canadian history that the military imperative the Intercolonial (a government-sponsored eastern railway) was intended to meet was a role taken instead by the privately owned, western Canadian Pacific Railway. The causes and course of the North West Rebellion by Louis Riel's Metis in 1885 have been well documented elsewhere, and need not be recounted here. But note should be made of the supporting role played by the Intercolonial.

It should also be noted that the federal government was quick to realize the strategic importance of the railway, as the *Rifleman On Line*, a web-based history of the Queen's Own Rifles, notes:

"Militia soldiers from across Canada answered the call to arms. The head of the CPR, W.C. Van Horne, promised Prime Minister MacDonald [sic] that he would transport all of the troops to Saskatchewan on the condition that he was allowed to do all the planning without interference from the army staff."

This Peto-like condition was quickly met, but it cannot be said that Van Horne acted with Peto-like efficiency, despite the fact some 3,000 soldiers—with the requisite number of horses and artillery pieces—were mobilized within days of call-up:

"The trip to the West was, for many, the hardest part of the campaign. The CPR line was not complete. There were four major gaps along the north side of Lake Superior. At some of these gaps the CPR had sleighs to carry the men and equipment but at others the men were required to march across the frozen lake. Even in areas where there was track the men suffered. There were not enough passenger cars, so open flat cars were used to transport the men through the frozen night. Eventually they made it to Port Arthur, where passenger cars were waiting. From there the run to Qu'Appelle Station was uneventful." *(Rifleman)*

With Riel returning from exile as an American citizen, and with American emissaries from Minnesota known to be on the scene, Canadians once again had reason to suspect Manifest Destiny was being exercised. Indeed, the debate about an intercolonial railway was initiated in large part by settlers in the Red River area, who sent Sandford Fleming to London in 1863 to press for Imperial funding for a railway. The defence of the northwestern territory had always been a high priority with Westminster.

Whether or not this was foremost in the minds of Maritimers of the day is unclear, but their response was prompt, if somewhat grudging, as Pierre Berton has suggested:

"The last troops to leave, on April 12, were those of the composite Halifax Battalion. They were called out after almost two weeks of controversy, some bitter attacks by Nova Scotia civilians and merchants, and a great many defections in the ranks. The threads that tied the Maritime Provinces to the rest of confederated Canada were tenuous. The following year (1868) a Liberal government would sweep back into power in Nova Scotia with an increased majority on a platform that included secession from Confederation. Few Maritimers thought that the North West had anything to do with them. Until this moment it had not occurred to them that they might have to commit their young men to the defence of the interior of the continent. They had always looked seaward, and their attitude was conditioned by the need to defend the coast of British North America.

'Why should our volunteers, and especially our garrison artillery, be sent out of the province to put down troubles in the North West?' one man wrote to the *Morning Chronicle*. 'Nova Scotia has nothing to do with their affairs; let Canada West look after their own matters.' "

This analysis is not entirely correct, as the preceding history has documented; certainly Nova Scotia's senior statesmen were aware of the defensive imperative of the Intercolonial. The reaction to the call to service in the North West, however, may be more of a matter of a lesson that each following generation has to re-learn, since many, if not most, of the men being called to arms were not alive at the time the Intercolonial was negotiated and established. Nevertheless, Berton contends this was not an isolated opinion:

"On April 2, after the government had ordered the 66th Battalion to stand ready to move, a representative delegation of businessmen from dry-goods stores, boot and shoe shops and grocery and drug firms demanded that a composite battalion be formed and only a certain number of men from the 66th be taken. It was from that unit that most of their employees came. Many Halifax merchants bluntly announced that if their men turned out for duty, they would be fired."

This should not be taken as proof that Nova Scotians were adamantly opposed to defending the far-flung margin of the continent, since volunteers did indeed answer the call to duty. In fact, as the Haligonians boarded their train at the city's grand Intercolonial station on North Street, citizens turned out in a patriotic display, as the *Morning Chronicle* of Monday, April 13th reported:

"Here were enacted scenes of mingled humor and pathos, while some of the sights were extremely touching. At the drill shed and on the way

---

the bands had kept up a constant strain of music, playing 'Far away,' 'We're off in the morning train,' 'Home, sweet home,' 'The girl I left behind me' and other appreciative melodies, keeping up the spirits of the lads and men.... The eyes of many a parent were wet with tears and little girls plaintively sobbed for their fathers and brothers."

The *Chronicle* proudly sent a special correspondent with the soldiers, riding the train all the way to Quebec and reporting;

"The train consisted of eleven cars and two locomotives, the two forward cars being the quartermaster's and for baggage, eight second class for the volunteers and a first class in rear for the officers.... A slight accident to the coupling gear between the rear locomotive and the front cart caused a detention at Richmond of fifteen minutes to repair it. One or two small scrimmages between some recruits and others of the 66th, who happened to have a little liquor with them, occurred on the road, but the disputes were quelled by the officers."

The newspaper's man on the scene was duly impressed with the Intercolonial's on-time performance, noting:

"The actual running from River du Loup to Chaudiere Junction, 120 miles, was done in 4.18... If the Grand Trunk exhibits the same activity in forwarding the troops the Haligonians will reach the scene of operations with such speed as to surprise themselves, and also let us hope the enemy."

He was less than impressed, however, by the performance of the Grand Trunk, which took over conveyance of the troops at Chaudiere Junction:

"By some unexplained action of the Ottawa military authorities and the Grand Trunk officials, the receipt of an order by the Grand Trunk to push the train through to Ottawa without stoppage was not wired to Col. Bremner. When the troops reached Montreal they were informed of the order, and then forwarded to Ottawa supperless. They had only one meal to-day and two yesterday. Although the men are prepared to bear hardships, if necessary, they deem such severe training impolitic, as the exhaustion and confinement is telling upon their general health."

Small wonder then that Maritimers should so love the Intercolonial, and come to regard it as their railway. The battalion's officers shared equally in the hardship:

"No Pullman was attached to the train, and the officers experienced considerable difficulty in disposing of themselves in their car, which was more crowded than any of the others."

Sir Robert Borden, the anti-confederate who became a Canadian Prime Minister watched troops leave Halifax to fight the rebels in the Northwest, and discovered a stirring passion for the new country.

The *Chronicle's* entire account of the trip from Halifax to Ottawa has been reproduced in Appendix Two of this work. It provides a vivid description of a soldier's life on the move in the railway age.

Among those moved by the passion of the event, as Morton notes, was a young lawyer who would go on to play a significant role in the future of the Intercolonial, and whose life would be irrevocably entwined with that of the railway's military role:

> "The young Robert Borden, a Nova Scotia anti-confederate, discovered his first stirring Canadianism as he watched fellow Haligonians entrain for the North West."

He would not be the first to feel the growing passion, nor would it be the only time that the Intercolonial played a part in the maturation of the nationalist spirit. In fact, it would be stirred three times in the span of less than 30 years. In the aftermath of the North West rebellion, Canada's domestic military policy focused again upon the militia role that had once proven to be so contentious in earlier times. This shift proved to be less than successful, as Morton notes:

> "Militia politics made less sense at the end of 1895 when Canada found itself involved in the worst Anglo-American war scare since 1861. The issue was an obscure border dispute between Venezuela and British Guiana but anti-British speeches were popular on the eve of an American election. At the climax of the crisis, the newest British gener-

al, W. J. Gascoigne, found himself without a staff, a plan and, thanks to a fierce but unrelated Canadian political crisis, a minister of militia. Like some of his predecessors, Gascoigne was appalled by Canadian insouciance in the face of imminent war."

He need not have worried. The collapse of the stock market, and warnings to the contrary from his own admirals and generals, obliged US President Grover Cleveland to abandon any thoughts of waging war, and accept a compromise:

"In Canadian military history, 1896 was a decisive year. In the aftermath of the Venezuela crisis, both the British and the Canadians did some overdue thinking. Reflecting on the possible war, the British army decided that its plan would have been to land troops at Boston or New York 'and make a vigorous offensive gesture.' Certainly no army would be sent to Canada." *(Morton)*

This shift in British policy appeared to put an end to the accepted military imperative of the Intercolonial Railway, for Britain was now ready, if necessary, to take the offensive on US soil, rather than ship troops to Canada to take up a defensive posture. It is this philosophy that laid the foundation for another ironic twist in the history of the railway; that it should reverse its role, and send Canadian troops in defence of the empire's interests overseas. The first opportunity to manifest this reversal came in the South African war of 1899-1901.

The so-called Boer War was made necessary, from Britain's point of view, to demonstrate to Europe, and most especially to the growing German power, that the empire was united and its resolve was strong; to engage England in war meant taking on Australia, India, and Canada—however reluctant Canadians may once again be to involve themselves in distant combat.

After a brief political crisis within two weeks of war being declared between Britain and the Old World-like settlers of Orange and Transvaal states, Canada mustered a contingent of 1,061 volunteers that left Quebec City on October 30th 1899, aboard the *SS Sardinian*, just in time to beat the seasonal freeze-up of the St. Lawrence.

Among the contingent were men from New Brunswick and Nova Scotia, who rode the Intercolonial from Saint John and Halifax, as described by James H. Birch Jr., in his book *War in South Africa*:

"Throughout the lower provinces more men desired to become 'The Soldiers of the Queen' than could be accepted, and great was the disappointment of those who had to remain at home. Offers for service came pouring in from Saint John, Fredericton, Woodstock, Saint Stephen, Newcastle, Chatham, Moncton, Sackville, and other places in New Brunswick; from Halifax, Truro, Yarmouth, Pictou, and elsewhere in Nova Scotia; while such was the feeling in little Prince Edward Island

The Dominion Atlantic Railway's locomotive, decorated to honour Annapolis Valley volunteers bound for the Boer War via the Intercolonial's track to Halifax.

(Nova Scotia Archives and Records Management Service #N-10152)

that the whole contingent might have been obtained there without much difficulty. In Saint John, the City of the Loyalists, where many of the leading citizens are the descendants of that sturdy stock, the New Brunswickers, numbering nearly one hundred strong, had a magnificent send-off.

The line of march from the parade grounds to the railway station, a distance of about one and a half miles, was crowded with enthusiastic thousands, who were evidently determined that this old city should not be outdone by anyone in its appreciation of the readiness of the boys in red and blue to uphold the national honor. From windows, roofs and every point of vantage, cheer after cheer went up as, with swinging stride and true soldierly men, they swept along.

From one of the windows of the Fusiliers' clubroom there streamed out an immense British flag, which called forth the most tumultuous cheering, while the playing by one of the bands of 'The Soldiers of the Queen', called forth round after round of applause. As the procession swept along Charlotte, down King, and up Dock Street, it seemed as if the entire population was outdoors, and as the familiar strains of 'Auld Lang Syne' floated out upon the evening air, for the shadows were now beginning to gather, the excitement knew no bounds...

The scene at the depot was one to be remembered, but not described. The immense building was packed with the representatives of all classes, ages, and sexes, while thousands were outside and around, anxious to have a part in the imposing pageant. The soldiers were to enter by a side door, and a strong force of police were on hand to keep open a narrow path to the cars. But when the band struck up the National Anthem, and the cheers from without indicated the arrival of the boys, the surging crowds came together with a rush, the pathway was closed, and band instruments, policeman's batons, ladies hats, and soldiers' uniforms were one wild medley of confusion."

Confusion also reigned upon the arrival of the New Brunswick men, as the Halifax *Chronicle* of January 10th 1900 reported;

"The train on which the St. John, Sussex and Moncton volunteers came arrived at Richmond at 2.30 and at North street later on. Owing to the uncertainty of the time of arrival, the hour first announced being 12.30, there was not a big crowd on hand to greet the volunteers and the people who did go up were divided between Richmond and North street station, it having been reported that the troops would detrain at Richmond with their horses.

But the horses did not come with the men and the latter came right into North street. Among those who met the train at Richmond and got on board were Capt. Curren, superintendent of militia stores, and Recorder MacCoy.

On arrival at North street the soldiers were drawn upon the platform and made a fine appearance. Most of them wore Hussar uniforms but there were some in artillery and few in infantry uniforms. All the cavalrymen came from Sussex, excepting four who came from Moncton.

Major Borden was in charge of the party and, accompanied by Capt. Curren, marched them to the exhibition grounds. Major Borden left again yesterday afternoon for Canning and will bring the Kings Hussars volunteers to-day.

There was no demonstration at North street when the quota arrived and citizens present thought there might have been a militia band in attendance to play the men to the quarters.

Car Conductor Hamilton, who came over with the volunteers, said the send off at the St. John depot last evening was a tremendous one."

Recruits from the Maritimes once again travelled the Intercolonial Railway, and volunteers from the rest of Canada rode the same rails when the second contingent left from Halifax on January 21st 1900.

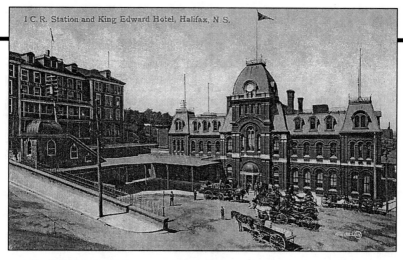

I.C.R. Station and King Edward Hotel, Halifax, N.S.

Halifax's North Street station seen in a Valentine Company postcard of 1910; it saw the departure and arrival of troops for the Northwest Rebellion, the Boer War and the First World War prior to its devastation by the explosion of 1917.
(Jay Underwood collection)

The Halifax *Morning Chronicle* reported on the arrival of the volunteers on January 8th:

"It is now possible that there will be a change in the arrangements for accommodation of the contingent. It is understood that an effort has been made to have the men, or most of them, quartered at Wellington barracks, but that the military authorities have not decided to shift the Leinsters, though they have offered to give up one floor of the big barrack to the Canadians, the overflow to go to the dockyard. It has been suggested if the mounted rifles go by the *Montezuma*, about 350 men might be placed in the barracks, and about 200 at the Exhibition grounds, between three and four hundred of the artillery would also be at the fair grounds. About 900 horses can be placed in the horse stalls and cattle sheds."

On January 9th, the *Chronicle* noted:

"The transport steamers *Montezuma* and *Laurentian* at the railway piers, and *Pomeranian* at Cunard's, attracted hundreds of citizens to the vicinity of the piers yesterday...

At last a detailed announcement is made regarding the dates at which the first quotas of the South Africa contingent will arrive in

Cape Breton artillery officers who rode the Intercolonial to Quebec, then back to Halifax for departure to South Africa. They are identified as (rear, from left) Lieutenant McMullin, Surgeon-Major O'Neil, Major Crowe, Lieutenant Ingraham. (Front from left) Lieutenant Downing and Captain McDonald. This illustration was taken from the Halifax Morning Chronicle *and computer-enhanced by the author.*

Halifax. The Sussex and St. John volunteers, under Major Borden, will arrive here on Tuesday evening and will be quartered at the Exhibition grounds. The Kings County Hussars will join the New Brunswickers on Wednesday evening, when the party will number about 37. Nothing respecting the time of arrival of the rest of the troops was given out here up to yesterday morning....

The Winnipeg and Manitoba dragoon troop will be the first of the contingent outside the provincialists to arrive here. They are expected on Friday evening or Saturday morning. The first troop thereof is B squadron of the BC Dragoons, 42 men and 44 horses enrolled at Winnipeg, and the second troop will be the Manitoba Dragoons, 46 men and 33 horses enrolled at Portage La Prairie, Verdun, Brandon, Yukon and Winnipeg..."

These units would form the regiment known as the Royal Canadian Dragoons, and would include three men who would receive the Victoria Cross for their bravery in action at the Komati River on November 7th 1900. For the record, it should be noted the vessel *Montezuma* was declared a health hazard (due to sickness among the crew) and was replaced by *Milwaukee*.

In what can only be described as a classic understatement, the *Chronicle* concluded:

> "It is expected the I.C.R. will be somewhat crowded for accommodations, and sleeping and passenger cars available at this end are being forwarded."

These men formed the two small battalions of mounted rifles and three batteries of field artillery, 1,320-strong, that comprised the second Canadian contingent, but in an ironic twist, several of the volunteers had to ride the Intercolonial's rails twice. The *Morning Chronicle* makes note of the incident:

> "The Halifax applicants who were given places in the artillery divisions of the Canadian contingent paraded at the drill shed at 5 o'clock Saturday and left North street at 6 o'clock on a special train to join the Sydney quota at Truro, thence to Quebec... The Halifax artillery recruits have received pay at the rate of 75 cents per day and substance pay at the rate of 60 cents per day up to the time of their arrival at Quebec."

It must have been a strange sight; the Halifax quota consisted of only four men, one of whom was an English mining engineer who had spent time in South Africa. Two of the men had previously served in artillery regiments. The *Chronicle* added this note about the "special train," in its following edition:

> "The Halifax quota to join the Sydney artillery volunteers left on Saturday afternoon for Truro on a special train. The train was not made up specially for the four volunteers, but the cars were needed up the line and the time was convenient for both railway and volunteers..."

Once mustered in Quebec, the men immediately returned to Halifax. They would become members of "E" Battery once in South Africa. Other Canadian volunteers would follow. The arrival of the Winnipeg volunteers was awaited with much anticipation, as the *Chronicle* of January 15th reported:

> "The Regina and Winnipeg volunteers arrived at Richmond at 2 pm Saturday, where they detrained and proceeded to their quarters at the exhibition grounds.
>
> Lieut. Col. Irving, Capt. Wynne, Capt. Curren and Dr. Jones, with Recorder MacCoy and W.F. Pickering were among those who were at the station to meet the train, and there were about a hundred citizens besides. The train consisted of fourteen cars, and every car was decorated with British and Canadian flags. The engine was likewise decorated, and on the cowcatcher a big Union Jack was draped.... Major Clapham, of the CPR, said they were given good send-offs right along

Sergeant Arthur H. L. Richardson of Lord Strathcona's Horse, received his Victoria Cross at Wolve Spruit, July 5th 1900.

(Lord Strathcona's Horse [Royal Canadians] Museum & Archives)

Lieutenant Hampden Z. C. Cockburn of the Royal Canadian Dragoons, was awarded the Victoria Cross for his action at Leliefontein, November 7th 1900.

(Royal Canadian Dragoons Archives)

Sergeant Edward J. Holland, of the Royal Canadian Dragoons, was one of three members of the regiment to earn the Victoria Cross at Leliefontein, November 7th 1900.

(Royal Canadian Dragoons Archives)

Lieutenant Richard W. Turner, Royal Canadian Dragoons, received his Victoria Cross for bravery at Leliefontein, November 7th, 1900.

(Royal Canadian Dragoons Archive)

the line and he mentioned Bathurst, Newcastle and Campbellton as particularly strong in their enthusiastic welcome and send-off. Major Clapham expects Nos. 7 and 8 trains will leave Regina on Monday morning.... The special conveying the detachment left Regina on the 7th and reached Winnipeg on the morning of the following day.

At the latter place ten palace horse cars, containing 147 horses, were added to the train, most of these animals being the private property of the officers and men.

Major Clapham was in charge of the train and looked after the interests of the men from the time they left Regina and Winnipeg, until their arrival in this city."

Perhaps the most storied regiment to pass through Halifax was Lord Strathcona's Horse, raised privately in western Canada by Donald Smith, a promoter of the Canadian Pacific Railway. The 400 men left Halifax aboard the *Monterey*, among them was another hero who would be awarded the Victoria Cross.

Also embarking for South Africa via Major Robinson's Path, were soldiers of New Brunswick's North Shore, through which the railway ran, who had been denied their opportunity to participate in quelling the northwest rebellion, as the on-line history of the Royal New Brunswick Regiment notes:

"In 1885, the New Brunswick Provisional Battalion was formed as a composite of all the regiments in the province, and was slated for service against the rebels in North-West Canada. Although the unit was speedily organized and readied for duty, the capture of Riel made the action superfluous. It was disbanded on 26 May, and the men returned home to their regiments without seeing action.

The situation was different, however, in 1899. 'G' Company, 2nd (Special Service) Battalion, Royal Canadian Regiment of Infantry was recruited from the Militia of New Brunswick. It was one of the two farthest forward companies at the capture of Paardeburg, and it brought home the regiment's first battle honour: SOUTH AFRICA, 1899-1901, 1902."

At the height of the preparations the *Chronicle* published the following report:

MUNITIONS OF WAR
Big Train Load of Supplies
Arrived for Transport

Pier 3, at deep water, presented a warlike appearance yesterday. A train load of supplies and munitions of war arrived this morning and was run into the shed, occupying both tracks. Ten or twelve box cars are loaded with supplies, the nature of which could not be ascertained. About thirty gun carriages and ammunition wagons are on flat cars and carefully covered with canvass.

The train is strictly guarded by a sergeant, corporal and six privates of the Leinsters, and the main doors of the shed are closed. Amongst the supplies are a gatling gun and ammunition and a large lot of revolvers.

The steady tramp of the guards up and down the shed and the long array of formidable-looking gun wagons be more of suggestion of war perhaps than anything yet seen in the way of preparations.

The transport *Laurentian* has been handed over to the government by Contractor Keefe and it is probable that her portion of the supplies will be put aboard tomorrow, though it is not likely she will take all which has come in.

The work of fitting the *Pomeranian* is progressing amazingly. The horse stalls are already nearly finished and the work on deck is progressing very rapidly. The quarters for new men aft are also being pushed rapidly toward completion.

It is stated that guard will be kept on all stores and supplies which come in until they are put aboard the ships.

Enquiries of the freight department elicited no further information as to the nature of the contents of the cars which will be gazed at curiously until unloaded."

The mobilization would prove to be a dress rehearsal for a greater conflict, an exercise that would give the Intercolonial some expertise that would render invaluable service in the First World War, with a schedule that would be mirrored in an eerie manner.

The first contingent left for South Africa from Quebec City aboard *SS Sardinian* on October 30th 1899, but over the next three years all other contingents would leave from Halifax, with the troops delivered by special trains.

The second contingent left Halifax in three phases, on the *SS Laurentian* January 21st 1900, the *Pomeranian* on January 27th, and *Milwaukee* on February 21st.

The third contingent, Lord Strathcona's Light Horse, left aboard the *Monterey* on March 17th 1900. The fourth contingent, a field hospital unit and the Canadian Mounted Rifles, left aboard *SS Manhattan* on January 14th 1902, and January 28th aboard *SS Victoria*.

The fourth contingent, the mounted police force comprised of squadrons from across the country, left aboard *HMS Montfort* on March 1st 1901. The final contingent left aboard three ships; *Cestrian* (May 8th 1902) *Winifredian* (May 17th) and *Corinthian* (May 23rd).

The Intercolonial stood ready to welcome the first Boer War veterans home when the steamer *Idaho* arrived in Halifax on November 1st 1901, with 400

Soldiers arriving in Halifax from South Africa saw the Intercolonial's North Street Station decorated for the occasion.
(Nova Scotia Archives and Records Management Service #N-9274)

men from the first contingent which had left Quebec in October of the previous year.

In peacetime the "free passage" of troops, a benefit initiated by the Nova Scotia Railway, was taken to the extreme, and was not without its abuses, as Stevens notes:

> "In March 1881 the General Officer commanding the Imperial garrison at Halifax used his pass to transport fourteen officers and their ladies to Ottawa for a vice-regal ball. Pottinger thought that this was a bit thick and as these soldiers had no votes he ruled that thereafter the General's pass could only be used by specified nominees."

David Pottinger was the Intercolonial's general manager, who waged a long battle against political interference and outright corruption in railway operations. The incident was typical of a litany of abuses and excess that plagued the Intercolonial and promulgated the mythology of its incompetence, recounted in great detail by Stevens. Politicians, pundits and the public alike all contributed in some way to this myth, and in doing so, pushed the military imperative into the background, until, as with its soldiers, Canadians came to treat the railway with the "hated in peacetime, loved in war" mentality that still pervades civilian thinking today. It was not as though there had not been ample warning. Almost from the moment Robinson proposed the route, there had been mutterings to the effect that the railway was "a cow that would never raise a calf," and as late as 1867, Fleming himself had warned:

> "A Military Railway between Quebec and Halifax, with a Commercial Railway between Montreal and St. John.
>   It cannot be done. As well try to mix oil and water."

As late as 1892, New Brunswick's A. G. Blair, a former premier and later to be Laurier's minister of railways and canals, (quoted by Donald Mackay in *The People's Railway*) had lamented:

> " ... if other than high state considerations had influenced the location it would now be enjoying a most successful career."

That "high state consideration" was the military necessity, and it made its value obvious in the greatest measure in support of the war which historians generally agree brought Canada into the international community as a nation in its own right.

CHAPTER SIX

The Shining Hour

THE CAUSES OF THE FIRST WORLD WAR NEED NOT BE DISCUSSED here; it suffices to say the Great War was to sound the death knell of the Intercolonial Railway. Oddly, Stevens' "definitive" history of the creation of Canadian National Railways devotes a mere two paragraphs to the impact of the war on the Intercolonial—a period he calls he railway's "shining hour"—and he begins with two misstatements:

> "And now, at long last the Intercolonial was destined to fulfil the purpose for which it had been built. Nearly fifty years before, the route had been chosen with a view to military security; in 1914 it became a strategic route of incalculable value."

Firstly, the route had been chosen more than sixty years previously, by Major Robinson; Sandford Fleming had merely validated that endorsement and taken credit for it. Secondly, the railway had not been intended to transport troops eastward to fight a European power, but westward to fend off American aggression. Stevens was right in suggesting the railway's value was "incalculable."

The full role of the Intercolonial during the First World War is difficult to establish, for its military imperative would in some part be usurped by the opening of Wilfrid Laurier's National Transcontinental Railway line from Montreal overland (roughly Robinson and Fleming's central route) to Moncton (completed in 1915 except for the bridge at Quebec City), and—after US entry into the war in 1917—the Canadian Pacific's line, through Maine from Montreal to Saint John.

It is certain, however, that a large number of the 619,636 Canadian soldiers who served in Europe from 1914-1918 embarked at Halifax, and arrived there by way of the Intercolonial's rails. Stevens' history, however, quoted some differing figures:

> "From August 4th 1914 to March 31st 1919 the Intercolonial in addition to its regular services handled 1,081 troop trains, conveying 691,262 of all ranks. Freight shipments rose from 5,082,484 tons in 1915 to 8,177,862 tons in 1918."

Canadian National's work on the topic, *Canada's National Railways: Their part in the War*, unfortunately does not distinguish between the constituent railways in the Canadian Government Railways system at the time, but does separate Canadian Northern from the pack. In this respect, the numbers of troops, and volume of munitions carried by the Intercolonial cannot be determined without factoring in the Prince Edward Island Railway. CN instead chooses to label all the railways under the Canadian National banner, even though that railway did not exist at the time of the war (the book was published in the 1920s by Canadian National, perhaps in an effort to stir public support for the new, controversial entity by invoking still simmering patriotic passions.)

CN does, however, acknowledge that the Intercolonial was probably the first of Canada's railways to learn that the nation was at war:

> "The first intimation.... came on that fateful Sunday August 2nd, 1914—the memorable day when a solemn hush pervaded the whole world, while men waited to know whether for the British Empire it should be peace or war. On that day, a message was received by the Passenger Traffic Manager at Moncton from Brigadier General Biggar, Ottawa, asking that two trains with artillerymen and guns, on their way from Prince Edward Island to Petawawa Camp, should be turned back. Great Britain had declared war and Canada was in it."

From that day onward for almost five years, the railways and the military were in constant communication. CN, ignoring the experiences of the Northwest Rebellion and the Boer War, suggests the railways were unfamiliar with the transportation of troops, and in order to move them quickly, and safely, the system of giving trains a special number was instituted:

> "Serial Number One, therefore, was given to the special train which ran from Toronto to Halifax on February 5th, 1915. It carried nurses and military engineers.... Thereafter, specials were forwarded incessantly. By the end of that month of February, twelve trains, carrying 4,195 troops, had been moved from Montreal to Halifax. During the remainder of the year 1915, one hundred and thirteen special trains with 14,000 troops were operated; and this was only a mere foretaste of what was to come in the succeeding three or four years. In 1916, 455 trains carrying 195,524 soldiers were moved to Halifax. In 1917 there were 309 special trains and 117,136 soldiers carried. In 1918, 294 specials with 102,847 troops. The United States had then entered the war and some

American troops were being rushed through Canada. The movement generally was at its height. In one month, eighty-two special trains with 33,754 men were moved from Montreal to Halifax. On one day of this month (April 26th), fourteen thousand men were carried."

This boast was first made by L. B. Archibald, Superintendent of Parlour, Sleeping & Dining Cars, Halifax in the October 1915 issue of the *Canadian Government Railways Employees Magazine*. In the article (see Appendix Seven), Archibald describes in detail the logistics behind a troop train movement, providing stark contrast with the almost casual arrangements undertaken in 1885:

"When a movement of troops is to be made. The Militia Department advises the Passenger Department of the Intercolonial giving the number and class of men, the stations between which the movement is to be made and the starting time. The Sleeping and Dining Car Department is then instructed to provide the necessary first-class sleeping cars for the use of the officers, and also to provide the necessary dining, commissary and table cars for use of both officers and men. The Superintendent of Car Service is called upon to furnish the necessary colonist cars for use of the men. All cars for this movement are then given a thorough cleansing.

The number of troops to be moved on one train varies but 40 to 50 officers and 500 to 550 men would be an average. For their transport, the following cars would be required, and the train made up in the following order behind the locomotive: 1 baggage car, 1 commissary car, 1 table car, 10 colonist cars, 1 first-class dining car and 2 first-class sleepers—16 cars, which is about all a first-class passenger locomotive can haul and make time."

The service would have made Wellington proud:

"For a train as above described, where three or four meals were served on the trip from Montreal to Halifax, about 1,000 lbs. of beef, 150 lbs. of sausage, 150 lbs. of bacon, 75 lbs. of lamb, 150 lbs. of fresh fish, 400 loaves of bread, 140 lbs. of butter, 40 doz. of eggs, 80 qts. of milk, 35 lbs. of oatmeal, 15 bus. of potatoes, 1 bus. of carrots, 1 bus. of turnips, 1 bus. of onions, 6 lbs. of tea, 150 lbs of sugar, 50 qts. of cond. coffee, 50 lbs. of rice and 80 lbs. of cheese would be required.

From this it can be seen that when the Canadian soldier travels, he brings his appetite along with the rest of his equipment. Nothing is too good for him."

Clearly the Intercolonial's contribution was of monumental proportions. It is less clear what proportion of CN's grand total of troops was carried solely by the Intercolonial:

Sketch of soldiers aboard their train: "Sunday at Windsor Junction is about the last word in isolation." From CN's book **Canada's National Railways: Their part in the War.**

"The total number of soldiers moved during mobilization was 462,379, on 1,191 special trains, while on the regular trains, 351,619 military passengers were carried—a total of 813,998."

These figures are tallied in Appendices Four and Five, at the end of this work.

Following the necessary observance of secrecy surrounding troop movements, the ports of departure were given code names. Halifax was known as "Uncalm," Saint John was "Undeclined." Montreal was designated "Untrap." The movement of these troops did not take place without some incident. CN notes some transport ships were often delayed by U-boat scares:

"When that happened, there would be some unusual excitement to the boys and girls at some lonely spot some distance down the line from Halifax. The troops trains would all be held up, it not being desirable to bring them into the city until the men could be embarked. One Sunday, four trains carrying United States troops were held up at Windsor Jct. And they were joined soon after by three or four others containing Canadian soldiers.

Sunday at Windsor Junction is about the last word in isolation; and when the soldiers looked out on the sea of rocks surrounding them, their feelings may be imagined. It was at times like these, that they seized the opportunity to cover the cars with chalked inscriptions, which became so familiar on troop trains. "Berlin or Bust", uncomplimentary remarks about the Kaiser, and notes of defiance from this battalion on its way to settle with him, were the most common sentiments."

What the soldiers thought of Windsor Junction, Nova Scotia, can only be guessed, but it is clear from the writer's description that he had never visited the village, where the Intercolonial and the Dominion Atlantic tracks met. Nova Scotia and New Brunswick units, however, made immediate use of the line at the outbreak of the war, participating in the creation of the first Canadian contingent, as described in various unit histories, such as *No Retreating Footsteps*, Will Bird's history of the Nova Scotia Highlanders:

> "On organization of the First Canadian Contingent in 1914, the 93rd Cumberland Regiment supplied volunteers to the 13th Battalion, while the 76th Colchester and Hants Rifles, and the 81st Hants Regiment supplied men for the 14th and 17th Battalions.
>
> The three Nova Scotia units, the 76th, 81st, and 93rd, subsequently contributed men to the 25th, 106th, and 193rd battalions of the C.E.F. The 25th battalion served in the 5th Brigade of the 2nd Canadian Division from September 1915, to the Armistice, and made a great name for itself as one of the foremost raiding units on the Western Front. The 76th, 81st, and 93rd also supplied personnel to the Halifax Composite Battalion, a militia unit which garrisoned Halifax Fortress and provided guards for the Internment Camps at Halifax and Amherst."

Likewise New Brunswick's North Shore provided its share of early volunteer soldiers, as the on-line history of the Royal New Brunswick Regiment notes:

> "When the regimental system was cast aside at the outbreak of the First World War, the men of eastern New Brunswick joined the numbered battalion of the Canadian Expeditionary Force and went off to war. Thus the 2nd Battalion, RNBR perpetuates the 12th Battalion, 26th New Brunswick Battalion, 55th New Brunswick and Prince Edward Island Battalion, 132nd North Shore (A Company in Campbellton, B Company in Chatham, C Company in Newcastle and D Company in Bathurst), 145th Battalion, and 165th French Acadian Battalion.
>
> With the notable exception of the 26th, all of these battalions had the misfortune to be broken up to reinforce the Canadian Corps and never saw action as concrete units. The 26th Battalion, however, became part of the 5th Infantry Brigade of the Second Canadian Division and served in France and Flanders from 1915 until the Armistice. This unit did yeoman service throughout the war, fighting in almost every major engagement in which the Canadians saw action on the Western Front. It accumulated 21 battle honours, won 266 decorations and awards, and lost of one of its commanding officers, LCol AEG MacKenzie, DSO, to enemy fire at Arras."

The first Canadian contingent embarked for Europe at Quebec, in a flotilla of 33 ships which gathered in convoy in the Gaspe and was escorted across the Atlantic by the Royal Navy. Other contingents would follow, a great many from Halifax and Saint John by way of the Intercolonial. This was not simply because of winter's influence on the St. Lawrence.

When German U-boats began appearing in the Gulf of St. Lawrence, a relatively enclosed body of water for all its evident size, the Department of Defence and Militia switched ship movements from Quebec to Halifax and Saint John, where more open water made wolf-pack hunting less successful for the Germans. A millennium website, which includes a history of Halifax-Dartmouth, notes that the city and its railway bore the brunt of mobilization for the First World War:

> "The enlistment rate at Halifax during the great conflict was one of the highest in Canada. Most of the half a million Canadians who ventured to the front passed through Halifax and boarded their transports at Pier Two."

This massive invasion may have been partly responsible for the increased capital expenditure the Intercolonial sought from the federal government, as *Canadian Railway and Marine World* reported in March of 1915:

> "The estimates laid before Parliament recently ask for the authorization of the following expenditures on capital account, among others:- Dock and wharves, $30,000; new terminal facilities, $3,000,000 (which includes a revote of $750,000); to increase accommodation and provide new machinery, $3,500 (revote), and for Willow Park service, $39,500 (revote)..."

Willow Park was the site of the Intercolonial's Halifax roundhouse and repair shops, and was devastated by the explosion of 1917. It remains to this day as the Canadian Armed Forces' supply depot in Halifax, although it is no longer connected by rail. In that same year, on May 2nd, the *Ocean Limited* (which is still the world's oldest continuously scheduled passenger train) began daily fast service between Halifax and Montreal. The Bathurst *Northern Light* observed:

> "New and thoroughly renovated equipment, with the most powerful engines, will help make the journey of twenty-five hours between the City by the Sea and the Canadian metropolis a pleasant experience."

This is not to suggest those comforts were passed on to the men in uniform. Among the thousands of soldiers who shipped out from Halifax was John Cannon Stothers, who joined the 170th Battalion (Mississauga Horse) and went overseas in October of 1916 aboard H.M. troopship *Mauretania*.

John Cannon Stothers.
(Courtesy Steven Stothers)

His letters home are posted on grandson Steven Stothers' web site, and one, which describes his trip on the Intercolonial, is reprinted as Appendix Three to this work.

"Dear Mother: Somewhere in Quebec, Sunday, October 22nd, 1916

It is some time since I really wrote you a letter. I've lived so much in the past few days that to write an account of it that would do it justice would take pages—perhaps reams.

Oct 23 . . . . I was interrupted last night by a bunch of the boys gathering around for a little sing-song which continued till "lights out". We are now into New Brunswick I think. Every little village we have passed through so far has been distinctly French in appearance. The first building in each village is the R.C. Church. They seem to go in strong for beautiful architecture in their churches even though their houses and buildings are not up to a very high standard—-much like our own 25 years ago.

This morning we saw a man ploughing with a team... one horse and one ox. Reg Topp is on this train as he got transferred with his pals of "D" company of the 170th. A week ago Sunday...

Friday night was the last night we spent in Camp Borden and on Sat. about 2 p.m. we entrained, mistakes were made in our arrangements for entraining and the men of the different platoons were not kept together in all cases. The result was that when we got to Union Station there was a great deal of confusion, and a few of the men did not meet their friends...

The train is bumping so much that I can hardly write. The scenery resembles that of Northern Ontario only is on a smaller scale. The rocks and mountains are not so bare and glaring as those along C.P.R. in Northern Ontario. We must detrain at Campbelltown, N.B.

We have just been off the train for an hour's route march at Campbelltown [sic], N.B. We got our limbs stretched and had a look at the place and the inhabitants and found everything good. The people on one street threw apples at us and caused a little disorganization of the ranks but the officers were the only ones to take exception to any such disregard for military etiquette.

There is a big river here and just beyond it a great hill lit up by the sun whereas where we are is under a cloud. The view is simply wonderful... and everybody is sitting up to take notice.

We should be in Halifax tomorrow morning about 3 or 4 o'clock. Our time is now one hour slower than the time here."

The time difference was significant to the railway of the day. Atlantic Time was also known as Intercolonial Time. By way of a footnote, eighteen members of the Stothers family enlisted to fight in the Great War. All survived the terrible ordeal.

At the end of the bumpy ride were the troopships, which took soldiers aboard as soon as the wheels of the carriages stopped turning. Perhaps with a captain's pride, the master of the troop ship *Olympic*, quoted by Robert H. Gibbons in *The Glory That was... Olympic* (Sea Classics, March 1973 Challenge Publications) noted:

"On March 23, 1916, the *Olympic* sailed for Halifax to pick up Canadian troops. A special feeling grew up in Halifax for the liner and when she was in port, the newspapers would announce 'Old Reliable in Port Again.' Commodore (Sir Bertram) Hayes [captain of the ship] recalls:

'Until they reached the docks they would not know by what ship they were going. As the train entered the docks they would all be hanging out of the carriage windows, and the first men who caught sight of her four funnels would yell, 'OLYMPIC,' or 'The Old Reliable,' and a cheer would go up that made the hearts of all on board glow inwardly.'"

Olympic made ten round trips to Halifax, ending January 12th 1917. The sudden influx of soldiers such vessels created did not come without its adverse effects, as a Halifax municipal web site notes:

"Debauchery has a long and illustrious history in Halifax. WWI, like other wars, squeezed the wild side of Halifax into the open, and created a kind of underground economy for the bootlegging of booze, the sex trade and 'moral blight' generally. Whenever the garrison was a hive of activity, relations between soldier and civilian occasionally buckled. The King's men were treated lightly by the authorities and seemed almost above the law, but on Dominion Day of 1916, Temperance was the victor. No less than 150 liquor wholesalers and retailers were put out of business and stuck with a surplus of illegal stock, their employees out of work. But Prohibition effectively pushed the supply and demand for booze underground."

As the website—perhaps philosophically—notes, the sobering influence of Prohibition did not last:

"On a day in May, an unruly mob of sailors broke into City Hall and smashed everything in sight over a shoplifting charge brought against one of them. The servicemen's riot of 1918 is one of many examples of the acrimonious relationship between soldier and civilian that has characterized the life of the garrison."

This rather sordid aspect of the city's history finds a more positive chord in the memoirs of David Blythe Hanna, the transplanted Scot who was the administrative genius of MacKenzie and Mann's Canadian Northern Railway. Writing of his experience in the Railway War Board from 1914-1918, Hanna, who would become the first president of Canadian National Railways, said of the Intercolonial:

"The Intercolonial, in a wonderful and totally unforeseen way, justified its building as a political railway. One is the more delighted to say this, because of a somewhat different tone that has perforce been discernible in one's allusions to some aspects of its administration from its earlier to its latter days.

For three years our Atlantic ports absolutely saved the situation, as far as Canada's sustained support for the war was concerned. Until the United States followed our example, in April, 1917, the short-line military access to the Atlantic ocean during the winter was not open to Canada. We couldn't reach Portland by the Grand Trunk, or Saint John, freely, by the C.P.R., because either movement meant using a foreign neutral for military purposes. The Intercolonial, therefore, was our true approach to Europe.

But the Intercolonial ran only from Montreal; and troops and supplies had to come from all over Canada. There could not be efficient movement from and to Montreal without co-operation in all the country between Montreal and Vancouver and Prince Rupert. The four main Canadian railway systems for war purposes were, therefore, operated as one vast national system. The Intercolonial in winter and spring was only the small end of the funnel. In summer, as Halifax was the nearest port to Britain, and the submarine menace made the shortest possible sea voyage more important than short land journeys on this side of the Atlantic, the Intercolonial was also in extensive use.

In several vitally important respects the Intercolonial was more consequential than the other lines combined. It had to receive a larger proportion of wounded and returning troops than any of them. The first provision for hospital trains fell on the Intercolonial; and the 'fish trains' were its peculiar care...

'Fish trains' carried British gold to be minted at Ottawa, most of it to be sent to the United States to pay for war material. 'Silk trains' carried Chinese coolies who were brought across the Pacific to work behind the trenches in France and Flanders. Between July, 1917, and April, 1918, sixty-seven 'silk trains' entered Halifax carrying 48,708 coolies."

The transport of the Chinese labourers was perhaps the least glorious of the Intercolonial's wartime feats, representing the deep-seated racism displayed toward Asians that persisted and manifested itself in the internment of Japanese Canadians during the Second World War. CN describes theses events, in the 1920s, with an almost innocent glee:

"They had to be carried in secrecy, in conformity with the general policy with which all war operations were conducted; and they had also to be carefully watched, lest they should escape en route. The head tax of five hundred dollars would have to be paid for any Coolie escaping; and as one Chinaman, to the eye of the average white man, is as much like another as are two peas, identification and recovery would have been difficult, if not impossible. Indeed, there is a story that a slippery Coolie did escape from a train passing over the prairies. The guard, who was responsible, was worried, but not dismayed. He dashed down and 'commandeered' the first Chinaman he met, and carried him off as a substitute for the one he had lost."

The CN book also notes that a troopship ready to leave Halifax was delayed for two days while enough rice was found to put aboard to feed the Chinese labourers. The fact that guards were necessary at all, suggests these labourers were not always willing workers. Hanna notes:

" ...the coolies, even when they could be kept behind blinds, were not as interesting as the boxes of gold, of which the public knew nothing, and about which observers along the route were mystified indeed."

Not all of the "fish trains" passed through unnoticed, however. The Moncton *Daily Times* of August 30th 1915 noted:

> "A special train passed through Moncton Friday night containing near-
> ly $20,000,000 in gold (700 boxes) and securities worth about
> $25,000,000, being the second largest shipment from London to
> strengthen British credit in the United States. It arrived in New York yes-
> terday morning. The train was made up of steel cars and had 38 guards
> aboard, and on the way to New York was preceded by a pilot engine
> and a car."

But what would a military railway's service be without its share of cloak-and-dagger operations? CN's official version of its war record notes there were many other such secret trains used on the Intercolonial:

> "Secrecy in the movement of troops was, of course, observed at all
> times; but occasionally trains [sic] would be run over the road, which
> was certainly not a troop train, because it would consist of only two or
> three cars. No doubt some of you who read this have heard those spe-
> cials hurrying by in the night, or have seen them flashing past by day,
> and have wondered who or what was in such a hurry.
>
> Even the trainmen, who were conducting the mysterious passen-
> gers, and the despatchers who were securing them the right of way and
> double assurance of safe operation, wondered who the mysterious
> passengers were, who never relieved the tedium of a long journey by
> so much as a peek through the heavily curtained windows.
>
> Generally such trains were carrying statesmen on special mis-
> sions—statesmen of Europe, often going to the United States; of
> Canada, going about at home or bound abroad; or, occasionally, after
> the United States entered the war, potentates of that country. For
> instance, on one occasion, Premier Robert Borden, attended by mem-
> bers of his cabinet, passed through Moncton on a mysterious special.
> The utmost secrecy attended the movements of this train. No one was
> allowed to see or recognize the occupants, while the train was passing
> through; although the news afterwards came out that when they
> reached Halifax they went directly on to the warship which was waiting
> to convey to Great Britain."

Borden made three such trips to Britain; the first in 1915 saw him raise Canada's manpower commitment from 150,000 troops to 250,000. The second came in 1916, to the Imperial Conference in London. The third trip took place in the spring of 1918 when Borden insisted upon, and won, the right for Canada to participate in planning the conduct of the war. It was one of those pivotal moments when Canada indelibly established its national identity, and secured its place as an equal partner in Imperial affairs. The official version continues:

> "On another occasion, a number of Italian representatives landed at Halifax from a warship, and were sent to Washington, under conditions of the most profound secrecy. A party of diplomats from the United States came through from Washington, and boarded a warship at Halifax. Mystery trains came to be rather common as the war progressed."

The record allows that British statesman A. J. Balfour was one of the passengers on a clandestine train, as he travelled to Washington via Halifax to entreat the US Senate and Congress to assist in the struggle.

In assessing the Intercolonial's role, John Castell Hopkins takes a more dispassionate view than either Borden or Hanna. In his 1919 work *Canada at War*, he infers the wartime service rendered by the Intercolonial to the Empire was a just return for British investment in Canada, and in particular, Canadian railways:

> " ...if railways, such as the Intercolonial, had to be constructed, at a period when Provincial credit was poor and inter-Provincial unity a dream, Great Britain guaranteed the loans to a total amount of $25,000,000...
>
> If the Dominion wanted to build great canals, or construct a Canadian Pacific, or a Canadian Northern, or a Grand Trunk Pacific, the money was readily obtained in London at a rate of interest and with a facility which no small nation not under the British flag, and not having British power and stability to guarantee its position, could possibly have commanded..."

The railways reciprocated on October 24th 1917 by forming the Canadian Railway Association for national defence, as Hopkins notes:

> " ...with the object of formulating in detail a policy of operation for all or any of the railways, for the co-ordinating of industrial activities toward the prosecution of the War, and for rendering the most efficient possible service to the national cause. It was hoped that through heavier loading of cars, elimination of unnecessary train service, the co-operative use of all facilities to the best advantage, the country's needs might be better served, and, of course, the convenience of the Railways also."

By then it could be argued the Intercolonial had already done its duty. What is remarkable about the Intercolonial's wartime service—and is often overlooked in popular histories—is the railway's safety record during a period when special troop trains were run amid the regular civilian passenger and freight trains. As the American experience in the Spanish-American War had shown, without a high degree of co-ordination, accidents were bound to occur, often with fatal results. The Intercolonial apparently did not experience a single mishap, unlike the system in Great Britain, where one accident alone—the Quintinshill wreck of May 22nd 1915—resulted in the deaths of 215 officers and men of the 7th Royal Scots Regiment, two employees of the Caledonian Railway, and serious injuries to 191 soldiers in the special troop train. Eight people died in the express train, and 54 were injured. Two other passengers died in the local train also involved in the wreck. The incident is best described in L. T. C. Rolt's classic work *Red For Danger*:

> "The troop train had suffered the worst; indeed, as a train it had ceased to exist at all… When the Carlisle brigade left the still smouldering remains at 9 a.m. the next morning after twenty-three hours continuous duty the fifteen coaches of the troop train, four coaches of the express, five goods wagons and all the coal in the engine tenders had been completely consumed…
>
> The precise number of men who lost their lives in the troop train was never established, for the roll of the Royal Scots was lost in the accident."

It cannot be said that the Intercolonial ran without mishaps, especially in the severe winters of 1916-17 and 1917-18. Most of the incidents involved extra freights, the most serious being a collision between regular passenger train 506 and a derailed series of ballast cars on the National Transcontinental Railway near Edmundston, NB on March 6th 1917. About the same time, there was a collision near Montreal involving a Canadian Government Railways troop train, with no loss of life, as the Moncton *Daily Times* recorded on March 6th 1917:

> "A heavily laden east-bound troop train was derailed in the Southwark yard about a mile east of St. Lambert, Quebec station a day or so ago, breaking the engine from the tender, which set the automatic air breaks [sic] on the twelve coaches, brought the train to a standstill after one coach had left the rails and several others had side-swiped a light engine standing close to a cross-over. No one was reported injured. Both engines were slightly damaged and were taken into the round-house, while the baggage car and the first three colonist-cars, all loaded with troops, were also somewhat damaged, having broken windows and scraped sides. These were taken back to Point St. Charles.

The troop train in charge of an I.C.R. engine and crew was going at a fair rate of speed on the main east-bound track when it took a switch to the cross-over which, for some unexplained reason, was left open. The engine jumped several feet as soon as it struck the frog at the end of the cross-over, and broke from the tender, landing on both rails of the west-bound track. The baggage car just cleared a little engine which was standing back of the frog on the west-bound track, but left the rails. The next car side-swiped the light engine, breaking its windows and scraping considerable paint and woodwork off, but neither car nor the next left the rails, although they rocked alarmingly.

Scare rumours spread

The automatic airbrakes worked so effectively that only a few soldiers in the forward cars were aware of what had happened, and no one was injured or seriously shaken up. Rumour was soon busy spreading the report that as many as thirty-five were injured or killed. Some of the soldiers in the rear cars continued their card games until told of the accident, when they hurried up to view the damage and assist in removing the baggage from the derailed car. This was placed alongside the track, and after a few hours delay, the new cars were procured and the troops proceeded eastward."

In November of the same year, in similarly severe weather, a local express from Levis, QC bound for Campbellton, NB ran into a stalled freight train at Montmagny, QC. Earlier that month the *Maritime Express* from Halifax to Levis derailed at L'Islet, QC, but there were no injuries or deaths reported in either case. Extreme winter weather played roles in many of these upsets.

The most devastating wreck in the region occurred post-war, in December of 1918, involving troops returning from Europe on a train on the National Transcontinental line, east of Edmundston, NB, described graphically by the Toronto *Globe* in its January 3rd 1919 edition:

"With every possible care and attention to alleviate their suffering, the forty-odd soldiers from Toronto and vicinity who were injured late Tuesday evening when a Transcontinental troop train jumped the track some distance east of Edmundston, were brought to this city, arriving about 4:00 a.m. to-day. The men who escaped injury on the train when it was derailed were also brought here. All will be taken to Toronto over the Canadian Pacific Railway. The first train left at 3:00 this afternoon with the uninjured men, while those hurt in the wreck left at 7:00 o'clock this evening on a specially fitted hospital train of the C.P.R.

Two hospital cars, with doctors and nurses, were attached to the train to carry the worst cases. The train carrying the uninjured men is

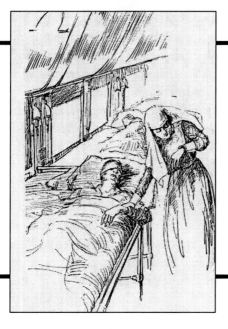

On board a hospital train. This sketch is from CN's book Canada's National Railways: Their part in the War.

expected to arrive at Toronto about noon Friday, while the hospital train will cover the distance between Quebec and Toronto in twenty hours, it having the right of way, and so is due to arrive at 3:00 p.m.

At the Discharge Depot the Canadian Press learned that none of the men injured is in danger.

Colonel Marriott, Commanding Officer of the Discharge Depot, with Major Labbe, second in command, have been on the job since the first reports of the wreck came in Tuesday evening, getting everything in ship shape to assure the comfort of the men.

Canadian Government special train No. 1174, with the injured and others arrived here at 5:30 this morning from Glendyne, Quebec, with four hundred and twenty-six uninjured but badly shaken up, and fifty-four injured. The bodies of the three killed were left at Glendyne, Quebec for inquest.

Arm Hacked Off to Release Him

No. 3,010,613, Private Olsen whose right arm was hacked off above the elbow, to release him from the wreck, was left in the hospital at Edmundston.

Toronto Soldier's Story

Private G. A. Phillips of Toronto, one of the injured, related his experience to the Canadian Press. He says that the accident occurred about 15 miles east of Edmundston on Tuesday afternoon, while their troop train was travelling at a fast clip. He says that of the thirteen cars in the train, ten were ditched, one of them completely over-turned. The three cars that remained on the track were the dining car and the provision cars. There was a strong wind, with snow. A biting cold caused suffering to the wounded, but help soon came, and the wounded were placed inside what remained of the cars that were not smashed. All the boys that were uninjured took a hand in helping out the injured, and soon, with the debris of the coaches, a number of open fires were roaring, bringing comfort to the men. A relief train came out from Edmundston, and, after its arrival, all worry and discomfort disappeared.

Other Toronto injured men here are: D. Sinclair, R. Tracall, A. Robb and E. Walios. They are only slightly injured."

The efficiency of the Intercolonial at this time was due both to the ability of its staff and Sir A. H. Harris, the Canadian Pacific executive who oversaw the co-ordination of the transportation system between Canada and Britain throughout the conflict.

There was more to the Intercolonial's wartime service than troop and munitions trains, and the occasional run of bullion, as the New Brunswick *Albert County Journal* reported from Moncton on July 25th 1917:

"Five train-loads of wounded men, and women and children, sent back from England by the imperial authorities, passed through the city Saturday night and Sunday morning. The first hospital train came through about 9:00 o'clock Saturday night, and the second about 2:00 o'clock in the morning. The other trains arrived later Sunday morning, and some of them were met by bands. The Maritime men were of course left behind for discharge at the port of embarkation, and some of them passed through by regular trains on Sunday en route to home in Upper Canada and the west. Private O'Brien, of Petitcodiac, a member of the 26th and home on two months' furlough, passed through the city on the C.P.R. yesterday afternoon. Many of the returned women are English who were living with their husbands in the west and followed them to Great Britain after they enlisted. There were also quite a number of the Canadian-born on the trains."

As important as it was, Halifax was not the lone focal point of the Intercolonial's wartime activity. CN notes that Moncton, the headquarters of the Canadian Government Railways in the region also played a key role in the effort to defeat the Germans:

"The stay of troop trains there was necessarily longer than at most places; and there was scarcely one of Canada's famous regiments which did not march through its streets... All troop trains were halted

Moncton's train station. Ninety per cent of all Canadian troops in the First World War passed through here, and the city was the headquarters for the Intercolonial Railway. This is a postcard view circa 1910.

(*Jay Underwood collection*)

there long enough for a thorough inspection, and all cars were cleaned, watered, and gassed. The engines and cars were changed, and orders given for a clear run to Truro and Halifax. This gave from a half to three-quarters of an hour for the men to relieve their weariness by a short route-march. It has been estimated that ninety per cent of the troops sent over-seas had the opportunity of marching through the streets of Moncton..."

Moncton by this time had become the junction for the Intercolonial, the Canadian Government Railways, and the National Transcontinental Railway. The large yards built for the NTR were invaluable for the preparation of the motive power and rolling stock needed to keep the troops and munitions rolling.

The Moncton shops also did sterling work in a humanitarian capacity, producing hospital cars in record time over the 1916-17 holiday season. The CN history notes:

"The first two cars built were more or less experimental. Eight more were quickly built, with the improvements and changes which inspection suggested. The Military Hospitals commission was so pleased with the work of the Moncton mechanics, that it immediately ordered another eight cars, which were completed in thirteen days."

The railway co-ordinated the movement of its hospital trains with the same precision as its special troop trains:

> "When the wireless station at, let us say, Pennant, not far from Halifax, picked up word from a homeward-bound hospital ship that she had so many wounded on board, it was at once passed along to the railway authority, and a vestibule-car hospital train, consisting of the special equipment set apart for the service, was run down to the side of the ship when she arrived."

The cars were state of the art, for their time, as the CN history notes:

> "The medical and commissary fittings of the car were very complete. Each car had a small kitchen, fitted with gas heater, sanitary sink and ice box, with ample accommodation for the dietitian to do her work. Toilet facilities were well arranged, and there were lockers for linen, medical supplies, and so forth. The cars were equipped with Baker heaters, and lighted by electricity, with auxiliary gas light. Electric fans were provided for each car. With the natural beauty of the mahogany finish, but with all unnecessary upholstering and carpeting removed, they were not only sanitary, but an attractive conveyance.... The exterior finish was in the standard dark green color used on cars of Canadian National Railways. A large red cross on a circle of white was painted on either side of the cars, with the words 'Military Hospital' in gilt letters."

On these trains were men who thoroughly deserved the distinction of being called a hero, for facing the insidious perils of trench warfare, bombardment, assaults and gas attacks. Many heroes did not return (see Appendix Six.)

Sterling wartime service came with a high price for Halifax and the Intercolonial, a payment that was made in blood on December 6th 1917, when two vessels collided in the city's harbour. The story is recounted on the City of Halifax's tourism website:

> "Around eight that morning, the Belgian relief ship *Imo* left its mooring in Bedford Basin and headed for open sea. At about the same time, the French ship *Mont Blanc* was heading up the harbour to moor, awaiting a convoy to accompany her across the Atlantic. A convoy was essential; this small, barely seaworthy vessel was carrying a full cargo of explosives. Stored in the holds, or simply stacked on deck, were 35 tons of benzol, 300 rounds of ammunition, 10 tons of gun cotton, 2,300 tons of picric acid (used in explosives), and 400,000 pounds of TNT. "

*A view of the Richmond yards c1910, looking north toward
Pier 6. It was from here that troops embarked for their
voyages to South Africa and Europe. This area was
devastated by the explosion of 1917.*

(Jay Underwood collection)

This lethal mix of explosives had been loaded onto *Mont Blanc* in New York, and the ageing ship had reached Halifax without prior incident:

> "The *Mont Blanc* drifted by a Halifax pier, brushing it and setting it ablaze. Members of the Halifax Fire Department responded quickly, and were positioning their engine up to the nearest hydrant when the *Mont Blanc* disintegrated in a blinding white flash, creating the biggest man-made explosion before the nuclear age. It was 9:05 am...
>
> Over 1,900 people were killed immediately; within a year the figure had climbed well over 2,000. Around 9,000 more were injured, many permanently; 325 acres, almost all of north-end Halifax, were destroyed."

Lost immediately in the explosion was the ICR station's covered passenger platforms (then under control of Canadian Government Railways) on North Street, where so many soldiers had arrived just days before. It was there that Canadians bound for the Boer War had embarked seventeen years previously, and the Halifax militia had entrained for the North West Rebellion barely three decades earlier.

The railway's yards and piers were destroyed, track was torn up, rolling stock and locomotives were scattered by the terrible wind. The immediate casualties included twelve brakemen, six engine crews, and five track workers. A total of about sixty railwaymen were killed. Also lost to the military were carloads of horses bound for the Western Front as pack animals. Out of this calamity came a story of heroism, and the salvation of an Intercolonial train

Vincent Coleman, the railway's hero of the Halifax Explosion. His watch was found in the wreckage of the shed at Richmond, its hands frozen at the time of the blast.
(Nova Scotia Archives and Records Management Service)

due into town at any moment. Michael Bird recounts the incident, in *The Town That Died*:

"In the outer office of the Railway Yardmaster, 200 yards away from where the *Mont Blanc* lay burning, Chief Clerk William Lovett and Train Despatcher Vincent Coleman were discussing the fire when the door was thrown open and the sailor.... burst in.

"Everybody out!" he shouted. "Run like hell! Commander says that bloody ship is loaded with tons of explosives and she'll blow up for certain." Then he was gone again and the door slammed behind him.

For a second neither man moved and the only sound in the office was the ticking of the clock on the wall and the muted roar of the billowing flames outside. Then Lovett leapt for the telephone and got through to the C.G.R. Terminal Agent's office on Cornwallis Street.

"Mr. Dunstan? This is Bill Lovett. There's a steamer on fire against Pier 6 and we've just been told by the navy that she's carrying explosives and is likely to go up any minute.... Right... No, he's not here at the moment.... Just Coleman and me.... Yes, we're clearing out now."

Lovett and Coleman made for the door together. They had left the office and were making their way across the tracks when the despatcher stopped and turned back.

"What do you think you are doing?" demanded Lovett. "We've got to keep moving."

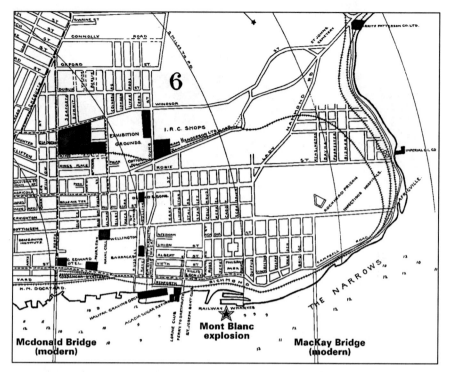

A map of the Intercolonial Railway yards in Halifax. The site of the Mont Blanc *explosion, at Pier 6 adjacent to the Richmond yards, has been marked in this detail from a city plan of 1910.*

(NSARMS/Ian Cranstone)

"I've just remembered. There are trains due in shortly. I must telegraph through to Rockingham and Truro to have them hold everything up."

Before his companion could say anything further, Coleman ran back toward the office. Once there he seated himself at his desk, reached for the telegraph key and began to send out his message."

Bird makes note of the final minute before the blast:

"At his desk in Richmond, Vincent Coleman just managed to complete his warning message with ' ...munition ship on fire in the harbour—Goodbye' and then the sixty seconds were past. Time had run out for Halifax."

Historians of the explosion disagree on the exact details of Coleman's story. The train due in was said to be late, and may have missed the devastation anyway, but it is Coleman's sacrifice and deliberate attempt to save the train, whether or not it was necessary, that made him a hero.

***Pier 8, lined with wrecked boxcars in the aftermath of the
December 6th explosion in 1917. The area was destroyed as thor-
oughly as if it had been bombed from the air by an enemy force.***
(Nova Scotia Archives and Record Management Service #N-17145-1)

Coleman's actions produced at least one grateful survivor, who was quoted
in the Moncton *Transcript* of December 7th 1917:

> "Conductor Gillespie, when went to Halifax on No. 14 Express on
> Thursday morning, arrived in Moncton this morning in charge of No. 9
> Express from Halifax. Conductor Gillespie had a narrow escape from
> death. His train was running on time, but was held fifteen minutes by
> the despatcher at Rockingham. He says that the explosion blew the
> windows out of the train at Rockingham, some 4 miles from Halifax. All
> the crew of No. 10 are safe."

Clearly not even a catastrophic explosion could prevent the Intercolonial from
getting Express No. 9 out on time! The newspaper may have erroneously
reported the number of Gillespie's train, since it was in all likelihood No. 10
and not No. 14. The No. 10 train was one of the first conveyances used in the
aftermath of the blast, as Janet Kitz explains in *Shattered City*:

> "The night express train from Saint John, New Brunswick, the No. 10,
> had been about ten minutes late that morning, pulling into Rockingham
> soon after nine. As it approached the suburb, about two miles north of
> Richmond, there was an upheaval, and all the windows were smashed.
> Luckily no one was hurt. The engine driver proceeded cautiously until
> the track was impassable. Soon all the passengers got off the train to
> see how they could help. The conductor decided the best thing to do
> was fill the train with injured and homeless and head back to
> Rockingham."

At about 1:30 that same day, the train was ordered to return to Truro, picking
up medical help at Windsor Junction. At Truro the victims were taken from the

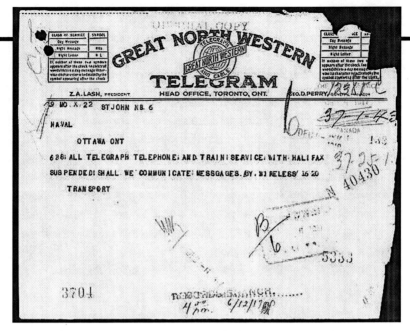

*The official telegram to Naval Headquarters, Ottawa,
December 6th 1917, advising of the explosion at Halifax. The
telegram says train service had been suspended, but this was not
accurate. The Intercolonial had trains running the next day.*
(National Archives of Canada)

train and given shelter. It would be the first wave of an exodus that would see
similar flights of mercy to Kentville, NS, and as far north as Antigonish, NS.

The activity of the Intercolonial after the explosion was worthy of any railway on a front line. As Kitz has noted, this was due in part to the swift action
of key employees:

> "W. A. Duff, assistant chief engineer of the Canadian Government Rail-
> ways, had stayed at the Queen Hotel. After the explosion he borrowed
> a car and drove to North Street Station to inspect the railway property...
> The further north Duff travelled the worse the situation became. Several
> times he turned back to drive seriously wounded people to hospital,
> but he finally decided that communication with the outside world was
> more important."

On arriving at Rockingham, Duff began the very necessary task of sending telegraph appeals for help to towns along the line as far as New Brunswick. Duff
did not act alone, and in fairness the Dominion Atlantic Railway deserves as
much credit for its part in the relief effort. George Graham, the chief executive

officer of the DAR had been in his private car at North Street Station when the *Mont Blanc* went up in smoke and flames, and his own escape from injury was miracle enough for one day.

As soon as word reached Moncton, CN's history notes:

> " ...the General Manager, Mr. C. A. Hayes... equipped a special train with aid of all sorts, human and material. Expert officials in all departments, medical aid, supplies and nurses were on the first special. It was followed by three others, with officials, fire and wrecking equipment, repair crews and plant, and food. From all quarters of the system, help and expert advisers were gathered to the solution of this new problem in Canadian railroading. The above force applied itself for the succeeding weeks, day and night, until order was once more restored and the service again in running condition.
>
> This, of course, did not hold up the transportation of troops."

This latter statement is not entirely true. Lost in the blast were about sixteen per cent of all the passenger cars in use on the Eastern seaboard at the time, and at least seventy per cent of the hospital cars. This would put a severe strain on the railway's ability to carry troops to the docks, and the returning injured away to hospitals in the outlying towns.

One of the first relief trains into the city came over the DAR tracks from Kentville, bringing more doctors, nurses and medical supplies to assist an already overwhelmed hospital system. Within a day of the blast, five relief trains had been sent to the city from the Annapolis Valley, and as far away as Amherst, New Glasgow and Sydney. Sir John Eaton, president of the prestigious Eaton's retail chain, sent his personal train stocked with food and supplies, while expresses would later arrive from as far away as Boston.

That train faced its own set of problems, as Kitz recounts:

> "On the way from Saint John to Halifax, people stood at every station, eager to board the train. Doctors and nurses were given preference, and soon every place was filled. Snow and gales also met the train, and heavy drifts caused stoppages. Then the engine broke down, delaying it even further. On Folly Mountain, difficult terrain about seventy-five miles north of Halifax, the railway line was completely blocked. When the purpose of the train was made known, every man in the area got to work, shovelling ramming and using brute force. Amid loud cheers, the train finally got through. It arrived in Rockingham early on the morning of December 8 and made its way slowly around the city, along the barely finished tracks to the South End Station, therefore avoiding Richmond."

The ICR passenger station at North Street was ruined by the blast of 1917, and sixty people died when the roof covering the platforms was blown in. The main building continued to serve as headquarters for the railway, despite having windows blown out and walls cracked. This photograph was from a series of postcars published by Underwood & Underwood.

(Jay Underwood collection)

The effect of the explosion on the Intercolonial could well be the topic of a single work, suffice it to say the impact was immediate and devastating. The entire railway from Richmond to North Street (that section now bounded by the Macdonald and MacKay bridges) was destroyed. Richmond station, a collection of wood-frame buildings, was erased. The massive platform roof of North Street station was torn open, and the carriages beneath it ruined by falling debris. The great stone structure would not fall, and would continue in service for some time thereafter, but it never regained its past glory. It was fortunate for the war effort that new piers had been completed in 1914, at a cost of $1.25 million, and were located in the south end of the city, escaping the force of the blast. As the CN history notes:

> "It is scarcely too much to say that had this pier not been available at Halifax, the embarkation of troops would have been seriously hindered and delayed, if not rendered impossible."

The Halifax cutting from Fairview to Greenbank had been the focus of a political storm, as Pierre Taschereau notes in *Halifax Field Naturalists News*:

The ICR roundhouse at Richmond, destroyed by the explosion of 1917. Located on the waterfront near the Pier 6 explosion site, the structure was augmented by a second roundhouse on the other side of the hill that is Fort Canning.

(Nova Scotia Archives and Record Management Service #N-14053)

"Hopes for an enlarged ocean railway terminal had been simmering in the Halifax business community since before the turn of the century. These were encouraged by politicians from time to time. Robert Borden's statement that 'the terminals at Halifax should be improved' in his August 18, 1903 speech on government railway policy was taken as a promise, and became a key plank in his election campaign of 1912. Well before the actual plan for a railway and shipping terminal at Greenbank near Point Pleasant Park was announced with great fanfare at a Board of Trade luncheon on October 30, 1912, there was a good deal of speculative real estate activity in areas expected to be subject to expropriation.

Reactions to the announcement by the Hon. Frank Cochrane, Minister of Railways and Canals, were positively ecstatic in Conservative circles whose newspaper, the *Halifax Herald*, sang lyrically of 'a new Halifax'. The opposition quickly dubbed the Prime Minister's plan 'Borden's Folly', and its papers, the *Morning Chronicle* and the *Daily Echo*, thundered against the plan's less desirable features and predicted it would force up the tax rate as well as dislocate the whole life of the city.

Criticism centred on the railway approach to the new terminal. The route chosen by F. W. Cowie, the federal government engineer, called

The Intercolonial Railway yard at Richmond was Ground Zero for the explosion in 1917. The railway employees worked with military efficiency to reopen the yard within days of the devastating blast.

(Nova Scotia Archives and Record Management Service #N-14016)

for a double track line branching off the Intercolonial Railway (ICR) at Three Mile House, Fairview, on Bedford Basin, curving southwest, around the city and running through the most attractive residential district bordering on the Northwest Arm. Here were 'country estates' of the city's wealthy and influential citizens whose spacious lawns and tree-lined carriageways, even one or two of their residences, would be demolished by the steam-shovels carving out the roadbed for the railway tracks.

The idea of running a branch line this way from the ICR was not new. As early as 1896 it was proposed to have electrical trains on such a route, down to the People's Heat and Light Company's Works on the Northwest Arm.

Liberal supporters, led by the *Morning Chronicle*, thundered furiously at 'scandals' and at all the drawbacks, mustering experts to prove the navigational hazards of an ocean terminal so near the mouth of the harbour, requiring a breakwater."

The city's military establishment were to oppose the plan on much the same grounds as it had the extension of the track from Richmond to North Street in

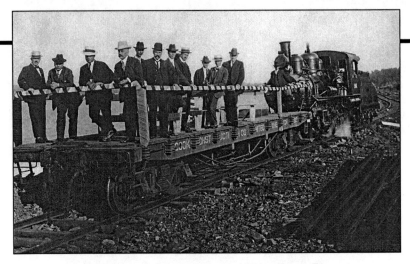

*Prime Minister Sir Robert Borden rides a flat car
ahead of a contractor's locomotive as he inspects the
construction of the Intercolonial Railway extension
to the new port of Halifax in 1916.*
(Nova Scotia Archives and Records Management Service)

the 1870s, and down to the deepwater terminals at Pier 2, where as many as 300,000 soldiers embarked for Europe:

> "The naval and military establishment complained that the plan contravened legislation safeguarding its rights, and would interfere with communication between the Citadel and the Harbour defences, thus obstructing defence in the event of attack from the sea."

Halifax's unfortunate circumstances were to prove Borden's foresight correct, and gave the Intercolonial the infrastructure it would need in time of such a dire emergency:

> "That the work had gone doggedly during the war years was to prove providential after the Halifax Explosion on December 6, 1917, destroying the North Street Railway Station and the lines leading to it. Construction crews worked furiously around the clock to put up temporary train sheds at the proposed site of the new South End Terminals and to ready the lines so that relief trains carrying medical personnel and supplies could be routed around the devastated area and brought within reach of the city centre. But for that line, relief workers, medical supplies, food, and the hundreds of other necessities would have been much slower reaching the wounded and homeless.

David Blythe Hanna: the first president of Canadian National Railways saluted the Intercolonial's response to the First World War.

The first official passenger train, the *Maritime Express*, steamed out of the still incomplete new station on December 22, 1918, carrying a distinguished group of governmental and business dignitaries bound for Fairview, thus ceremonially inaugurating the new service."

From an operational point of view, the explosion of 1917 proved that the Intercolonial Railway could have lived up to its military expectations had it been attacked directly by enemy forces.

It is doubtful German saboteurs could have wreaked such enormous damage on any part of the line, but by its ability to rebound from the explosion, the railway proved it could mobilize its manpower and machinery with all the efficiency of a military operation, even in such extraordinary circumstances.

D. B. Hanna had a fond remembrance of the railway, still fulfilling its military imperative in the aftermath of greater devastation than any enemy of Canada might have thought of inflicting: As it was, the Intercolonial's last act as a railway fulfilled both a military role and a peaceful intent:

"Halifax was blown to pieces by the war (1917 Explosion). But her recovery from the worst disaster that has befallen any Canadian city was swift and courageous. With troops going or coming, on many of the biggest steamers afloat—the *Olympic* was the greatest ferrier of valour the world has ever seen—there was promptitude and skill in every movement out and in. During demobilization Halifax was used in summer as it had been during hostilities, in the interest of speed. On the morning of July 9th, 1919, the *Olympic* docked at No. 2 pier at 7:15. The

H. M. T. "OLYMPIC" LEAVING SOUTHAMPTON

"THE SHIP THAT BROUGHT ME HOME"

Left SOUTHAMPTON, July 2nd ;   Arrived HALIFAX, July 8th, 1919

1914 - Canadian Expeditionary Force - 1919

MONS	ST. ELOI	NEUVE CHAPPELE	YPRES 2	FESTUBERT	GIVENCHY	LA BASSE	LOOS
PLUGSTREET	ST. JULIEN	YPRES 2	THE SOMME	COURCELETTE	VIMY RIDGE	HILL 70	
BASCHENDALE	AMIENS	ARRAS	CAMBRAI	VALENCIENNES	OCCUPATION OF MONS. NOV. 11		

The RMS Olympic, *"Old Reliable" to the Canadian troops that sailed on it from Halifax to England during the First World War. On one such call, it took 17 special trains to get all the soldiers onto the railway and headed for home in western Canada. This postcard was issued to soldiers on the ship's last voyage as a troop carrier in 1919.*

(Jay Underwood collection)

first special train, Intercolonial to Montreal, thence C.P.R., to Vancouver, pulled out at 7:40, the next at 8:02 and the third at 8:15. The eleventh special from the *Olympic*, brought the total of men disembarked up to 5,430, and left at five minutes past eleven."

CN's official history offers more detail, noting that by this time, handling of such great numbers of men had become somewhat routine for the Intercolonial:

"The '*Olympic*,' (that great White Star liner, which during the war carried troops between Halifax and Great Britain with the regularity of a ferry, and escaped all the dangers of the route) arrived in Halifax on July 8th 1919. She docked at Pier Two, at 7:15. The first special, No.1587, with 550 of all ranks, pulled out at 7:40 routed via Canadian National Railways to Montreal, thence via C.P.R. to Vancouver. Special No. 1588 left at 8:02 via the same route for Calgary and Medicine Hat; No. 1589 left at 8:15 with 258 of all ranks for St. John, N.B.; No. 1590 at 8:35 with 380 for Winnipeg and Port Arthur; No. 1591 at 8:50 with 327 for Edmonton, Regina and Brandon; No. 1592 at 9:05 with 372 for London and Hamilton; No. 1593 at 9:42 for Toronto with 542; No. 1594 at 10:00 with 491 for Kingston, Montreal and Quebec; No. 1595 at 10:20 with

501 for Toronto, Kingston and Montreal; No. 9596 [sic] at 10:45 with 492 for Ottawa, Montreal and Quebec; No. 1597 at 11:05 with 455 for Montreal."

The *Olympic* was a sister ship to the ill-fated White Star liner *Titanic*. Some of the victims of that fatal 1912 sinking are buried in Halifax. The reference to special train No. 9596 (actually No. 1596) is obviously a typographical error.

It can be argued that the Halifax Explosion made the Intercolonial's integration into what would become Canadian National Railways inevitable from a political point of view. In that single day, the railway went from being a relatively successful venture in public ownership to a liability facing massive capital reconstruction costs, and thus no better than the Canadian Northern or Grand Trunk railways as far as the politicians seeking a solution to Canada's "Railway Problem" were concerned. Indeed, Hanna's tribute notwithstanding, it would be the Intercolonial which became the universal symbol for the failure of Canadian National's constituent railways, rather than the more deserving Grand Trunk—a British-controlled private venture that had rarely paid its shareholders the dividend it had been created to generate.

The Intercolonial became a military asset in every sense when it began to transport prisoners to and from internment camps during the Great War. This is one of the lesser-known aspects of the war in Canada, although there were two camps in the Maritime Provinces, both in Nova Scotia—one at Halifax, and the other at Amherst.

The Amherst internment camp was established in 1914 in the Malleable Iron Foundry buildings close to the heart of town, and immediately adjacent to the Intercolonial's line as it arcs through the town before crossing the Tantramar marshes. The foundry had its own spur off the main line, a convenient entry into the camp, which was surrounded by barbed wire. Over the course of the war, it housed about 835 prisoners at a time; the majority of them were seamen. According to a brochure produced by the Cumberland County Museum:

"The first prisoners arrived from Halifax on April 17, 1915 aboard armed trains. A total of 640 sailors of the captured vessel *Kaiser Wilhelm der Grosser* were transported from the Halifax Citadel where facilities were not large enough for their containment."

HMS *Highflyer*, a Hermes class cruiser, had caught the German ex-liner turned armed merchant raider refuelling at sea, and sunk her off the West African coast at Rio del Oro in August of 1914.

Other inmates were German civilians, removed from other communities in Canada for the sake of security, but not all arrived at the camp via the Intercolonial. Photographs at the Cumberland County Museum show prisoners

The Amherst internment camp. This view, taken as the old foundry buildings were being demolished after the war, shows the proximity of the Intercolonial's main line.
(Cumberland County Museum)

aboard a vessel, probably at Pugwash, NS. They were housed according to the rules of conduct stipulated by the Hague Convention of 1907. They were put to work locally:

> "During the summer of 1916, prisoner labour was used at the Nappan Experimental Farm, clearing forest for farm land. Other groups worked on the maintenance of the Canadian National Railways... " *(Cumberland County Museum)*

As innocent as it may sound, having the prisoners work on the railway was a technical violation of Article Six of the Hague Convention:

> "The State may utilize the labour of prisoners of war according to their rank and aptitude, officers excepted. The task shall not be excessive and shall have no connection with the operations of the war."

Under the terms of the convention, the prisoners were to have been paid "at the rates in force for work of a similar kind done by soldiers of the national army, or, if there are none in force, at a rate according to the work executed." CN's history of the war lists more than 5,000 of its employees who served in the

German Navy prisoners pose for their photograph after arriving at the Amherst internment camp. The track into the old foundry complex can be seen in the rear.
(Cumberland County Museum)

army during the war, an indication that manpower on the railway was at a premium and making the use of prisoner labour a necessity.

It was while fulfilling its role as prison transport that the Intercolonial carried its most famous—some might say notorious—passenger. Lev Davidovitch Bronstein had been living in New York in March of 1917, when he heard that some of his compatriots in Russia were planning to overthrow the unpopular tsar and end Russia's disastrous war with Germany.

Bronstein was no stranger to the troubles in Russia. He had been imprisoned by the tsar and sentenced to exile in Siberia for his part in the revolutionary activity that had been threatening to topple the monarchy even before Nicholas came to the throne. Bronstein, who by that time had taken the name Leon Trotsky, escaped from Siberia and sought shelter in France and Spain before taking his wife and two children to the United States, where in January of 1917 he began editing the émigré newspaper *Novyi Mir* (New World) and participating in anti-war rallies.

On hearing of the revolution's imminent outbreak, he boarded the Norwegian ship *Christianiaffjord* bound for Europe, but go no farther than Halifax, when he and five other Russians were arrested and taken as agents of

***Canadian guards pose by the tracks at
the Amherst internment camp.***
(Cumberland County Museum)

the German government, intent upon toppling the Russian government, Russia still being an ally of the British at the time.

Trotsky was put aboard an Intercolonial train and sent to the Amherst internment camp (typical of his emotionally-loaded rhetoric, Trotsky calls it a "concentration" camp in his 1930 autobiography *My Life*) where he was imprisoned and made friends with soldiers of the very regime he had despised for its aggressive imperialist prosecution of the war.

In his own words:

> "The police left my wife and children in Halifax, the rest of us were taken by train to Amherst, a camp for German prisoners. And there, in the office, we were put through an examination the like of which I had never before experienced, even in the Peter-Paul fortress. For in the Czar's fortress the police stripped me and searched me in privacy, whereas here our democratic allies subjected us to this shameful humiliation before a dozen men."

His stay was short-lived. He was released April 29th 1917 and taken by the Intercolonial back to Halifax. By May of that year he was aboard another train, this time arriving with some triumph in Petrograd (St. Petersburg) to join his friend Vladimir Lenin, to oversee the ouster of the tsar, and the creation of the Soviet Union.

Len Davidovitch Bronstein, also known as Leon Trotsky, the Russian revolutionary leader arrested in Halifax and taken by Intercolonial train to the prison camp at Amherst, Nova Scotia.

Trotsky makes no comment about his train ride to or from the Amherst prison. He would gain greater notoriety for his military policies in the Russian civil war that followed, and for his role as People's Commissar for Military and Naval Affairs, and the founding of the Red Army. He was assassinated in Mexico City in 1940 after running afoul of Josef Stalin.

• • • • • • •

On December 20th 1918, the Governor-General-in-Council issued the order instigated by the policies of Sir Robert Borden, putting the Intercolonial Railway under the control of the government-appointed board of directors of Canadian Northern Railways, and the Intercolonial ceased to exist. The order contained the first official use of the name "Canadian National Railways" from which the Intercolonial could not escape, despite doing so earlier when it became part of the amorphous Canadian Government Railways system. As if in tribute to its years of service, the new railway adopted the Intercolonial's slogan "The People's Railway," and barely more than 40 years of public service in peace and war faded into history.

As with its opening, when there was no ground-breaking ceremony and no golden spike driven. The Intercolonial officially closed quietly and with as much dignity as an old soldier can muster.

But, even in "retirement," Major Robinson's Path remained faithful to its cause. The line was used again, by Canadian National in 1939-45, in the service of the empire, supplying troops, munitions and materiel to Great Britain. Its most recent stint of active service was during the 1990-91 war in the Persian

Gulf, when European armies, notably British and German, removed tanks and armoured cars from the great training ground at Suffield, Alberta, over the path (at least from Moncton to Halifax) for shipment to Saudi Arabia, in preparation for the liberation of Kuwait.

Even today, CN's yards at Rockingham, on the Bedford Basin, sometimes hold trains of military vehicles both in- and outward bound for Alberta or Europe. The 2005 edition of the *Canadian Trackside Guide* notes CN occasionally runs two military trains, following the path, at least as far as Moncton, over the line surveyed by Major Robinson. Train U75311 is listed as an "Army Schedule" between Dartmouth, NS to Edmonton, AB. Train U75441 is listed as a "Military Move" from Shiloh, AB to Halifax.

Perhaps the Intercolonial's best epitaph was penned by C. P. Stacey in the *Backbone of Canada*:

> " ...the Intercolonial's value to Canada could not be measured for in dollars. It was one of those great projects essential to an independent Canadian nationality which have been forced upon this country by the proximity of the United States and which have been carried out by government because private enterprise could not or would not do the job that was required."

APPENDIX ONE

Major Robinson's Report

Halifax, Nova Scotia, August 31, 1848

THREE principal lines or routes for a trunk line of railway present themselves for consideration; and by combining portions of two of these lines together, a fourth and fifth route may be formed.

1st. Commencing at Halifax and crossing the Province of Nova Scotia to a port in the Bay of Fundy, from thence by a steamer to St. John, in New Brunswick, and then by Fredericton along the St. John River, to the Grand Falls.

From the Grand Falls by the best practicable route across to the mouth of the Riviere du Loup, on the St. Lawrence, and by the right bank of the St. Lawrence to Quebec.

The distance by this route would be as follows:-

	Miles
Halifax to Windsor	.45
Windsor to Annapolis	.85
Annapolis to entrance Bay of Fundy	.11
Across Bay of Fundy to St. John (by sea)	.45
St. John to Fredericton	.65
Fredericton to Woodstock	.62
Woodstock to the Grand Falls	.71
The Grand Falls to the mouth of the Riviere du Loup	.106
Riviere du Loup to Quebec	.110
Total distance Halifax by the St. John River to Quebec	**600**

This line may be termed a Mixed route—by railway and steamboat.

2nd. Commencing at Halifax and running to Truro at the head of the Bay of Fundy, thence over the Cumberland Mountains to Amherst, then along the coast from Bay

---

Verte to Shediac, thence by a north-westerly course, crossing the Rivers Richibucto and Miramichi above the flow of the tide, so as not to interfere with the navigation.

Then by the valley of the North-western Miramichi to Bathurst, on the bay Chaleurs, along the coast of this Bay to the Restigouche River, and by it and the valley of the River Metapedia to the St. Lawrence, and by the right bank of the St. Lawrence to Quebec.

The distance by this route would be as follows:-

	Miles
Halifax to Truro	55
Truro to Amherst and Bay Verte	69
Bay Verte to Shediac	26
Shediac to the Miramichi River	74
Miramichi River to Bathurst	56
Bathurst to the Eel River, near Dalhousie	48
Dalhousie to the mouth of the Metapedia River	30
Metapedia River to the mouth of the Naget River, near the St. Lawrence	86
Along the St. Lawrence from this point to Quebec	191
Total distance by this route	**635**

This, for the sake of reference, may be called the Halifax and Eastern or Bay Chaleurs route, through New Brunswick to Quebec.

3rd. Commencing at the harbour of Whitehaven, near Canso, at the northeastern extremity of Nova Scotia, thence along the Atlantic coast to Country harbour and valley of the River St. Mary, thence by or near to Pictou and along the northern shore to Bay Verte.

From Bay Verte to or near to the Bend of Peticodiac, thence across to Boistown and northerly to the Restigouche River, crossing it several miles to the east of the Grand Falls.

From thence by the most direct and practical course to the Trois Pistoles River, along the right bank of the St. Lawrence to Quebec.

The distance by this route would be nearly as follows:

	Miles
Whitehaven to Country Harbour	40
Country Harbour to St. Mary's Valley and Pictou	64
Pictou and along coast to Bay Verte	77
Bay Verte to Bend of Peticodiac	40
Peticodiac to Boistown	80
Boistown to the crossing of the Restigouche River	115
Restigouche River to Trois Pistoles, by Kedgwick and Rimouski Vallies	105

Along the St. Lawrence to Quebec..131
Total distance from Whitehaven by Boistown to Quebec........**652**

This may be termed the Direct route.

4th. Combining the Halifax route through Nova Scotia, and the Direct route through the centre of New Brunswick.

The distances will probably be as under;-

	Miles	
From Halifax by Truro and Amherst to Bay Verte as per Route No. 2 124		In Nova Scotia
Bay Verte to the Bend of Peticodiac, Boistown, Restigouche River, as per route No. 3................................235		In New Brunswick
By the Kedgwick and Rimouski, to the mouth of the Toreadi..75		|
Mouth of the Toreadi to the crossing of the Trois Pistoles River 30		In Canada
Along the St. Lawrence River to Quebec 131		|
Total distance from Halifax to Quebec by this route...........**595**		|

5th. Combining the Whitehaven route through Nova Scotia, with the Eastern or Bay Chaleurs route through New Brunswick to Quebec, the distances will be as under:-

	Miles	
From Whitehaven by Pictou and the North Coast to Bay In Verte, as in route No. 3...181		In Nova Scotia
From Bay Verte to the Bay Chaleurs, and mouth of the Metapedia, as in route No. 2 234		In New Brunswick
Mouth of the Metapedia River to the mouth of the Naget 86		In Canada
Along the St. Lawrence to Quebec.......................................191		|
Total distance from Whitehaven to Quebec by this route....**692**		|

Thus the distances will be as under:-

	Miles
1st. By the mixed route, Halifax to Annapolis, the St. John to Quebec the distance will be..600	
2nd. By the Halifax and Eastern, or Bay Chaleurs route to Quebec 635	
3rd. By the Direct route, Whitehaven, Boistown, and Quebec 652	
4th. By the Halifax, Truro, and Boistown, to Quebec............................595	
5th. By the Whitehaven, Bay Verte, and Bay Chaleurs to Quebec.......692	

The first line fails in the most essential object contemplated by the proposed railway viz., a free and uninterrupted communication at all times and seasons of the year, from the port of arrival on the Atlantic terminus in Nova Scotia to Quebec.

The intervention of the Bay of Fundy is fatal to this route.

In summer the transhipment of passengers and goods to and fro would be attended with the greatest inconvenience—loss of time and additional expense; whilst in winter it would be even still more inconvenient, and liable to be interrupted by storms and floating masses of ice which then occur in the bay.

In the case of the conveyance of troops, transport of artillery and munitions of war, the crossing the bay would at any time be most objectionable, and if suddenly required in critical times might be attended with the worst consequences.

Commercially too, it would destroy the fair prospect of the proposed line from Quebec to Halifax competing successfully with the route by the Gulf of the St. Lawrence, and with rival lines in the neighbouring States.

But there are also other serious objections to be offered against it.

Passing through New Brunswick and on the right bank of the St. John River, as it must necessarily do, to the Grand Falls, it would be a considerable distance, both before and after the reaching that point, run along and close to the frontier of the United States.

In case of war, therefore, or in times of internal commotion, when border quarrels or border sympathies are excited, this line, when most needed, would be the most sure to fail, for no measures could be taken which would at all times effectually guard it from an open enemy and from treacherous attacks.

The passage across the Bay of Fundy so close to the shores of Maine, would invite aggression, and require a large naval force for its protection.

The engineering difficulties as the line approaches the Grand Falls from Woodstock would not be easily overcome.

The space between the St. John River and the Boundary Line becomes gradually contracted to a width of not more than two to three miles, and the country is broken and rough, whilst the banks of the St. John are rocky and precipitous for many miles below the Falls.

From the Grand Falls to the St. Lawrence, a distance of more than a hundred miles, the country is so far known to make it certain that there is very difficult and unfavourable ground to be connected, which would require careful explorations and extensive surveying.

This intervention of the Bay of Fundy, therefore, and the proximity of this line for a considerable distance, to the frontier of the United States, was so objectionable and fatal to this route, that the attention of the officers and the exploring parties was, after a slight examination of the country between Halifax and Annapolis, directed in search of other and more favourable lines.

To understand the comparative advantages possessed by the *other* routes, as well as to be able to weigh the objections which may be raised against each, and afterwards determine from their relative merits, which *is the best direction for the proposed line to take*, it will be necessary, previously, to give some description of the country through which the lines pass, the present amount and distribution of the population, and the engineering difficulties which were met along the lines examined.

As it will be seen in the end, that only one of the lines, viz., the second, has been explored and carried out *successfully* from its terminus on the Atlantic quite through to Quebec, it may be perhaps considered superfluous to enter upon the discussion of rival lines, but the object to be gained by doing so, is to show that so much has been done and is known of the country as to render further explorations for new lines unnecessary, because, if completed, they would not likely to be recommended in preference to the one which will be proposed for adoption.

The distance from the Atlantic coast of Nova Scotia to the bank of the St. Lawrence is about 360 miles in a straight line. Intersecting the country which must be traversed by any line of railway and crossing its course at right angles, are *five great obstacles* which have to be either surmounted or avoided.

1st is a broad range or belt of high and broken land which runs along the Atlantic shores of Nova Scotia, from Cape Canso to Cape Sable. The breadth varies from about twenty miles in its narrowest part to fifty or sixty miles in other places. Its average height may be about five hundred feet. The strata of which it is composed consist of granite, slate and a variety of rocks, hard and difficult to cut through. The characteristic features of the surface are rugged and uneven, and therefore very unfavourable for railway operations. No useful minerals of the metallic kind have been found in it, in quantities sufficient to work to advantage.

Valuable quarries of stone for building purposes are abundant, but these will be found everywhere nearly along the proposed line.

This formation is estimated to cover nearly two-thirds of the surface of Nova Scotia. It is generally speaking unfavourable for agriculture, the timber on it is stinted in growth, and it is an object of some importance to pass through it and leave it behind as soon as possible.

If a line be drawn from the head of the estuary of the Avon, near Windsor, to the Great Shubenacadie Lake, and then across the Stewiacke River, along the upper parts of the streams in the County of Pictou, to the Gut of Canso, all the portion lying to the south of this line belongs to this formation, and all to the north of it to the more favourable and highly valuable formation of the carboniferous system.

The narrowest and shortest line by which this range or belt can be crossed occurs at Halifax, and at the same time, owing to a favourable break in the chain, at the lowest point in altitude; the summit level through it not exceeding ninety feet.

The Halifax line (route No. 2) is clear of it in twenty miles. Before the same can be done by the Whitehaven and direct line (route No. 3), it must follow the coast for upwards of thirty miles, as far as Country Harbour, and then a further course for upwards of another thirty miles; involving in this distance two if not three tunnels, and must surmount a summit level of 400 feet.

---

2. The second great obstacle is the Bay of Fundy. This stated, is fatal to the first route. By the other routes it can be turned and avoided.

3. The third obstacle is the range of Cobequid Hills. These extend all along the north shore of the Bay of Minas and very nearly across, but not quite, to the shore at the Straits of Northumberland. In breadth the range preserves nearly an uniform width of about 10 miles. In altitude the hills average from 800 to 1000 feet. The lowest point, after a careful survey, was found to be at the Folly Lake, 600 feet above the sea. This range can be avoided and passed by the Whitehaven and direct route, but must be surmounted and crossed over by the Halifax and eastern line (route No. 2.)

The prevailing rocks are granite, porphyry, and clay slate, in the upper portions; along the shore of the Bay of Minas and on the northern side, the formation is of the red sandstone and the coal measures.

This range abounds with the most valuable minerals of which a large mass of specular iron ore, of unequalled richness, occurs close to the line, and only requires facility of carriage for bringing coals to the spot, to be worked with profit.

A large portion of this tract still remains ungranted, and timber of excellent growth, with abundance of the finest stone for building purposes, are to be met with, and still belonging to the Crown, can be had for the expense of labour only.

4. The fourth obstacle is the broad and extensive range of highlands which occupies nearly the whole space in the centre of New Brunswick from the Miramichi River north to the Restigouche. Some of these mountains rise to an altitude exceeding 2000 feet.

The Tobique River runs through them, forming a deep valley or trough, which must be crossed by the Direct line, and increases greatly the difficulty of passing by them.

The lowest point of the ridge, overlooking the Tobique River, at which any line of railway must pass, is 1216 feet above the sea. Then follows a descent to the river of 796 feet in 18 miles, and the summit level on the opposite ridge or crest between the Tobique and Restigouche waters, is 920 feet above the sea, or a rise of 500 feet above the point of crossing the Tobique water. These great summit levels which must be surmounted form a serious objection to this route.

The Eastern line by the coast avoid this chain altogether. The greatest summit level along it will not be above 368 feet, while the distance by each from the province line at Bay Verte to the Restigouche River (the northern limit of New Brunswick) will be as nearly as possible the same, there being only a difference of one mile in these two routes through this province.

The rocks composing this chain of mountains are granite, various kinds of slate, grauwacke, lime stone, sandstone, &c.

5. The fifth and last obstacle to be overcome and which cannot be avoided by any of the routes, is the mountain range running along the whole course of the

River St. Lawrence in a very irregular line, but at an average distance from it of about twenty miles. It occupies with its spurs and branches a large portion of the space between the St. Lawrence and the Restigouche River. The rocks and strata composing the range are of the same character and kind as the Tobique range. The tops of the mountains are as elevated in the one range as in the other.

The exploring parties failed in finding a line through this range, to join on to the direct line through New Brunswick, but succeeded in carrying on the Eastern or Bay Chaleurs route, owing to the fortunate intervention of the valley of the Metapedia River.

The line which was tried and failed, was across from the Trois Pistoles River by the heads of Green River, and down the Pscudy, or some of the streams in that part running into the Restigouche River.

A favourable line from the Trois Pistoles was ascertained along the Eagle Lake and Torcadi River, as far as the Rimouski, and it is probable that by ascending this river, and descending the Kedgwick River, this line, Route No. 4, could be completed.

But it is most improbable that it could compete in favourable grades with the Metapedia.

It will be allowing it sufficient latitude to suppose it will be equal in engineering merits, and that if accomplished, it will give the route No. 4 and apparent advantage of forty miles in distance.

A very striking characteristic in the Geological formation of North America, and which has been noticed in the writings of persons who have described the country, is the tendency of the rock strata to run in parallel ridges in courses north-easterly and south-westerly.

On referring to the General Map No. 1, and confining the attention more particularly to that portion of country east and north of the St. John River through which any line must pass—this general tendency cannot fail to be remarked.

The River St. Lawrence—the main Restigouche River and intermediate chain of mountains—the Tobique River and mountains—all the streams in New Brunswick (the main trunk of St. John and branch of the Miramichi excepted).

The Cobequid Range, the Bay of Fundy, and the high and rocky range along the Atlantic shore have all this north-east and south-western tendency.

It will be evident, therefore, that any line from the coast of Nova Scotia to the St. Lawrence has a general direction to follow, which is the most unfavourable that could have occurred for it, having to cross all these mountain ranges, streams, and vallies at right angles nearly to their courses.

The line explored for the direct route through New Brunswick were obliged on this account to keep the elevated ground crossing the upper parts of the streams.

By doing so, a line was found to the Restigouche which may be considered just within the limits of practicability, but having very unfavourable summit levels to surmount.

And the peculiar formation of the strata and general course of the vallies and streams renders it most improbable that any further explorations to improve this direct line through New Brunswick would be attended with much success.

Very fortunately for the Eastern line, one of the branches of the north-western Miramichi presented itself as an exception to the general tendency, and enabled that line to reach the coast of the Bay of Chaleurs.

The distance across in a direct line from the coast of Nova Scotia to the St. Lawrence has been stated at about 360 miles, forming the difficult and unfavourable portion of the line. When the St. Lawrence mountains are passed, then the tendency of the strata and courses north-easterly and south-westerly becomes as favourable for the remaining 200 miles along that river, as it was before adverse.

The general character of the ground between the St. Lawrence River and the mountains, is that of irregular terraces or broad vallies rising one above the other by steep short banks, having the appearance as if the river had at some former period higher levels for its waters.

The streams run along these vallies parallel with the course of the St. Lawrence until meeting some obstruction they turn suddenly off and find their way over precipices and falls to the main river.

Having described such of the physical features of the country which form *obstacles* in the way of the lines under consideration, it is proper next to describe those features and other resources which are advantages and should be *sought* for by competing lines.

The geological systems which prevail through the intermediate country to the mountain ranges are the carboniferous and new red sandstone.

They include large deposits of red marl, limestone, gypsum, free stone of excellent quality for building purposes, and extensive beds of coal. Indications of the latter are met with in abundance from the banks of Gay's River (twenty miles from Halifax), up to the Restigouche River, and along the shores of the Bay Chaleurs.

Wherever these systems and minerals are found, a strong and productive soil favourable for agricultural pursuits and settlements, is sure to accompany them.

The surface of such a country too is generally low or moderately undulating, and therefore the more of such a district that a line can be led through, the better for it.

In Nova Scotia this formation occupies its northern section, and amounts to nearly one-third of its whole area. It then extends all over the southern and eastern parts of New Brunswick.

In this respect, therefore, the Route No. 2 has a decided advantage.

The greatest and most valuable coal-field is that of Pictou.

It is situated on the south side of the harbour. The exact extent of the bed is not known, as it is broken by a great (geological) fault. It occupies, however, an area of many square miles.

The coal is bituminous, of good quality, and the veins of most unusual thickness.

Mines in it are extensively worked, and large exports from them are made to the United States. Iron ore is abundant.

This is an advantage in favour of the Whitehaven and direct route.

The next great coal district is the Cumberland field, and it is second only in importance to that of Pictou.

It is supposed to extend from the Macon River, west of Amherst, over to Tatamagouche in the Straits of Northumberland.

Some mines in it have been recently opened, and promise to be very productive.

The Line No. 2 passes over this field for miles, and may be considered from that circumstance, as not being deprived altogether of an advantage possessed by the other route.

The *great* agricultural capabilities of the eastern counties of New Brunswick have been described in the reports of Mr. Perley, the Government Emigration agent, which were presented to the New Brunswick Legislature in February 1847, and ordered to be printed.

One most important objects to be attended by the construction of the railroad is the settlement of public lands, and the encouragement of emigration from the mother country.

As bearing very strongly upon this point in the choice of the best direction for the line, I subjoin the following extract taken from Bouchette's Work on Canada, vol. 1, page 331. It is a quotation made by him from "The Commissioners report of 1821."

"The Bay of Gaspe, and particularly the *Bay des Chaleurs*, are susceptible of the most improved agriculture. For the establishment of emigrants no part in Canada offers such immediate resources of livelihood as may be derived from the fisheries. It is a fact worthy of notice, that in the year 1816, when the lower parts of the province were afflicted with a famine from the destruction of the harvest by frost, no such inconvenience was experienced at Paspebiac, nor at any other lace within the level tract above mentioned."

The tract alluded to here is not clearly defined by the quotations, but it is supposed to mean the whole district along the south shore of the Bay Chaleurs.

This tends to show the effect produced by the vicinity of the sea, in moderating the temperature and saving the crops from untimely frosts. In this respect, therefore, the Line No. 2 has an important advantage over the one through the central and more elevated land of New Brunswick.

As the interior is approached, and the distance from, as well as the elevation above, the sea increases, the danger to crops from cold nights and early frosts also increases.

In the Madawaska Settlement, and on the Upper St. John River, great failures of crops have occurred from this cause, and wheat and potatoes are very liable to be destroyed.

From the Bend of Peticodiac to the St. Lawrence, a distance of upwards of 300 miles, the direct line would pass through a perfect wilderness, with not a single settler on the whole line, except a few at or near Boistown.

Leaving engineering difficulties for the moment out of question, the cost of construction would be materially increased by the extra difficulties attendant on the transport of necessary materials, and in supplying with food the labourers and others engaged on the line.

This disadvantage is not shared by the second route, which can be approached in numerous places along the Gulf shore by means of bays and navigable rivers.

The Direct line No. 4 will not have such advantages to present to settlers as the second. On the contrary, if adopted, it might be found necessary to incur expenses for the establishment of small communities along the line to repair and keep it open.

The facilities for *external* as *well* as *internal* communication, and other advantages arising from commerce and the fisheries, which will be developed by the Eastern line (and entirely wanting along the Direct route), will, it is fully expected, make its vicinity eagerly sought by settlers, and that it will, in the course of no very great length of time, lead to the extension of that long-continued village which now exists with but little exception from Quebec to Metis (200 miles), from the shores of the St. Lawrence to the Atlantic Ocean.

An important item bearing upon the consideration of the best route is the present distribution of the population in New Brunswick and Nova Scotia.

In illustration of this part of the subject, and to afford a better idea of the nature of the country than can be given by a merely outline plan, a model map has been prepared, showing the whole course of the lines (Routes No. 2 and 4) from Halifax to the St. Lawrence, and by the latter over the Trois Pistoles River, beyond which the line is continued through a level fertile and densely peopled district of Quebec.

The red line shows the proposed Route No. 2 The Halifax and Eastern or Bay Chaleurs line.

The black line shows the Direct route, No. 4, from the Bend of Peticodiac.

The yellow tint shows the present settlements.

The green is the wilderness of uncleared forest, unsettled, and the far larger portion of it still ungranted and waiting for occupation.

It must be premised that a branch railway from the city of St. John is contemplated to pass up the valley of the Kennebecasis, and connect with the main trunk at the Bay of Shediac.

The survey of this line, ordered by the Provincial Government, is in progress; and from the latest information received, the line promises most favourably.

The total population of New Brunswick has been estimated to amount, at the beginning of 1848, to 208,012, distributed in the proportions under:-

County of Restigouche		4,214	
"	" Gloucester	10,334	
"	" Northumberland	19,493	
"	" Kent	9,769	
			43,810
"	" Westmoreland and Albert	23,581	
"	" Kings	19,285	
"	" St. John	43,942	
			86,808
"	" Queens	10,976	
"	" Sunbury	5,680	
			16,656
"	" York	18,660	
"	" Carleton	17,841	
			36,501
"	" Charlotte	24,237	
	Total		208,012

Of these, the first four, amounting to 43,810, are on the line of the proposed Route No. 2, and will be entirely thrown out by the adoption of the other.

Campbellton, Dalhousie, Bathurst, Chatham on the Miramichi, and Richibucto —sea-ports and shipping places of consequence on the Gulf shore; all of them susceptible of the greatest development, will be left isolated and cut off.

These ports are ice-bound during the winter months; and railway communications will be to them of the greatest importance.

It will affect most materially the interests of the city of St. John, and the receipts upon their branch railway.

It will affect also sensibly the receipts of the main trunk line.

Along the south bank of the St. Lawrence, from Quebec to Metis, there are settled along it in what can only be compared to one continued village for 200 miles, 75,000 inhabitants.

Of these, also, a large population probably 12,000 in number, residing between the Rimouski and Metis River, will be deprived of the benefit of the Railway, if the Direct line be adopted.

To counterbalance the serious detriment which would thus be caused, this line would diminish the length of the branch line, likely to be made to connect it with Fredericton, which is the seat of Government, and contains about 6000 inhabitants.

The population of Nova Scotia may be estimated to be about, viz. :-

City of Halifax and County		40,000
County of Cumberland		10,600
"	" Colchester	14,900
"	" Pictou	30,300

County of Sydney and Guysborough	23,200
Remaining Counties	111,260
Total	230,200

The population of Cape Breton is estimated at 49,600

Of the above, if the Whitehaven and Direct route be adopted, the city of Halifax and county, amounting to 40,000, will be excluded from the benefit of the line.

If the Halifax and Eastern line (route No. 2) be adopted, then the population of Sydney and Pictou, amounting to 53,500, will be excluded.

To the population in the northern remaining counties (111,209), the Halifax route will be of essential benefit.

From the other routes, they would derive no advantage whatever.

It is now proposed to give an account of the explorations and their results.

The dotted lines on the General Plan, No. 1, show where these were made, and the courses taken.

In the season of 1846, the Cumberland Hills were very carefully examined; sections with the theodolite were made, and barometrical observations taken, to ascertain the lowest and most favourable point for crossing them.

The line which had been cut out and explored for the military road was followed from the Bend of Peticodiac to Boistown.

From Boistown the general course was followed, and levelled as far as the Tobique River, but the county was so unfavourable that new courses had to be constantly sought out.

A new line altogether was tried from the Tobique, as far as the Wagan Portage.

The result deduced from the observations and sections proved this line to be quite impracticable for a railway.

Whilst the line was being tried, other parties explored from Newcastle on the Miramichi River, over to Crystal Brook on the Nipisiguit, the vallies of the Upsalquitch and its tributaries, and as far as the Restigouche River.

The country at the upper waters of the Nipisiguit, and the whole of the Upsalquitch vallies, were found to be rough, broken, and totally impracticable.

The result of this season's labours went to show, that the best, if not the only route that would be likely to be practicable, would be by the North-west Miramichi to Bathurst, and then along the Bay Chaleurs.

During the winter, a small reconnoitring party (on snow shoes) was sent up the Metapedia Valley, as far as Metallis Brook, and they made their way across the country from thence to the mouth of the Torcadi River on the Rimouski.

Their report on this line was rather favourable, and had there been any necessity for it, it would have been more fairly explored the next season (1847).

As soon as this was sufficiently advanced to admit of the parties entering the woods, the explorations were resumed.

BUILT FOR WAR: Canada's Intercolonial Railway

A grade line was carried over the Cumberland Hills. It was cut out through the woods, from the foot on one side to the foot of the slope on the other, a distance of ten miles, and carefully levelled with a theodolite. This proved it to be quite practicable.

The exploration of the Eastern line was again taken up.

It was commenced at the head of the tide, on the south-west Miramichi, and was carried up the Valley of the North-west Miramichi over to and down the Upsalquitch River to Bathurst, and along the shores of the Bay Chaleurs to the Restigouche, up the Metapediac to the Metis, and along the bank of the St. Lawrence to the Rimouski and Trois Pistoles River.

The result of this exploration was so satisfactory, that the party engaged upon it, returned by the same route, surveyed it, and took the levels along it back to the Miramichi River.

An exploratory line was then cut through the greater portion of the flat and generally level country between this river and the province line at Bay Verte.

An examination of the country was made from the Trois Pistoles River along the St. Lawrence to Quebec; which, with what had been done in Nova Scotia, during this and the former season, completed the whole of one good and favourable line from Halifax to Quebec.

The details are given in the accompanying Report, Appendix No. 1, General Plan No. 1, Model Map No. 2, and Book containing exploratory sheets, No. 16, containing plans and sections of the whole route, and comprises the line recommended to be adopted.

Unwilling to abandon the direct route through the centre of New Brunswick, by which, if a line could be successfully carried out, the distance would be so materially shortened, as is apparent by the mileage given in route No. 4, it was determined to use every effort to decide either the practicability or the impracticability of such a line.

To this end large parties were employed the whole season.

One party explored, cut and levelled a line the whole way between the Napadogan Lake and the Restigouche River, a distance of ninety-six miles.

The line explored was a very great improvement upon the one of 1846.

It is considered to be so far satisfactory as to prove that a line for that distance can be found which would be within the limits of railway gradients.

The details are given in the Assistant Surveyor's report, Appendix No. 2, with three exploratory sheets, Nos. 17, 18, 19, containing plans and sections of the ground passed over.

A large party was engaged in trying to find a line from Trois Pistoles River on the St. Lawrence, through the Highlands to the Restigouche River, for the purpose of connecting on to the New Brunswick party. The winter overtook them whilst still embarrassed in the Highlands at the head waters of the Green River.

The dotted lines on the General Plan, No. 1, will show their attempts.

A line was tried up the valley of the Abersquash, but ended in a cul-de-sac. There was no way out of it.

A second line was carried from Trois Pistoles over to Lac-des-Isles, Eagle Lake; and by the Middle branch of the Tuladi River, the north-west branch and head-waters of the Green River were gained.

But this point was not reached except by a narrow valley or ravine of four miles in length.

A theodolite section was made of it, and it was found to involve a grade of at least one in forty-nine, and to attain that, heavy cuttings at one part and embankments at another would be necessary.

There is no occasion at present to enter upon the discussion of whether this should condemn a whole line, for having attained the forks; at the head of the main Green River, no way was found out of it and this explored line, like the first-mentioned, must be considered to have ended in a cul-de-sac also.

Further details are given in the report of Mr. Wilkinson, the surveyor entrusted with the more immediate charge of this part of the line, in Appendix No. 3, with sketches attached to it.

It is just probable that a line might be found by way of the Kedgwick River and the Rimouski as far as the mouth of the Torcadi River. From which to the Trois Pistoles, there was ascertained to be no difficulty.

But as the advantages in every way, except distance, are so much in favour of the Eastern line, it would only be incurring delay and perhaps useless expense in further explorations of this part of the country.

In the report there is a third route suggested for exploration and trial; viz., by one of the lower branches of the Green River and the Squattock Lakes.

Whether successful or not, it is liable to the objection of approaching the frontier of the United States.

There remains to be noticed the exploration for a line from Whitehaven on the eastern coast of Nova Scotia towards Pictou and Bay Verte.

This was rendered necessary in consequence of the suggestion made by Captain Owen, R.N., to make Whitehaven the Atlantic terminus of the railway.

The details of this exploration are given in the accompanying report, Appendix No. 4, and exploratory sheets Nos. 20, 21, 22 and 24.

Engineering difficulties and expensive cuttings occur on this route.

From the commencement in the harbour of Whitehaven the line must pass along a barren and rocky coast for upwards of thirty miles to Country Harbour, before it can turn off towards the interior. And it cannot do this and get clear of the sea-shore without the necessity of making a tunnel of about a mile in length through a ridge of whinstone.

Again, at the falls of the St. Mary's River there will be required a tunnel of a quarter of a mile, and a viaduct across a valley, of about 500 feet in length.

The summit level occurs between Lake Eden and Beaver Lake, and is 400 feet above the sea.

At Grant's Bridge on the East River, for nearly three miles in length, there would necessarily be several expensive cuttings through rocks of sandstone and lime-stone.

The length of this line from Whitehaven to Bay Verte is estimated at 181 miles.-From Halifax to the same point is 124.Leaving a difference of fifty-seven miles.

If the Direct route No. 3 could be established, it would add seventeen miles to the trunk line.

But as it is not supposed that Halifax, the capital and greater commercial city of the province, would in such a case allow itself to be excluded from the benefits of the proposed railway, then it would involve, in addition to this seventeen miles of trunk railway, a branch line of probably 90 miles.

Or if the Eastern Bay Chaleurs line through New Brunswick be added on to it, as in Route No. 5, then it will involve no less than fifty-seven miles extra of trunk line, and the same necessity for the branch line of ninety miles mentioned.

To compensate for such disadvantages it must be shown that Whitehaven has the *most paramount claims* to be selected as the Atlantic terminus in preference to Halifax.

The harbour of Whitehaven is 120 miles nearer to England by sea than Halifax.—Equivalent to, in ocean navigation by the steamers, ten hours.

This, it is readily conceded, is a very great advantage, and were there no draw-backs, or other considerations in the way, it would be quite sufficient to give that port the preference.

It is a well known fact however, that there is a time and season in the year when the Cunard steamers cannot keep their direct course to Halifax even, but are com-pelled by fields of ice, to keep to the southward, and sometimes pass to the south of Sable Island.

During this time, which occurs in the spring of the year, and may last for two or three months, there would be some risk in their making direct for the more north-ern port of Whitehaven. And if for these three months the steamers were obliged to make Halifax their port, then for that time the Whitehaven line would be useless.

In respect to the advantages which it is said to possess, of remaining open all the year round, it is not quite clear that it does so.

From enquiries made on the spot in the summer of 1847, Captain Henderson learnt that the preceding winter the harbour had been frozen over entirely, five to six inches thick, and that it was sometimes blockaded up and much incommoded by ice.

Subsequently, however, and during this winter when the objects of the enquiries made there in the summer became known, and the advantages of the Railway spoken of, a statement accompanied with affidavits was forwarded with a view to counteract the effect of the information given to Captain Henderson and the parties exploring there.

They tend to show that though the immediate entrance to the harbour may be, and generally is clear, yet that large quantities of floating ice find their way through the Gut of Canso, and by Cape Breton, which pass off in a southerly direction, crossing the direct path of steamers and vessels from Europe.

The coasting vessels keeping in shore are not so liable to be molested by it.

The harbour is admitted to be a fine sheet of water, but it does not and cannot vie with Halifax, either in appearance or capacity.

Referring to Lieutenant Shortland's report, who made a survey of it in obedience to the directions of Captain Owen, R.N., it appears that it is not free from the objection which is made against the Port of Halifax, and is its only drawback, viz., the prevalence of fogs.

Lieutenant Shortland says, "that in foggy weather the harbour (Whitehaven) is difficult to approach, especially to a stranger, as the soundings in shore are very irregular, and I have not been able to learn good indications of its vicinity to be gathered from the lead, so as to render its approach by that means certain; and Torbay, its immediate neighbour to the westward, is a dangerous place to get into.

"From the fishermen and small coaster I understand the currents round the point are uncertain and generally depend upon the wind, though the prevailing current is to the westward.

"I experienced this current in a boat when I visited the outer break, it was then setting to the westward, at the rate of one mile and a half per hour at least. I also perceived vessels in the offing setting rapidly in the same direction, the breeze was from the eastward and light, though it had previously blown hard from the same point.

"We also on our passage from Halifax to Canseau, during a fog, with the wind from the south-west, experienced an easterly current, but the land once made, the harbour is easily attained, especially by a steamer."

This can scarcely be considered a favourable report of its advantages as a harbour intended for the great Atlantic terminus.

Accommodation and safety for a fleet of merchantmen could be expected there, as is to be found in Halifax.

To make it a safe approach, Lieutenant Shortland continues thus:

"A judicious arrangement of fog signals and lighthouses with buoys, on the principal dangers, and a good survey with the sea-soundings well laid down, would make the approach in the night, or during fogs, attended with small danger to a careful seaman."

One of the undoubted results of the railway will be to make Halifax, if it be made, as it ought to be, the Atlantic terminus, the great emporium of trade for the British Provinces and the far west.

Whitehaven has not the capacity for this, and in winter it is evidently danger-ous for sailing vessels, and the selection of it as a terminus would be to exclude Halifax altogether, or to compel the formation of a branch railway of ninety miles in length, in addition to fifty-seven miles of trunk railway.

It involves also the necessity of making expensive arrangements, lighthouses must be built, depots for the supply of the steamers must be made, fortifications must be erected, and accommodation for a garrison provided. For the terminus of a great line of railway would need protection in time of war.

At present there are only a few fishermen's huts.

The probable saving of ten hours of time in an open voyage which varies even with the Cunard steamers, from nine to eighteen days, is not of such all absorbing magnitude as to entail by the choice of the terminus, such a fearful amount of extra expense and inconvenience to a whole province.

At a more advanced period, perhaps, when the provinces have attained all the prosperity they have a right to expect from this and other great works which would follow as surely as effect follows cause, then it may be time to consider the pro-priety of making a *branch* to Whitehaven.

Its selection now as the terminus would most materially affect the receipts to be expected from the traffic.

Whitehaven, therefore, with its longer and more expensive line of railway, full of engineering difficulties, passing for miles through a district of country, rocky, bar-ren, and unfavourable for agriculture, benefiting a comparatively small proportion of the inhabitants, to the exclusion of the capital and the greatest amount of the province;- or else involving the necessity of making a branch line of ninety miles in length is decidedly recommended to be *rejected*.

And the city and harbour of Halifax (one of the finest in the world) *is recom-mended to be selected* as the Atlantic terminus, for the proposed line of railway.

That part of the Direct route (No. 3 and 4), viz., the line from the Bend of Peticodiac by Boistown to the Restigouche and the St. Lawrence, crossing the range of New Brunswick mountains, having to surmount two summit levels of 1216 and 920 feet, causing heavy grades, and increasing materially the cost of transport; passing through a totally unsettled and wilderness country; involving greater difficulties in the transport of the materials necessary for its construction, and supplying food to the labourers engaged in its formation; excluding the towns and settlements on the Gulf shore, and so preventing the development of the vast resources of the country to be derived from the fisheries; and also inflicting a seri-ous loss to the interests of the main line, and to the intended branch from the city of St. John in New Brunswick, is, notwithstanding its one great advantage of diminished distance, recommended most strongly to be *rejected*.

And the Route No. 2, from Halifax to Truro, at the head of the Bay of Fundy, passing over the Cobequid Hills; and on or near to Amherst and Bay Verte, crossing from thence over to the Rivers Restigouche and Miramichi, above the flow of the tide, so as not to interfere with their navigation; then by the valley of the North-west Miramichi and Nipisiguit Rivers to Bathurst; then along the shore of the Bay of Chaleurs to the Restigouche River; then by the valley of the Metapediac over to or near to the River St. Lawrence; then by the route as shown in the General Plan No. 1, along the banks of the St. Lawrence to Riviere du Loup; and from thence continued through either the second or third concessions along the river until it approaches Point Levi, is recommended as the *best direction* for the proposed trunk line of railway from an eastern port in Nova Scotia through New Brunswick to Quebec.

It combines in the *greatest* degree the following important points:-

1st. The immediate prospect of direct [sic], as well as the greatest amount of remuneration for the expenditure to be incurred; the opening up a large field for provincial improvements for the settlement of emigrants, and by affording the opportunity in addition to *internal*, of *external* communication, by means of the Gulf of St. Lawrence and the Bay of Chaleurs, it will tend to develop in the highest degree the commerce and the fisheries of the Province of New Brunswick.

2nd. Passing along the sea-coast for a great distance, and capable of being approached at several points by bays or navigable rivers, it possesses the great-est facilities for construction, tending to reduce the expense and by its more favourable grades also the cost of working and subsequent maintenance.

3rd. By passing over a less elevated country, and at the least distance from the sea, there will be less interruption to be apprehended from climate, whilst the more favourable grades will increase the efficiency and rapidity of intercourse.

4th. Passing at the greatest possible distance from the United States, it pos-sesses in the highest degree the advantage to be derived from that circumstance of security from attack in case of hostilities.

The best general direction for the proposed trunk line of railway being admit-ted to be that of Route No. 2, viz., the Halifax and Eastern, or Bay Chaleurs route, some additional remarks may be made upon its peculiar advantages, as well as upon the few engineering difficulties which occur, and in explanation of the plans and sections forwarded.

The details of the plan are given in the Appendix No. 1. The plans referred to are the General Plan No. 1, the Model Map No. 2 (which should be stretched out on the floor to be properly viewed), and the book containing fifteen exploratory sheets of plans and sections which relate exclusively to this line.

The city of Halifax is situated on the western side of the harbour, whilst the best site for the terminus is on the opposite shore at Dartmouth.

The distance to Quebec from the latter will be four miles shorter than from the former; and one great advantage is, that its shore line is as yet comparatively free from wharves and commercial establishments, and an extensive terminus can be formed there at less expense and inconvenience than on the Halifax side, where the Government Dockyard and private establishments would interfere materially in the selection of a good site for it.

At Dartmouth it is expected that vessels entering the harbour will be able to unload at the railway premises, or probably into the railway cars, whilst an equally good terminus is to be had at Port Levi, opposite to Quebec. The same railway cars, loaded from the ships in harbour at Halifax, will thus, after running an *uninterrupted* course for 635 miles, be delivered of their contents into the boats if not the holds of vessels in the St. Lawrence. The same can of course be done from the River St. Lawrence to the vessels waiting in Halifax harbour.

Such an uninterrupted length of railway, with such facilities as its termini, will be, it is believed, unequalled in the world.

In the transmission of goods and merchandise this will be a most favourable point in competing with rival lines. The American railways, especially along the Atlantic States, are constantly interrupted, and passengers have to transfer themselves not only from cars to steam-boats, but sometimes from one set of carriages to another set, in waiting for them on opposite banks of a river.

In Nova Scotia the passage over the Cobequid Hills cannot be effected without heavy grades of 1 in 79 and 1 in 85; but as these occur, the one ascending and the other immediately descending, and only for ten miles, the inconvenience can be easily got over by affording an assistant engine for the goods' trains at that part. No engineering difficulties are expected to occur from this point up to the Restigouche River.

It is necessary, however, to make some remark in reference to the sections shown in the Book Exploratory, sheets 6 and 7, comprising that part of New Brunswick lying between Shediac and the North-west Miramichi.

The whole portion of the country is believed to be generally low and flat, with occasional undulations. The section run through it in the previous season of 1846, towards Boistown, confirmed this impression.

Its exploration and examination, therefore, was left to the last, and it was not until the really formidable-looking obstacles had been explored and successfully got over, that the attention of the parties was turned to it.

As at this time the season was rapidly closing, the exploring parties were directed to cut *straight* lines through it, as the best means of obtaining the general altitudes and a knowledge of the country. No attempt was made to contour the hills. The sections, therefore, in these two sheets are not grades for the railway, but of the ground passed over by the straight lines. With the exception of the immediate banks of the St. Lawrence, this is expected to prove one of the easiest portions of the line.

When the line reaches the mouth of Eel River, it cannot proceed direct on to Dalhousie, but must turn up the valley of that river.

Two courses are afterwards open to it, one to turn off through a valley, by which it can soon gain the Restigouche, the other to proceed on to the head waters of Eel River, and then turn down to that river. Which is the best of these two routes can be better determined when the detailed surveys of the route are made.

The most formidable point of the line is next to be mentioned,- this is the passage up the Metapediac valley.

The hills on both sides are high and steep, and come down either on one side or the other, pretty close to the river's bank, and involves the necessity (in order to avoid curves of very small radius) of changing frequently from one side to the other. The rock, too, is slaty and hard. From this cause, 20 miles of this valley will prove expensive, but the grades will be very easy.

About fourteen bridges of an average length of 120 to 150 yards will be required up this valley. There is also a bridge of 2000 feet long, mentioned in the detailed report as necessary to cross the Miramichi River.

But bridging in this country is not the same formidable affair that it is in England.

The rivers are nearly always shallow, and the materials of wood and stone, are close at hand.

The bridges in the United States, on the best lines, are built of wood on the truss-work principle, with stone piers and abutments.

On the Boston and Albany lines, and on many others in the New England States, the bridge generally used and approved of is known as "Howe's Patent Truss Bridge."

The cost of this kind of bridge, as furnished by the parties who have purchased the patent is as follows:

	Dollars	£	s.	d.	
For spans of 60 feet, single track, 11 per foot.	= 2	5	10	Sterling
100 feet "	18 "	3	15	0	"
140 feet "	21 "	4	7	6	"
180 feet "	27 "	5	12	6	"
200 feet "	30 "	6	5	0	"

The cost for double track would be about 55 per cent additional.

The price includes the whole of the superstructure ready for the rails, but not the piers and abutments.

The bridge over the Connecticut River at Springfield, is built on this principle; it has seven spans of 180 feet each, and the sill of the bridge is 30 feet above low water. On other lines the same kind of bridge is used, but no ironwork is permitted (the unequal expansion and contraction of this metal is objected to), and the addition of an arch is introduced.

A bridge built on this principle on the Reading Railroad, 1800 feet long, cost 40,000 dollars, equivalent to £8,330 sterling.

Soon after passing the valley of the Metapediac, the great obstacle of the St. Lawrence chain of mountains is got over, and the line may range away towards Quebec. Having, however, occasionally a river or a ravine to cross, whose passage requires consideration.

At the Trois Pistoles River, the stream in the course of ages has worn out a very awkward and deep ravine. The bank on one side is generally steep and abrupt, whilst that on the opposite is low and sloping away back for a long distance, before it again reaches the height of the table land.

The most favourable site for crossing it occurs at about eleven miles from the St. Lawrence, where the two banks become nearer to each other, and are more equal in height.

At this point the breadth of the stream is 100 feet at bottom. The width between the banks at top 500, and the depth is nearly 150 feet. The banks are rocky. Though formidable it is by no means impracticable.

On the New York and Erie Railway there is a bridge whose roadway is 170 feet above the bottom of the ravine, which it crosses by one span of 275 feet. Its cost was £5,200.

From Riviere du Loup to Quebec, the railway might but for the snow, be carried almost at surface level.

Through the whole of New Brunswick, for 234 miles, and through Lower Canada as far as Riviere du Loup, 167 miles, there will be found along the line abundance of timber and stone (including limestone) of the best quality for building purposes. There will be found also, in New Brunswick more especially, abundance of gravel for the superstructure.

In Nova Scotia, the railway will have to pass with but little exception through land which has been sold or granted away to individuals. The exception will be the other way in New Brunswick. It will be seen on reference to the Model Map, that it approaches the settlements between Bay Verte and Shediac, and skirts the Bay of Chaleurs.

In Canada from the mouth of the Metapediac to the Trois Pistoles, it runs through still ungranted land. But for the last 110 miles between Riviere du Loup, it runs through a densely settled country.

Until the detailed surveys are made, and the precise location of the line marked on the ground, it will be impossible to state precisely the exact number of miles it will pass through Crown land.

If the following estimate be taken, it will not much be out-

In Nova Scotia	15 miles
New Brunswick	200 "
Canada	160 "
Total	375 "

The following synopsis will show approximately the quantities of ungranted land in the counties through which the line passes:-

In Nova Scotia

	acres
Halifax County	780,000
Colchester	120,000
Cumberland	180,000
	1,080,000

In New Brunswick

Westmoreland County	301,000
Kent	640,000
Northumberland	1,993,000
Gloucester	704,000
Restigouche	1,109,000
	4,747,000

In Canada

Bonaventure	2,000,000
Rimouski	5,000,000
Kamouraska	500,000
L'Islet	600,000
Bellechasse	500,000
	8,600,000
Grand Total	14,427,000

The land for the railway will have to be purchased in Nova Scotia for nearly its whole course, and in Canada for the 110 miles mentioned.

The latter, it is expected, will cost very little more than the expense which it would be necessary to incur in cleaning, getting out the stumps, and preparing the wild lands for the railway.

No part of the line will ever be at any great distance from Crown Lands; but it will be a question of detail for this part as well for the Nova Scotia section, whether it will be more advantageous to cut and convey them the timber and materials required, or purchase them.

The direction of the proposed line being determined upon, the next points which present themselves for consideration are, the character of the road and method of construction.

In the first instance it is considered that one line of rails will be sufficient, but in taking ground for the railway and stations, and wherever the line passes, regard should be paid always to the prospect of its being made at some future time a double track. And in the anticipation of a heavy traffic, which there is a fair prospect of soon passing along it, and with a view to ultimate economy, as well as the saving of much inconvenience, it is recommended that the road (being intended for the great trunk line) should be constructed at once in a substantial and permanent manner, with a good heavy rail, capable of bearing high rates of speed for passenger trains.

On all principal lines of railway in the United States, the flat iron bar is everywhere being discarded, and the H or T rail, generally of 56 lbs to the yard, is being substituted for.

On several of the lines also a double track is being made, and the works constructed are of a more permanent character than formerly.

Much has been said in praise of the cheap method of making railways in America, and the advantages to be derived from it in new country.

As an example of this system and its practical results, the Utica and Syracuse railway may be here quoted.

This road is 53 miles in length and forms part of the Great Western Line, connecting Albany on the Hudson River, with Buffalo on Lake Erie—one of the principal lines in the country.

In its construction more than a usual amount of timber was used. For a considerable portion of its length (upwards of 19 miles) it passes through a deep swamp. Piles were drive into this, to support a long continued trestle-bridge over which the railway track was carried upon longitudinal bearers.

For the other 33 miles the grading was made in the usual manner by excavations and embankments: but the superstructure was of wood.

Upon the grading in the direction of its length, a small trench was excavated, and a sill of wood was firmly bedded in it. Where the sills abutted end to end, they were supported by a piece of wood, of the same section, laid beneath them. At right angles, to and upon the upper surfaces of the sills were spiked cross-ties, and again at right angle to the cross-ties, and immediately over the sills, were laid the longitudinal wood-bearers, to which the iron plates were firmly spiked. The centre of the rail and sill were in the same vertical plane.

Thus everything was done for economy: as much wood as possible being used. This railway for its construction and equipment cost on an average only £3,600 per mile.

It was thought worthy, in 1843, to publish an account of it in London, and it forms the chief subject of a volume, thus entitled "Ensamples of Railway making, which, although not of English practice are submitted to the Civil Engineer and the British and Irish Public."

The following Report is extracted from the Annual Statement of the Secretary of State to the Assembly of the State of New York, dated 4th March, 1847 :-

"The Syracuse and Utica Railroad has been opened for the transportation of passengers for the last eight years.

"The company having determined to relay the road with an iron rail of the most improved form, have contracted for a considerable portion of then iron necessary, and are proceeding with the intention of laying a substantial structure adequate to the proper performance of the business required.

	Dollars
"The present wood structure has cost the company	417,075.55
"The iron now laid thereon is the flat bar and will be useless, and therefore will be sold. It is hoped that there may be derived from the sale of it	80,000.00
"Leaving the sum of	337,075.55

which has been expended for the cost of the wood structure, which, in addition to a large annual amount for repairs, will be practically, worn out, sunk, and gone, when the new structure is laid and used. The new structure, it is supposed, will cost about the same as the former, towards which, it is hoped, the old iron will pay as above 80,000 dollars, leaving the sum of about 300,000 dollars to be raised by the company on its credit.

"This will, when paid, reimburse the capital of the company for the equivalent amount, which has been appropriated to the worn-out structure. In addition to the cost of the new structure, there will be required a considerable sum for new engines, cars &c. The demand upon the company for the transportation of property at the close of the canal, has entirely exceeded its capacity to do this business. Property destined for sale in the eastern markets, in large quantities, was stopped at most points upon the line of the railroad contiguous to the canal. Being practically confined to the winter months in this branch of business, it cannot be expected that the company could provide a supply of cars for this sudden and extraordinary demand, when they must stand idle and go to waste during two-thirds of the year.

"When the road shall be relaid with the proposed iron rail, the public will require that the trains shall be run with increased speed. In relation to this subject, it is deemed proper to refer them to the following suggestions contained in the report of this company made last year.

"Very great embarrassment is experienced from the fact that cattle are allowed to run at large, and to impede and so often delay the trains as at present. It is a serious matter, and unless more care shall be bestowed by the owners in restraining them, either at their own suggestion or in pursuance of some proper law to be passed, it will be found very difficult to make good time upon this line. A part of our business must always be done in the night, and it is then we experience the great hazard. The trains are frequently thrown off by them, and the danger to the persons in charge and to the passengers is imminent. The owners always insist upon pay for their animals destroyed, without reflecting upon the great damage that they cause to the property of the company, and the more fearful injury that might ensue the passengers. If the owners will not take care of them it is impossible to keep them off. In Massachusetts much less difficulty in this respect is experienced, for there, it is believed, a penalty is incurred by the owner of domestic animals that go upon the railroad. Our business is conducted with all possible care in this respect, and the enginemen suitably feel the risk of life and limb (which to them is almost as important) that they incur from the growing evil.

"A very proper law in this State has guarded the public and the company against direct wanton injury to the trains by individuals. It is submitted that *negligence* in allowing animals to run upon the railroad should be prevented by some suitable restraints."

Some of the inconveniences arising from a cheap railway may be learnt from this Report.

At this time the total amount spent upon its construction appears from the same report to have been 1,098,940 dollars, equivalent to £4,520 sterling per mile.

The new superstructure, it was supposed, would cost about the same as the former, viz., 417,075 dollars, or about £1640 sterling additional, which will make the price of this railway when completed as intended £5,960 per mile.

In other parts of the States where the trestle bridge or skeleton railways have been made, instances have been known of the locomotive slipping down between the rails, which have warped outwards.

With a view, therefore, to ultimate economy, and to save inconvenience and interruption to the traffic when once established, it is most strongly recommended that the line whenever commenced shall be at once properly and efficiently made.

In determining the form of the road it is necessary to bear in view that it will pass through a country everywhere liable to be obstructed by heavy falls of snow. It does not appear, however, from the results of inquiries made in the United States, that anything beyond inconvenience, and some additional expense in the cost of working the line, is to be apprehended from this cause.

The railway from Boston to Albany, which crosses the range of mountains between the Connecticut and Hudson Rivers, attaining them an elevation of upwards of 1400 feet above the sea, to which it ascends by a grade of about eighty feet per mile for 13 miles, traverses a country subjected to the same sort of winter as the British North American Provinces.

The average depth of snow in the woods is from 3 to 4 feet which is not much less than it is in the woods of New Brunswick and Canada.

In 1843, a year remarkable for the great number of snow storms which occurred, there was sixty-three falls of snow, but the traffic was not interrupted to any very serious extent, not more than two or three trips.

To keep the roads clear, two descriptions of snow ploughs are used, one for the double track and another for the single. In the former the *share* of the plough travels immediately over the inner rail, throwing the snow outwards from the track. It is first used on one track, and then runs back upon the other.

In the single line the ploughshare travels in the centre of the track, throwing the snow off at once upon both sides.

For the double track the snow plough weighs from 5 to 6 tons, and costs about 125. For the single track it is somewhat lighter.

The plough requires generally, when run without a train, two engines of 20 tons each, or with a train three engines.

When the fall of snow does not exceed a few inches, the small plough always fixed in front of the engine, consisting of an open frame work projecting about 5 feet in front and called a "*Cow scraper*," is found, when eased over, to be sufficient to clear the line. When the fall is deeper, the plough is used immediately after the snow has ceased to fall.

It can be propelled by three 20 ton engines through 3 feet of newly fallen snow at the rate of 6 miles an hour.

If the fall does not exceed 2 feet, it can travel at the rate of 15 miles an hour.

The drifts through which it is propelled are sometimes 15 feet deep, and from 200 to 300 feet long, and at others 8 or 10 feet deep, and from a quarter to half a mile in length.

The line of railway is marked in divisions of about 8 miles, to each of which eight or ten men are allotted, who pass along the line each day with small hand ploughs, picks, &c., clearing away the snow and ice which the trains collect and harden between the rails and the roadway.

It is found that the freezing of the snow or rain upon the rails does not impede the heavy engines, the weight of the forward wheels is sufficient to break it, and enable the driving wheels to bite.

Whenever, from local causes, the snow is found to drift on the line of railway, snow-fences are erected, which are found very effectual. They are simple board fences from 10 to 15 feet high, placed from 10 to 20 feet back from the railway.

In wet weather the rails become very slippery, but the difficulty is overcome and the wheels enabled to bite upon the steep gradients by the use of sand boxes, which are fixed in front of the engine and immediately over the rails.

These can be opened at pleasure by the engine-driver, and the sand is used wherever necessary.

The means thus successfully adopted to overcome the obstacles arising from ice and snow are employed much in the same way upon all the railways which are exposed to them.

In the year 1847 the expense incurred under this head (removing ice and snow) upon the western railroad in Massachusetts, was, according to the official return, 2,763 dollars, equivalent to £575 sterling.

Upon many of the other lines expenses under the same head are returned, but very much smaller in amount.

In places where the rails are not raised above the general level of the country, much greater difficulty is experienced in keeping the lines clear of snow than in parts where there are embankments.

From the foregoing it does not appear, therefore, that snow need be considered an insurmountable obstacle to the formation of a railway from Halifax to Quebec.

To obviate as much as possible, the liability to interruption from this cause, it is recommended that in the construction of the line, it be adopted as a principle, that the top of the iron rail be kept as high as the average depth of snow in the country through which the line passes.

In Nova Scotia this will require probably and embankment of 2 feet high, gradually increasing as it proceeds northward to the St. Lawrence an along the flat open country on its banks, to 5 or even 6 feet.

The whole of that part of British North America through which this line is intended to be run, being as yet free from railways, the choice of gauge is clear and open.

Without entering into and quoting the arguments which have been adduced in favour of the broad or narrow gauge of England, as it is more a question of detail than otherwise, it will be deemed sufficient for the present report to recommend an intermediate gauge. Probably 5 feet 6 inches will be the most suitable, as combining the greatest amount of practical utility with the least amount of increased expenditure.

With the object of proceeding on to the consideration of expense of construction, the proposed trunk line will be supposed to have a single track with one-tenth additional for side lines and turn outs, to have rail 65 lbs. to the yard, supported upon longitudinal sleepers with cross-ties, similar to the rail used upon the London and Croydon line, the wood to be prepared according to Payne's process, to have a gauge of 5 feet 6 inches, and as a principle, the top of the rails to be kept above the level of the surface of the ground, at a height equal to the average depth of the snow. For the best information as to the cost of making such a railway, reference must be made to the works of a similar character in the United States.

At about the close of the year 1847, there were in that country nearly 5,800 miles of railway completed or in progress. The average cost for those having a single track has been estimated at 22,000 dollars, equivalent to £4,166 sterling per mile. For the double track 32,000 dollars, or £6,666 per mile.

But the extreme differences which are to be observed in the cost of construction in the various States are so great, ranging from £1600 up to £24,000 per mile, that no criterion can be established from averages obtained from such discordant data.

The state of Massachusetts affords the best materials for accurate information.

All the railroad corporations are by law obliged to make annual returns to the legislature, and very valuable statistical information is thereby obtained upon railway affairs.

From the official reports for the year 1847, the following table has been compiled.

Name of Road	Length of road in miles	Total cost of road and equipment	Cost per mile	
		Dollars	Dollars	
Boston and Lowell	26	1,956,719	75,258	
Boston and Maine	73	3,021,172	41,385	
Boston and Providence	48 44½	2,545,715	53,014	
Boston and Worcester	14 36 36	4,113,609	70,318	
Connecticut River	2 38 38	1,167,156	70,318	
Eastern	20	2,937,206	30,714	
Fall River	42 49½	1,070,988	25,499	
Fitchburg	2	2,406,723	46,732	
Lexington & West Cambridge	6½	221,309	34,047	
Nashua and Lowell	14¼ 20	500,000	35,087	
New Bedford and Taunton	1 59	483,882	23,042	
Norwich and Worcester	7 37	2,187,249	33,140	
Old Colony	7	1,636,632	37,196	
Pittsfield and North Adams	19	446,353	23,492	
Western	118	6,982,233	59,171	
Total	683¾ 146¼	31,675,946		
Single Track	830			

Form of rail and lbs. per yard	Miles of single rail	Miles of double rail	Dividend for 1847	Cost per mile of single track, std.	Remarks
M. lbs.				£	
1½ 45 20 56 3¾ 63	None	26	8	7,830	
6m 45 lbs. Rest 46 to 60	68	5	9	8,069	
T or H 56-58	32¼	15¾	7½	8,316	
T or H 60-64	14	44½	8	7,583	Including Branches
H 56 lbs.	38	None	7	6,399	Do.
H and 57 lbs. Chair 46 lbs.	42	16	8	8,269	Do.
H 52-56 lbs.	42	None	–	5,312	
T 56 lbs.	46¼	5¼	10	8.835	Do.
56 lbs.	6½	None		7,093	
T 56 lbs.	1¼	13	10	3,822	
56 lbs.	21	None	8	4,800	Do.
T 56 lbs.	64¼	1¾		6,725	Do.
H 56 lbs.	44	None	6½	7,749	Do.
H 56 lbs.	19	None		4,894	Do.
56½ to 70	99	19		10,617	
	146½			7,950	Average for single track per mile.

This table comprises, with the exception of about fifty miles, upon which there occur some doubts as to what the account precisely embraces, the whole of the railroads at present completed in the State of Massachusetts. The table shows 683½ [sic] miles of railway, including branches, which have cost in their construction and equipment, 31,675,946 dollars, or £6,699,155 sterling.

There are 146 miles of double track. They have been taken at so much additional single track. A double track would not cost exactly twice that of a single one in its construction; but as these lines were made originally only with single tracks, and have been added to from time to time as circumstances would admit, it must have tended to increase the cost, and in calculating the average expense per mile, it is considered the result will not much be in error. The cost per mile it appears then has been £7950 sterling.

There is no other State in the Union which presents equally good data for making an approximate estimate.

The climate and nature of the country bears also a strong resemblance to that through which the Halifax and Quebec line will pass, and in this respect the analogy of the two cases is extremely favourable.

The New York and Erie railroad, 450 miles in length, now in course of construction, will, it is supposed from the latest information, cost £6,250 per mile, exclusive of equipment.

The estimate for the Hudson River railroad from New York to Albany, now in progress, is for the single track £7,440 sterling per mile.

The estimate for the Montreal and Portland line is about £5,080 sterling per mile.

For the Great Western Railroad in progress in Upper Canada, the estimate for that section of the line which would most resemble the Halifax and Quebec road is £5,638 per mile.

On referring to the table, it will be seen that all the lines have either the H or T rail, generally 56 lbs. to the yard.

The price of railroad iron in the States is very much greater than in England, or what it can be procured for in the British Provinces. It pays very high duty on importation into the States.

On some of the lines upwards of £15 per ton for rails has been paid. In England rails can now be bought for £8 or £9 per ton.

The advantage which the Halifax and Quebec line will possess over the lines in the table in respect of iron alone, may be estimated at £500 per mile.

When these lines were constructed also, the demand for labour was extremely great, and wages much higher than in the present day.

The average (of £7950) derived from the table, may therefore very fairly be reduced by several hundred pounds.

The Halifax and Quebec line will have also many advantages which the American lines had not.

The land for the greater portion of the road will not have to be purchased. Timber and stone will be had nearly along the whole line for the labour of cutting and quarrying.

Judging then from the analogy afforded by similar, or nearly similar lines in the neighbouring States, giving due weight to the considerations which have a tendency to modify the cost in the particular case of the Halifax and Quebec line, and forming the best estimate to be derived from the data obtained upon the exploratory survey, which, under the circumstances of a perfectly new country, only recently explored, and still covered with a dense forest, is all that can in the first instance be done; it is considered that if the sum of £7000 sterling per mile be assumed as the probable cost of the proposed line, it will not be far from the correct amount.

The total distance from Halifax to Quebec will be about 635 miles.

635 miles at £7000 per mile will be	£4,445,000
Add one tenth for contingencies	£ 444,500
	£4,889,500

Or, in round numbers, five millions.

It is estimated, therefore, that the cost for construction and equipment of the proposed trunk line, from Halifax, through New Brunswick, to Quebec, will amount to £5,000,000 sterling.

The question which presents itself next for consideration is a very important one, namely, the probable returns for such an expenditure.

The information to be afforded on this head can only be derived in a very general way, from a consideration of the present population and resources of the three provinces.

The direct communication between the two termini, Halifax and Quebec, is of a very limited nature.

By land it is confined almost to the conveyance of the mails. Passengers proceed generally by way of the United States.

By sea, in 1847, the communication was by seventeen vessels, which arrived at Quebec, having tonnage of 1257, and eighteen departed from that port for Halifax whose tonnage amounted to 1386 tons.

This amount of intercourse does not at the first view appear encouraging to expected receipts, but when it is made to appear that this limited intercourse arises entirely from the want of good means of intercommunication such as would be afforded by the proposed railway, it becomes a strong argument in favour of making the line, rather than against it.

The communication of the provinces with each other is cramped and restricted beyond measure by the same want.

By sea the amount of intercourse may be judged of by the return... furnished by the Quebec Board of Trade.

The chief elements which enter into, and upon which depends, the success of every railway enterprise, are population, agriculture and commerce.

At the extremities of the line, and for some miles along the St. Lawrence, there is an abundant population. External commerce there is in imminent degree. In that of agriculture its deficiency is great at present, but as there are millions of acres of good productive land only waiting for the hands necessary to cultivate them, and the means of access to which will be afforded by the railway, this very circumstance may be made to conduce to the advantage of the line, and pay a large portion of the expense of its construction.

The population of Halifax (the Atlantic terminus) is estimated at 25,000 souls. It is the capital of the province, the seat of government, and its commerce extensive. The value of its imports and exports is estimated at £2,500,000.

The city of Quebec, the other terminus, according to the census of 1841, contained (including the county which is not given separately) 45,000 persons.

But this city derives additional importance from its being the one great shipping port and outlet for all Canada. By its port passes the whole trade of the province. It may be regarded as the focus of commerce for a million and a half souls. The value of the imports and exports together may be estimated at £5,500,000 sterling, giving employment to a very great amount of shipping.

This immense trade is of necessity crowded into six months, the navigation of the St. Lawrence being closed for the remainder of the year.

In addition to these two great termini there are lying on each side of the line two most important tributaries, viz., the city of St. John and Prince Edward's Island. The former with a population in city and county together of nearly 44,000 persons, with a commerce of the value of £1,800,000 in exports and imports, giving employment also to a great amount of shipping. The latter with a population of 50,000 engaged principally in agriculture and the fisheries. The exports and imports of this island are about £200,000 annually.

Between the city of Quebec and the River Metis there are, settled along the south bank of the St. Lawrence, 75,000 inhabitants all engaged in agriculture. These people are French Canadians, and almost every family has a small farm and homestead.

A striking peculiarity of these farms is their elongated shape, the length being generally thirty times that of the breadth, oftentimes a greater disproportion exists. The houses and farm buildings are always built at one extremity, that which adjoins the road dividing one set of concessions from another. There are generally three or four lines of houses and roads running thus along the St. Lawrence.

The effect produced by this manner of parcelling out the land and building has been to form what can only be compared to one long and continued village for 200 miles.

For the first 100 miles out of Quebec, as far nearly as the Riviere du Loup, the proposed line of railway will run through the centre of this extended village, and with a train of moderate length, the last carriage will scarcely have cleared the door of one house before the engine will be opposite the other. For the second 100 miles it will leave these concessions and farms a little on one side, but still within reach. A more favourable disposition of a population (comprised of small farmers) for contributing to the *way traffic* of a railroad could scarcely have been devised.

In the country lying between the Restigouche River and Halifax, the inhabitants who will be near to the railroad will amount to about 100,000; making the population either upon or near to the line, including the two termini, 250,000 persons. But if the total population be taken within the area, which will be benefited *by*, and become contributors to the line, then it may be estimated at not less than 400,000 souls.

In a report of the Directors, made upon the New York and Erie Railroad in 1843, when the question of proceeding with that line was under consideration, one of the data upon which its future receipts was calculated was derived from population and relative distance. And using the data obtained from the working of one portion which had been completed and was in operation, it was calculated that 531,000 persons on a line of 425 miles in length, would return in *net* earnings to the railway 1,343,500 dollars, or 2½ dollars nearly per head, equivalent to 10s. sterling. As the railroad is not yet completed, the true result cannot yet be seen.

The net earnings of the railroads in Massachusetts for the year 1847 were 2,290,000 dollars. The population of that State, over whose area railways are everywhere extended, and the whole of which may therefore be considered as tributary to them, being at the time about £800,000. This gives 2¾ dollars per head, equivalent to 11s., or the same result nearly.

Applying the same ratio (of 10s. per head) to the 400,000 inhabitants who are within the area and likely to become tributaries to the Quebec and Halifax Railway, it would give £200,000 as its probable revenue.

The great staple of New Brunswick is its timber. For this all absorbing pursuit the inhabitants neglect agriculture, and instead of raising their own supplies they import provisions in large quantities from Canada and the United States. In the year 1846, New Brunswick paid to the latter for provisions alone, £216,000 sterling, whilst, in return the United States only took from them £11,000 in coals and fish.

Of Nova Scotia the great staples are timber and the products of the fisheries. The inhabitants import provisions also largely.

Canada is an *exporting* country, and capable of supplying the demands of both.

In the winter of 1847-48 the price of flour at Halifax and St. John was at 40s. per barrel, and it was being imported from the chief ports in the United States, even from as far as New Orleans in the Gulf of Mexico. At the same time at Quebec the price of flour was only 25s. per barrel. A very great difference, which, had the railroad been in existence, would not have occurred.

Another great source of revenue likely to be developed by the railway is that of coals, to be derived from the Great Cumberland Field.

Quebec and the upper country would no doubt take large quantities for their own consumption. Halifax the same for itself, and also for exportation to the United States.

Considerable returns would arise from the fisheries and from the products of the forest lying contiguous to the line, which would find their way by it to the shipping ports.

The country through which the road will pass possesses, therefore, *in itself*, elements which, when fully developed, cannot fail to realize large receipts.

But there are, exclusive of these, other and highly important sources for productive revenue.

Halifax may be considered to be the nearest great sea port to Europe.

Passengers travelling between England and the Canadas would adopt this railway, as the shortest and best line which they could take. Emigrants would do the same.

The mail, troops, munitions of war, commissariat supplies, and all public stores would naturally pass by it, as the safest, speediest, and cheapest means of conveyance.

If a straight line be drawn from Cape Clear in Ireland, to New York, it will cut through or pass close to Halifax.

The latter is therefore on the Direct route; and as the sea voyage across the Atlantic to New York may be shortened by three days nearly, in steamers, it is not improbable that on that account, when the branch railroad to St. John is completed, and other lines to connect on with those in the United States, the whole or the greater portion of the passenger traffic between the Old and New World would pass through Halifax, and over a great section of the proposed railroad.

But the great object for the railroad to attain, and which, if it should be able to accomplish, its capability to pay the interest of the capital expended would be undoubted, is to supersede the long and dangerous passage to Quebec by the Gulf of St. Lawrence.

To make *two* voyages in a season vessels are obliged to leave England earlier, and encounter the dangers of the ice in the Gulf, much sooner than it is safe or prudent for them to do.

The loss of life and property which has occurred from this cause, and returning late in the autumn has been enormous. It cannot be ascertained, but probably it would have more than paid for the railway.

An opinion may, however, be formed of it from the rates of insurance, which in the spring and autumn are as high as 10 per cent. A much higher rate than to any other part of the world.

The navigation of the St. Lawrence is closed for about six months of every year.

During the whole of this period all the produce of the country is locked up, and necessarily lies unproductive on the hands of the holders.

The surplus agricultural produce of the year cannot be got ready to be shipped in the season it is produced. In the winter of 1846-47 it has been stated on good authority, that 500,000 barrels of flour were detained in Montreal at the time when famine was raging in Ireland. As soon as the sea opened, there was a demand for shipping to carry provisions, that the ordinary course of the timber was deranged by it.

All this would have been prevented had the railway been then in existence.

For six months in the year then, the St. Lawrence would cease to be a competition with the railway, and large quantities of produce would be certain to be forwarded by it.

For the other six months of the year it would have also the following strong claims to preference;- rapidity of transport; the saving of heavy insurance; cheaper rate of freight from Halifax; vessels engaged in the Canadian trade could make three voyages to Halifax for two to Quebec.

The trade which is now crowded into six months, to the great inconvenience of everyone concerned, rendering large stocks necessary to be kept on hand, would be diffused equally over the whole year.

It is most probable that these advantages will be found so great, that only the bulky and weighty articles of commerce, such as the very heavy timber, and a few other goods will continue to be sent round by the Gulf of St. Lawrence.

If such should prove to be the case, then the proposed railway would have as much or perhaps more traffic than a single track could accommodate.

The cost of transportation, it is calculated, will not be too high on this line to admit of the above results being realised, and in that case, more especially if the capital can be raised at a moderate rate of interest, it is considered highly probable that it will even in a commercial point of view be a profitable undertaking.

From evidence given to the Gauge Commissioners in England, it appears that the cost of transport for goods on the undermentioned lines of railway was as follows:-

Great Western	.06 of a penny per ton per mile.	
Grand Junction	.13 "	"
Birmingham and Gloucester	.09 "	"
South Western	.10 "	"
London and Birmingham	.12 "	"
	.50	
	.10 Average ton per mile	

This is supposed to be gross weights, including carriages &c.

One fifth of a penny per mile per ton will be a liberal allowance for the net weight.

From a very carefully prepared document, extracted from a Report of the Commissioners appointed in 1846 by the Legislature of the State of New York, to locate certain portions of the New York and Erie Railroad, it appears that the cost of motive power on some of the principal railroads in the United States was 40 cents per train per mile, equivalent to 1s. 8d. sterling.

With the expected grades on the Halifax and Quebec line, it is calculated that an engine of good power, having the assistance of an extra engine for 25 miles of the distance will convoy 100 tons of goods at a moderate speed of 8 to ten miles an hour over the whole line.

	£	s.	d.
The total cost per train would then be			
635 miles, at 1s. 8d. per mile	52	18	4
25 miles at 1s. 8d. for extra train	2	1	8

Or 11s. per ton for the whole distance. Equal to .207 drs. per ton per mile, the same nearly as the average on the English railways.

At this rate the *actual cost* of carrying a barrel of flour from Quebec to Halifax will be only 1s. 1d.: and if it be doubled to pay interest on capital, then 2s. 2d. might be the price charged for its conveyance.

The freight of flour from Quebec to England may be taken at 5s. per barrel; from Halifax at 3s.

The difference in freight would therefore pay its transit by railway, and the difference in the rates of insurance would be to the profit of the owner; and the voyage being shorter, there would be less risk of its arrival in the market in a heated or deteriorated condition.

Provisions and all other articles whose value is great in proportion to their bulk, would be as advantageously forwarded by this route.

It is fully expected, therefore, that the railway will be able to compete successfully with shipping in the St. Lawrence even during the summer season.

But there is still another great and important source from which traffic may be expected, viz.,- from those vast and extensive regions in the far west, round the Lakes Huron, Michigan and Lake Superior.

By the completion of the canals along the River St. Lawrence, the produce of these lake countries now finds its way to the markets of Montreal and Quebec.

Lake cargoes, consisting of upwards of 300 barrels of flour can now pass from their ports down to Quebec without once breaking bulk.

Already produce which found its way to New York by the circuitous route of the Mississippi and New Orleans has been diverted to the channel of the St. Lawrence.

The extent to which this will take place it is not possible yet to calculate; but there is no doubt that large quantities of produce which formerly found its way to the Atlantic ports of New York and Boston, will be diverted to the St. Lawrence.

Of the enormous exports of provisions from the United States, the following will give some idea.

	In 1846	In 1847
Flour–barrels	2,289,476	4,382,496
Wheat–bushels	1,613,795	4,399,951
Corn–bushels	1,826,068	16,326,050
Meal–barrels	293,720	918,066

The greatest portion if not nearly all this immense produce of which the above forms only a *few items* in the *great account*, was received at the Atlantic ports from the far West. And it is for this most important and still increasing trade, that Montreal and Quebec will now, by means of the St. Lawrence canals, have the most favourable chance of a successful competition with New York and Boston.

It has been calculated that the cost of transport for a barrel of flour from the Lakes to New York was 5s. 1d. sterling; to Boston 6s., exclusive of charges for transhipment.

By the Quebec and Halifax line it is estimated, now that the canals are open, a barrel of flour may be delivered at Quebec for 2s. sterling, and carried to Halifax for 2s. 2d.; total 4s. 2d.

By the Montreal and Portland, 1s. 8d. has been estimated as the price per the railway, to which if 2s. more be added as freight to Montreal the price by that line will probably be only 3s. 8d. sterling per barrel. The Montreal and Portland will have therefore an apparent advantage over the Quebec and Halifax line, arising from its much shorter distance. But there are some drawbacks attending it, which may cause the preference to be given to the latter notwithstanding. The line passes through the United States.

A transit duty of 2½ per cent. *ad valorem*, has to be levied upon all foreign produce, and introduces the inconvenience of custom-houses and custom-house officers.

Portland is a foreign port, and is 100 miles by the sea farther from England than Halifax.

It has been seen in a former part of this report, when speaking of the Utica and Syracuse Railroad, how inadequate that line was to take all the traffic which was required to be forwarded by it, at the time that the Erie canal was closed.

The growing population and produce of the Western States are so gigantic, that it is probable there will be more than sufficient to employ fully, *both* the Montreal and Portland and the Quebec and Halifax Railroads.

From the forgoing remarks, it will appear then, that although no very good or precise estimate of the returns for the expenditure of five millions sterling can be given, yet that there are very good general grounds upon which to form an opinion, that ultimately, if not at once, the line will, in a commercial point of view, be a very productive one.

The Montreal and Portland, which will be the great competitor with that of the Quebec and Halifax line, is an enterprise of a purely commercial and local nature. As such, it is not likely shareholders will be contented, unless they receive what they have every right to expect—a high rate of interest for the expenditure they have incurred, and the risk they have encountered in the undertaking.

But with the Quebec and Halifax line it is very different. The enterprise is of *general interest*. It contains the prosperity and welfare of each of the three provinces, and the honour as well as the interests of the whole British Empire may be affected by it. It is the one great means by which alone the power of the mother country can be brought to bear on this side of the Atlantic, and restore the balance of power now fast turning to the United States.

Every new line of railway made in that country, adds to their power, enabling them to concentrate their forces almost wherever they please, and by the lines, of which there are already some and there will soon be more, reaching to their northern frontier, they can choose at their own time any point of attack on the long extended Canadian frontier, and direct their whole strength against it.

The provinces, therefore, and the empire having such interest in the formation of the Halifax and Quebec Line, it should be undertaken by them in common as a great public work for the public weal.

If so undertaken, the provinces supported by the credit of the mother country, could raise capital at a rate of interest which could not be done by any company of shareholders. And is to this advantage be added, the disposal for the exclusive benefit of the railway, of a portion of the wild lands along the line, and in the immediate country which it would be the means of opening to settlement and cultivation, then it is highly probable that it would be constructed for three millions sterling.

In a former part of this report it has been estimated that there are in the counties through which this line will pass, fourteen millions of acres of land yet ungranted, and therefore remaining at the disposal of the Provincial Government.

The ordinary price of an acre of wild or uncleared land is about 2s. 6d. to 3s. per acre. But where public roads are made through them, the value immediately increases, and it will not be considered an extravagant estimate, to suppose that the land along it, or in the immediate vicinity of the railway, will be worth £1 per acre.

For the construction of the Great St. Lawrence Canal, by which Canada has now the prospect of reaping such immense advantages from the trade of the western country, the Imperial Government guaranteed the interest on a loan of two millions sterling and upwards, at 4 per cent. This loan was easily raised, and a large premium per cent. was received in addition to it.

There can be little doubt that another loan of three millions sterling at the same rate of 4 per cent interest, could be raised upon the credit of the provincial revenues if guaranteed by the mother country. With this amount of capital and two millions of acres to be reserved, and sold from time to time, it is conceived the railway may be made.

Upon the strength of these two millions of acres and the loan as a basis, a large amount of *notes* might be issued in payment of the wages and salaries of the labourers and other persons employed on the work of the railway. They should be made receivable for taxes and customs duties. The amount authorized to be issued might be limited to the extent of the acres, and as these were sold an equal amount of the notes should be cancelled.

The issue of a number of notes which would pass current over the three provinces would be conferring a great benefit upon the community at large. The currency is not the same throughout and persons who travel from one province to another are now put to inconvenience and have to pay a discount upon exchanging the notes of one colonial bank for those of another. Advantage might be taken of the measure to assimilate the currency of the colonies to each other, and make it "sterling" the same as in England.

By a little arrangement also, these notes might be made payable at the chief ports of emigration in the United Kingdom; and in that case a very great convenience would be afforded to a large class of persons on both sides the Atlantic.

To remit small sums now, requires the intervention of bankers or agents. This has the effect upon persons resident in the settlements (and no doubt often also in the towns), of preventing their sending the assistance which they otherwise would do to friends at home. Many small notes would be put up, and sent in a letter, which now is never thought of, for want of the convenience.

In remitting sums from Halifax to England, the banks do not like to give bills at less than sixty days' sight. These notes would, therefore become a great public benefit, and there would be no fear of their being kept in circulation almost to any amount.

Upon the loan of three millions, the interest at 4 per cent. would amount to £120,000 per annum.

Of this sum it may fairly be assumed that for the conveyance of the mails between Halifax and Quebec, the Post Office department would be willing to pay annually an equal amount to what is now paid for the same service. This has not been officially obtained, but there are good grounds to suppose that it is nearly £20,000.

In the case, then, that beyond this the railway only paid its own working expenses, the sum of £100,009 would have to be made good out of the revenues of the provinces.

The proportion of this, or of whatever sum might be deficient to pay the interest on the loan, would have to be arranged; and it may, for the sake of illustration be supposed to be as follows:-

Nova Scotia	£20,000	Proportion	.2
New Brunswick	£20,000	"	.2
Canada	£30,000	"	.3
The Imperial Government	£30,000	"	.3
Total	£100,000		1.0

For the proportion guaranteed by the provinces, they would receive the benefits conferred by the railway in developing their resources, increasing the value of all property, promoting the sale and settlement of their wild lands, increased population and increased revenue.

For the proportion guaranteed by the Imperial Government, all Government officers, civil or military, troops, munitions of war, supplies &c., for the public service, and *emigrants* should be transported over the line at the cost price.

New Brunswick and Nova Scotia it is understood are most willing to guarantee the interest to the extent of their means, and in a fair proportion.

Canada having done so much already for the communications above Montreal, it is fully expected will not be backward in perfecting those below Quebec.

In the extreme case supposed above, viz., of the railway yielding no returns beyond working expenses, it is not conceived that either one of the provinces or the empire would not receive an equivalent in some other form for its direct contribution to make good the interest.

An account is at present being taken of the existing way traffic between Halifax and Amherst, by the commissioner appointed in Nova Scotia to collect statistics for the railway. The same is being done for that portion of the line along the banks of the St. Lawrence.

There is some reason to believe that these two portions of the line will be found to have sufficient traffic to pay over and above working expenses, the moderate interest upon capital of 4 per cent.

If such should prove correct, then the foregoing statement would be modified and stand thus:-

Total distance from Halifax to Quebec 635
Quebec to Riviere du Loup 110
Halifax to Amherst and Bay Verte..125
                                                                            235
Leaving unproductive still miles..400

If the total line can be done for £3,000,000 then the proportion for the 400 miles would be £1,889,600 or £2,000,000 nearly.

The interest for which would amount to £80,000

Deducting £20,000 for the conveyance of the mails, then the sum to be responsible for would be £60,000, which divided proportionally as before, would give for:

Nova Scotia	£12,000	Proportion	.2
New Brunswick	£12,000	"	.2
Canada	£18,000	"	.3
The Imperial Government	£18,000	"	.3
Total	£60,000		1.0

Therefore, for the responsibility (perhaps for assuming it only) of £100,000 or as the case may prove £60,000, the Quebec and Halifax Railway may be made.

But to look at this great work only as a commercial speculation and as yielding mere interest for the expenditure incurred would be to take the very limited view of the objects it is capable of achieving.

In the United States they are well aware of the increased value which internal improvements and communications give to property of every kind.

In those countries works have been undertaken for that object alone, not for the mere return which the work, whether railway, road or canal, would make of itself.

The indebtedness of the several States has been incurred almost entirely in making great internal improvements. And in the boldness and unhesitating way in which they have incurred debts and responsibilities for the purpose of developing their resources may be seen the secret of their unrivalled prosperity.

The State is in debt, but its citizens have been enriched beyond all proportion.

Most unfavourable comparisons are made by travellers who visit the British Provinces and the United States. And some have gone so far as to state that, travelling along where the boundary is a mere conventional line, they could at once tell whether they were in the States or not.

On the one side the State Governments become shareholders to a large amount in great public works, *lead* the way and do not hesitate to incur debt, for making what has been termed "war upon the wilderness;" employment is given, and by the time the improvement is completed property has been created and the *employed* become proprietors.

On the other side the Provincial Governments do not take the initiative in the same manner, and hence in the settlements and in the provinces generally, may be seen this marked difference in the progress of people who are identically the same in every respect.

Until the British Provinces boldly imitate the policy of the States in this regard and make war upon the "wilderness," their progress will continue to present the same unfavourable contrast.

The creative or productive power of canals, railways &c., may be traced in the history and progress of the State of New York.

The Erie Canal was commenced in 1817, and completed in 1825, at a cost of 7,143,789 dollars or £1,400,000 sterling. In 1817 the value of real and personal property in the city of New York was from official documents estimated at

£16,436,000 sterling. In 1825, it was estimated at £21,075,000 sterling. In 1829 the population of the State was 1,372,000 and in 1830 the population of the State was 1,918,000.

The canal was found so inadequate to the traffic, that between the years 1825 and 1835, a farther sum of £2,700,000 was expended enlarging it.

Making the total cost to that date £4,100,000 sterling.

It has been seen that in the city of New York

In 1817, the official value of real and personal property was	£16,436,000
1835	"	£45,567,000

Being an increase of 2 ¾ times in eighteen years.

For the State of New York

In 1817, the official value of real and personal property was	£63,368,000
1835	"	£110,120,000

Or an increase of nearly £47,000,000 sterling in the value of property attributed chiefly, if not entirely, to the formation of the canals.

In 1836, the amount conveyed to tide water by the canal was 697,357 tons.

And on the first of July of that year there had accumulated in the hands of the commissioners an amount sufficient to extinguish the whole of the outstanding debt incurred in its construction.

The net receipts from all the State canals, after deducting the expenses of collection and superintendance, for the year 1847, was £449,270. Villages, towns, and cities have sprung up along its course.

The population of the State was

In 1810	959,949
Was in 1845	2,604,495

In 1846, the value of real and personal property was estimated at £128,500,000

It will be seen from the above, therefore, that in addition to the wealth created for individuals, the canals produce a large annual revenue to the State.

The following extracts from the financial affairs and statistics of some of the States may be quoted in illustration of this part of the subject.

1847

Massachusetts

	Dollars
Total indebtedness of the State, 1st January, 1847	999,654
Credit of the State, *lent* to railroads	5,049,555
Total liabilities of the State	6,049,209

As security for the redemption of the scrip lent to Railroads, the Commonwealth holds a mortgage on all the roads, and also 3000 shares in the Norwich and Worcester and 1000 in the Andover and Haverhill.

Pennsylvania

	Dollars
Public property, canals and railroads at original cost	28,657,432

Maryland

	Dollars
Receipts from Baltimore and Ohio Railroad	42,402
Ditto from Canal Companies	11,550

North Carolina

	Dollars
Debt of State on account of Railroad Companies	1,110,000

Ohio

	Dollars
Debt contracted for the sole purpose of the construction of Public Works within the State	19,246,000
Canals, 820 miles in length cost	15,122,503
Net receipts in 1846, after paying repairs and expenses	408,916

In 1810 the population of this State was 45,865
In 1820 "   "   "   "   581,434
In 1840 "   "   "   "   1,519,467
or tripled nearly in twenty years, during the progress of her canals.

Michigan

	Dollars
Debt on 30th November, 1845	4,394,510

Total length of Railroads finished and *belonging* to the *State* 222 miles

This State was authorized to raise a loan of 5,000,000 dollars for internal improvements.
For the same purpose Congress granted to this State 500,000 acres of land.

In 1840 the population was   212,267
In 1845   "   "   304,278
or an increase of 50 per cent. nearly in *five* years.

Indiana

	Dollars
1st January, 1847, the Public Debt was	14,394,940

By the terms of the Act adjusting this debt, it is to be equally divided between the State and the Wabash and Erie Canal. Of this canal, which is to be 458 miles long, 374 miles are in Indiana; 174 of this portion are finished, and in operation. There remain 200 miles to be completed, upon which part of about $1,200,000 have been expended by the State. It is

---

estimated to cost the farther sum of 2,000,000 dollars to complete the entire canal. To cover this amount, the State is to transfer to trustees 963,126 acres of land adjoining to or in the neighbourhood of the canal.

The population of this State in 1811 was			24,520
"	"	1830 "	343,031
"	"	1840 "	685,086

or doubled in ten years.

Illinois

	Dollars
1847 Total Interest Improvement debt	8,165,081
Total Canal debt	6,009,187
	14,174,268

The population in 1830 was	157,455
" " 1840 "	476,283

or *tripled in ten years*.

	Acres
The sales of the Public Lands during one year (1845) in the United States amounted to	1,843,527

	Dollars
Producing	2,470,298

or an average of 6s. 7d. sterling per acre.

But to show the effect produced by a canal or railway passing through property, the following extract may be quoted from the Report of a Board of Directors of the New York and Erie Railroad Company in February 1844.

"The Board find that they have omitted one description of property which has heretofore been considered of great value, but the right to most of which has been lost to the company by failure to complete the road within a certain period; the most valuable of which consisted of 50,000 acres of wild land in Cattaraquas County, near Lake Erie, and one-fourth part of the village of Dunkirk.

"An offer in writing was made in 1837 by responsible parties to take these donations and pay a further sum of 400,000 dollars, provided certain portions of the railroad were completed within a specified time.

That is, about 8 dollars, or 33s. 4d. sterling acre.

In Michigan 461,000 acres were granted by Congress for the endowment of a university. These lands were selected in sections from the most valuable of the State. The minimum price of these was at one time 20 dollars or £4 6s. 8d. sterling per acre, but became lower afterwards: 17,142 acres, the quantity sold up to 30th November, 1845 brought £2 9s. per acre.

69,000 acres devoted to schools were sold for £1 7s. per acre.

Such then, are some of the results of making "war upon the wilderness."

In New Brunswick there are, according to an official Report of the Surveyor-General, dated 15th December, 1847, 20,000,000 acres of which about 6,000,000 are either granted or sold, and 3,000,000 may be considered barren or under water; leaving, therefore, at the disposal of the Government, 11,000,000 of acres of forest land fit for settlement.

Of the 6,000,000 granted or sold, only 600,000 acres are estimated as being actually under cultivation.

By a statistical table published by W. Spackman, London, there are

	Acres Cultivated	Acres Uncultivated	Acres Unprofitable	Total Acres
England	25,632,000	3,454,000	3,256,400	32,342,000
Wales	3,117,000	530,000	1,105,000	4,752,000
Scotland	5,265,000	5,950,000	8,523,930	19,738,000
Ireland	12,125,280	4,900,000	2,416,664	19,441,944
New Brunswick	600,000	16,400,000	3,000,000	20,000,000

Population of	England	14,995,508
"	Wales	911,321
"	Scotland	2,628,957
"	Ireland	8,205,382
"	New Brunswick	308,000

In Ireland there appears to be from the above table 17,000,000 acres of ground fit for cultivation, and it has a population of 8,000,000 to support.

In New Brunswick there is an *equal amount* of ground to cultivate, and it has only a population of 208,000 persons.

If the land yet uncleared and fit for cultivation be added which remains in the northern section of Nova Scotia, and again between the boundary of New Brunswick and the River St. Lawrence to thee east of Quebec, then there would be a quantity of nearly equal to that of England itself, supporting a population of 400,000 souls.

It is not too much to say that between the Bay of Fundy and the St. Lawrence, in the country to be traversed by the proposed railway, there is abundant room for all the surplus population of the mother country.

Of the climate, soil and capabilities of New Brunswick, it is impossible to speak too highly.

There is not a country in the world so beautifully wooded and watered.

An inspection of the map will show that there is scarcely a section of it without its streams, from the running brook up to the navigable river. Two thirds of its boundary are washed by sea; the remainder is embraced by the large rivers—the St. John and Restigouche.

For beauty and richness of scenery this latter river and its branches are not surpassed by anything in Great Britain.

Its lakes are numerous, and most beautiful; its surface is undulating, hill and dale, varying up to mountain and valley. It is everywhere, except a few peaks of the highest mountains, covered with a dense forest of the finest growth.

The country can everywhere be penetrated by its streams.

In some parts of the interior, for a portage of three or four miles, a canoe can float away either to the Bay Chaleurs and the Gulf of St. Lawrence, or down to St. John's in the Bay of Fundy.

Its agricultural capabilities, its climate &c., are described in Bouchet's Works, in Martin's British Colonies, and other authors. The country is by them, and most deservedly so, highly praised.

There may be mentioned, however, two drawbacks to it, and only two.

The winter is long and severe; and in summer there is a plague of the flies.

The latter yield and disappear as the forest is cleared; how far the former may be modified by it experience only can show.

For any great plan of emigration or colonization, there is not another British colony which presents such a favourable field for the trial as New Brunswick.

To 17,000,000 of productive acres there are only 208,000 inhabitants.

Of these 11,000,000 are still public property.

On the surface is an abundant stock of the finest timber, which in the markets of England realize large sums annually, and afford an unlimited supply of fuel to the settlers.

If these should ever become exhausted, there are the coal-fields underneath.

The rivers, lakes and sea-coasts abound with fish.

Along the Bay Chaleurs it is so abundant that the land smells of it; it is used as manure, and while the olfactory senses of the traveller are offended by it on the land, he sees out at sea immense shoals darkening the surface of the water.

For about the same expense five emigrants could be landed in New Brunswick for one in the Antipodes. Being within a fortnight by steam from London, any great plan of colonization could be directed and controlled by the Home Government.

In case of distress or failure, it would be long previously foreseen; the remedy or assistance could be applied; or, if beyond these, there would be the upper country and the far west always open, and ready to receive the colonists.

The present limited population being so generally engaged in the pursuit of the timber trade and in the fisheries, there is the richest opening for agriculturists.

New Brunswick annually pays to the United States upwards of £200,000 for provisions and other articles which she can raise upon her own soil.

Nova Scotia does very nearly the same thing.

Whilst within a few miles reach of their own capitals, there is abundance of land for agricultural productions, these two provinces are *dependent* for large supplies of food upon the United States.

Flour is imported from as far as New Orleans.

Wheat grown in the valley of the Mississippi is shipped at St. Louis, and imported into New Brunswick. It is ground into flour at the mills of St. John, and furnishes a large share of the bread eaten by the labourers of that city.

There exists, therefore, a good market already on the spot for agricultural produce; and it would be a strange anomaly, indeed, if a country situated within three or four weeks' sail of the markets of England, could not compete with the growers of produce in the valley of the Mississippi and the countries round the great lakes in the far west.

One thing, however, is greatly to be deprecated, that is any sudden or large emigration without previous preparation.

Before wheat or food of any kind can be grown the forest has to be removed, and that is the work of time and hard labour, during which those engaged in it must be fed from other sources.

With some little previous detailed surveying, the proposed railway can be commenced both at the Quebec and Halifax ends as soon as decided upon and carried on for miles. During which time the further detailed survey necessary for the remainder of the line, and particularly the portion through the wilderness, might be made, and the line actually marked and cut throughout.

This line, when cut, would form a basis for laying out extensive blocks of land, and dividing them into allotments for settlers.

It will be unnecessary in this Report to recapitulate all the good effects produced upon every country in which railways have been established; but some may be mentioned.

They have become necessary to the age, and that country which has them not must fall behind in the onward march of improvement and in the development of its resources. And the longer it is suffered to do so, the greater and more unfavourable will be the contrast which it will present to the world.

Already in this respect the British Provinces of Nova Scotia and New Brunswick are far behind their enterprising neighbours.

One of the most immediate effects of making this railway would be to place them in a position of equality. They are now *dependent* upon them for food.

At the closing of the navigation of the St. Lawrence, if the United States were merely to prohibit the exports of provisions from their own harbours, the consequences would be serious to these two provinces. Canada could not supply them.

In May 1847, when the exploratory parties were being formed at Fredericton and provisions were being forwarded to the woods for their use, there was a scarcity of flour at St. John's. It was said that sufficient for only two or three days'

---

consumption remained in that city. The price rose considerably, and the scarcity was only averted by the arrival of some cargoes from the United States, intended for Eastport.

The railway, had it been established, would have prevented such a state of things, and may save it for the future.

For the want of such a communication, Nova Scotia now finds it easier and more advantageous, notwithstanding a heavy duty of 20 per cent. against her, to export her great staple of fish to the States, than to Canada; whereas if the railway were made, it would pass on to the latter, where there would be an extensive market for it, and flour would be received in turn.

Halifax would become the grand emporium of trade for the British provinces.

With the assistance of the electric telegraph, an order from Quebec could be received in a few minutes, and the articles wanted could be sent off by the next train.

As the vessels now arrive in fleets in the spring, and again in the autumn, it is a matter of forethought and consideration to the merchant of Canada to know what he shall provide himself with.

To the intending emigrant it will afford him the choice of any month in the year to set out for his new country, and if by means of friends previously settled in his place of abode has been chosen, he can time his arrival so as to have the shortest possible time to wait until his own crops are ready to supply him with food.

Arriving now as thousands annually do in the spring when the seed-time is at hand, and the land uncleared, they lose the valuable opportunity of that year's crop, and have to wait over, existing perhaps, upon their little capital for nearly eighteen months, until the succeeding harvest comes to them. To all such emigrants nearly a year may be saved.

Surprise has sometimes been expressed that out of so many who yearly land in the provinces, so many pass on and become settlers in the States.

To the poor man his labour is his capital, and he must transfer himself to the place where employment is to be found.

The proposed railway would be such a work as would engage thousands in its immediate construction. While the stimulus and new spirit it would infuse into the whole community, now cribbed and confined as it were to their own locations, would give rise to branches and other works which would employ additional thousands.

It has been seen that the population of some of the Western States have doubled and even tripled themselves in the course of ten years.

The population of New Brunswick is now only 208,000. Her revenue in 1847 was £106,000 sterling, or 10s. per head.

There is no apparent reason why, if the same facilities of employment and land for settlement were afforded, that her progress should not be also very great.

Every emigrant, induced to settle and remain in the country, may be calculated as producing 10s. annual revenue to the province.

If the formation of the railway increased the population of New Brunswick by 10,000 persons only, then her proportion of the guaranteed interest would be covered from that cause alone.

The same might occur also to Nova Scotia and Lower Canada.

It may be asked what is to become of the labourers employed on the railway during the winter. This is the season when lumbering or cutting of timber commences. They might engage in it also. But with the wages earned in the summer, they should be incited to purchase small lots of ground of about fifty acres each.

The labours of the season over, or suspended upon the railway, they could most advantageously employ themselves in clearing, logging and improving their own lots. This they could do to such an extent that in the spring the women and older children could burn the logs off and put in some sort of crops for food, such as potatoes, Indian corn &c.

Mechanics might either so the same if railway work could not be found for them, or find employment in the towns.

Another great effect of the railway would be to enhance almost immediately the value of all real and personal property. The effects produced by the Erie Canal in doubling and nearly tripling that of the City of New York has been stated.

Villages and towns would, no doubt, spring up in its course the same as on the canal. The railway would give them birth. Agriculture and external commerce would support and enrich them.

But if, by its means, the navigation of the Gulf of St. Lawrence is spared, what an amount of human suffering and loss of life will it not save.

The losses from shipwreck have been great, but not equal to that arising from protracted voyages and crowded emigrant ships.

In 1847, 89,738 persons emigrated to the British Provinces, of whom 5,293 persons perished at sea, and 10,000 are said to have died after their arrival.

This was a most unusual year, and it is to be hoped by every friend of humanity, that anything like it will never occur again.

No human means could have saved all this loss of life, but there is no doubt, a less protracted voyage and a more favourable time than the spring of the year in the St. Lawrence would have prevented some of the fatal results.

The railway established, the passage may be shortened, and the time of emigration may be selected at choice.

Troops are annually moved to and from Canada. About the close of the navigation in 1843, a transport, having the 1st Royal Regiment on board, was wrecked in the mouth of the St. Lawrence. The men got safely to shore, but there were no roads or means of getting away from that place. By the personal exertions of one of the officers, whom made his way through the woods on snow-shoes to the nearest settlements, and thence to Quebec, information was given of the wreck, and a steamer sent down to take them off. But for this, the consequences must have been that the regiment would have to winter there in the best manner they could.

Embarking and disembarking at Halifax, all danger and inconvenience from the Gulf navigation would be avoided. Time and expense would be saved, and the season might be disregarded.

The mails to and from Canada could pass over British territory *exclusively* and they would be received at Quebec before the steamer reached Boston, and at Montreal about the same time as it arrived at that port.

In a political and military point of view, the proposed railway must be regarded as becoming a work of necessity.

The increasing population and wealth of the United States, and the diffusion of railways over their territory, especially in the direction of the Canadian frontier, renders it absolutely necessary to counterbalance, by some corresponding means, their otherwise preponderating power.

Their railway communications will enable them to select their own time and their own points of attack, and will impose upon the British the necessity of being prepared at *all points* to meet them.

It is most essential, therefore, that the mother-country should be able to keep up her communications with the Canadas at all times and seasons. However powerful England may be at sea, no navy can save Canada from a land force.

Its conquest and annexation are freely spoken of in the United States, even on the floors of Congress.

Weakness invites aggression, and as the railway would be a lever of power by which Great Britain could bring her strength to bear in the contest, it is not improbable that its construction would be the means of preventing a war at some no distant period.

The expense of one year's war would pay for a railway two or three times over.

The following extract from the report of Lord Durham, her Majesty's High Commissioner and Governor-General of British North America in 1839, is so apposite and just, and bears so strongly upon the subject under consideration, that it is conceived no better conclusion can be made to this Report than to insert it.

"These interests are, indeed of great magnitude; and on the course which your Majesty and your Parliament may adopt with respect to the North American colonies, will depend the future destinies, not only of the million and a half of your Majesty's subjects who at present inhabit those provinces, but of the vast population which those ample and fertile territories are fit and destined hereafter to support. No portion of the American continent possesses greater natural resources for the maintenance of large and flourishing communities. An almost boundless range of the richest soil still remains unsettled, and may be rendered available for the purposes of agriculture. The wealth of inexhaustible forests of the best timber in America, and of extensive regions of the most valuable minerals, have as yet been scarcely touched. Along the whole line of sea-coast, around each island, and in every river, are to be found the greatest and richest fisheries in the world. The best fuel and the most abundant water-power are available for the coarser manufactures, for which an easy and certain market will be found. Trade with other continents is favoured by the possession of large number of safe and spacious harbours; long, deep and numerous rivers, and vast inland seas, supply the means of easy intercourse, and the structure of the country generally affords the utmost facility for every species of communication by land. Unbounded materials of agricultural, commercial, and manufacturing industry are there. It depends upon the present decision of the Imperial Legislature to determine for whose benefit they are to be rendered available. The country which has founded and maintained these colonies at a vast expense of blood and treasure, may justly expect its compensation in turning their unappropriated resources to the account of its own redundant population, they are the rightful patrimony of the English people,—the ample appanage which God and nature have set aside in the New World for those whose lot has assigned them but insufficient portions in the Old."

And if for great political objects it ever become necessary or advisable to unite all the British provinces under one Legislative Government, then there will be formed on this side of the Atlantic one powerful British State, which supported by the Imperial power of the mother-country may bid defiance to all the United States of America.

The means to the end, the first step to its accomplishment, is the construction of the Halifax and Quebec Railway.

WM. ROBINSON
Captain, Royal Engineers, Brevet-Major.

August 31, 1848

Major-General Sir John F. Burgoyne, K.C.B.
Inspector-General of Fortifications
    &c.   &c.   &c.

APPENDIX TWO

From the Halifax *Morning Chronicle*, April 13th 1885

OFF TO THE WAR
The Halifax Battalion Starts
At Noon on Saturday

THE PARADE AND DEPARTURE
Exciting Scenes and Incidents
An Eventful Day in Local History—Happenings En Route

A war in Canada has been a rare thing in the last hundred years. Peace and plenty have almost reigned supreme. It is a still rarer occurrence, however, to have the militia of this province called out for active service. Two years ago this spring the Lingan riots caused the ordering out of a portion of our local forces. But the volunteers drafted on that occasion got no further than Cunard's wharf. Not so in the present instance. Two weeks ago, all but a day or two, the word passed from mouth to mouth among the citizens that the Riel rebellion had assumed proportions that warranted the ordering out of the 66th battalion to hold itself in readiness for marching. Drill was at once began and kept steadily up till the firing of the three guns on the calm evening air of Friday last. Up to this time many members of the composite battalion cherished the idea that they would never be required to take up arms in their country's defence. By many it was thought that the whole thing would eventually dwindle away, that the insurgents would be put down without the aid of Nova Scotian skill and muscle. But one disaster crowding upon another necessitated the calling out of more troops, and the Halifax men being next on the roll, were fixed upon as the successors to those who had gone before. To many the summons was a decided relief. To be held in suspense for a fortnight is anything but agreeable and the substitution of direct knowledge for anxious expectancy fired the men with a zeal that had hitherto been unknown.

The day of embarkation broke bright and cheerful. As the sun began to pour his rays through the windows of the drill shed the citizen soldiers could be seen resting on their guns, cheerfully chatting about the one eventful topic of the hour. When the swelling tones of St. Mary's bell called together the worshippers of early morn, people could be seen wending their way in the direction of the drill shed from every quarter. The night before, the order had been given for every man to be in his place at half-past seven. But the hour was too early for such a command to be punctually observed. In hundreds of homes the parting formalities had to be gone through. The admonitions and affectionate caresses of the mother who, perhaps, was giving her only boy to the god of battle, the fond farewells of the wife whose husband might never return, and the brother and sister who saw their dearest relatives about to face the stern realities of war, all delayed the gallant soldiers from being at hand at precisely the appointed moment. However, the sad partings were soon over, whatever little nick-nacks or luxuries were to be taken had been snugly tucked away in the small compass of a soldier's kit, and the men were nearly all assembled. By nine o'clock the great bulk of the battalion had fallen into line, and those who had not arrived on the scene were being hunted out by a picket, who were successful in getting hold of several tardy volunteers, who either intended holding back altogether, or thought that by being late they might be left behind. At this time the crowd outside had grown to immense proportions, the street being lined on both sides for hundreds of feet with a dense throng, every one of whom was eager to get a view of the battalion as it marched away. The shed itself was literally packed, and proved to be a tight fit for the whole strength of the expeditionary force and the large concourse of friends who had gathered to bid a farewell blessing and a God-speed to the Halifax battalion. On the door was a strong force of police, headed by Deputy-Marshal McDonald, who were driven to their wits ends to keep out the great throng that pressed for admittance. And notwithstanding their vigilance quite a number gained an entrance who had no right to be there, being carried through the door by the pressure of the crowd and jumping through the open windows. The idea was to start the men at 8.30, but a great deal of work had to be done and a good many annoying detentions had to be put up with. The chief cause of delay was the payment of the men. When word was received Friday afternoon to start the troops at once the banks were closed, and no money could be obtained until a little before ten Saturday morning, when a draft of $4,000, which had been previously telegraphed, was cashed at the Bank of Montreal. After the money had been secured it took some little time to pay it out, each captain distributing the earnings to his men from a huge roll of notes. Quite a number had their pay left to their families, while others took it to use as pocket money en route. To every two men a bag was served out, in which were placed the needful knives, forks, spoons, etc. When they had all been given out they were forwarded to the depot on teams. Before starting the entire battalion was inspected by Colonel Bremner and staff, every man individually, in order to see that all were fully supplied with the necessary equipment. The examination, although somewhat critical, resulting every man passing muster. During the whole morning the wives and sisters were flitting in and out of the ranks, presenting their loved ones with a variety of good things, and some of them with tear-dimmed eyes and others with smiling faces were saying "good by," "take care of yourself," "be sure to write" and many other injunctions and much tender advice. At length everything had been attended to and no further preparations were necessary. But the greater part of the morning had slipped away and not until quarter to eleven were the doors cleared of the crowd and the troops in the order of the several companies, marched through the portals of the building. Heading the gallant four hundred were the Royal Irish rifles band, and the bands of the 63rd rifles and 66th Princess Louise fusiliers. Following the musical corps were Lieut.-Col. Bremner, Major MacDonald, Adjutant Kenny, and other staff officers; the two companies of the garrison artillery, the three companies of the 66th and the three 63rd companies. Preceeding the procession was a squad of police, who had all they could do to keep the way open, both sides of the road being packed with an unbroken line of spectators. As the troops filed down Spring Garden road on to Barrington street the air seemed to become suddenly filled with hosts of flying handkerchiefs. From every house step and window, from the steps of the stately St. Mary's cathedral and from the balcony of the academy of music these fluttering streaks of white were constantly waved. And thus it was over the whole route. From Barrington street the column proceeded down Salter to Hollis, marching in fours. When George street was reached the brilliant cavalcade wended its way up the hill and passed through Granville street into Water street. From thence it rounded the corner of Jacob street, going up the whole length of that thoroughfare, when it turned into Brunswick street, and proceeded to North street, when it made its final detour, moving straight down to the depot. Along the entire route the streets were thronged with thousands of people. Every coign of vantage was occupied, and from hundreds of windows the fair sex dangled their delicate kerchiefs, while cheer after cheer arose with pleasing spontaneity.

At North street was one of the most remarkable scenes ever witnessed in this city. The actual withdrawal of our militia for active duty, an event without a parallel in provincial annals, had so deeply impressed itself upon the people that everyone who could possibly go determined to see them off.

As a consequence the heroes were greeted with an enormous mass of humanity, as they marched down the hill. From every surrounding housetop, window, step, vehicle or whatever elevation it might be, thousands of eyes reviewed the cortege as it trooped along to the tune of inspiring music. On the street and the pavilion fronting the depot were thousands upon thousands of men, women and children, while the building was circled with a throbbing mass of humanity. Inside the station every nook and crevice was absolutely jammed with a mixed assemblage of mankind, filled with the intense excitement of the moment. As the troops entered the side door, every man with his musket resting on his shoulder, round after round of cheers burst forth, while a myriad of handkerchiefs waved from fair hands a hearty adieu. The cars had been arranged on the centre track, and through the western gate the troops were marched in the best order they could. Instantly upon the men entering the building the crowd pressed eagerly forward to get a closer view of the departing soldiers. The most indescribable confusion ensued. Several police were stationed at the gate but small as the entrance was, it became narrower and narrower as hundreds of people jostled and pushed and squeezed and elbowed each other into the very smallest space. Within the railing confusion was worse confounded. Where ten could comfortably stand twenty were compelled to remain, and for a half hour it was with the most difficulty that one could move one way or the other. Here were enacted scenes of mingled humour and pathos, while some of the sights were extremely touching. At the drill shed and on the way the bands had kept up a constant strain of music, playing "Far away," "We're off in the morning train," "Home, sweet home," "The girl I left behind me" and other appreciative melodies, keeping up the spirits of the lads and men. But inside the depot the bands were resting the greater part of the time, and the lack of inspiriting airs and the presence of a host of weeping friends, caused many a heart to feel truly sad and many a lump to rise in the throats of the manly fellows. Mothers, wives and sisters were present in great abundance, and it seemed as if their affectionate farewells would never cease. The eyes of many a parent were wet with tears and little girls plaintively sobbed for their fathers and brothers. After a while the platform became passable, and then began the handshaking from the car windows, which was kept up till the train departed. At length "All aboard" was shouted by Conductor Gunn, and every one who had friends among the departing made a final effort to say good by. A father reached down from a car window, and drawing his little girl up the side, affectionately kissed her. Others threw kisses from where they were standing and exchanged the last adieux; the band struck up "Auld Lang Syne" and the Halifax battalion slowly moved out of the depot. With one accord a great shout went up from the vast multitude that lined the track from the station to the bridge and along the railing on Campbell road, which was followed by another and another and mingling with the music of the bands and the explosions of the torpedoes that had been laid along the track, sent off the gallant band of citizen soldiers with an enthusiasm that will never be forgotten. For a few minutes the crowd watched the speeding train, with the officery in their gay uniforms on the rear platform, and then wended their way homewards, some indifferent, many sorrowful, but all feeling that the return of our volunteers will be looked for with the greatest concern, and that occasion will be no less memorable than the period of their departure.

The trip to Truro

The train consisted of eleven cars and two locomotives, the two forward cars being the quartermaster's and for baggage, eight second class for the volunteers, and a first class in rear for the officers. The journey to Truro was without extraordinary incident, but one or two delays on the road caused a late arrival, the town not being reached till half-past three. A slight accident to the coupling gear between the rear locomotive and the front car caused a detention at Richmond of fifteen minutes to repair it. One or two small scrimmages between some recruits and others of the 66th who happened to have a little liquor with them occurred on the road, but the disputants were quelled by the officers. Some of the men amuse themselves in singing and a few in dancing to the time of Jock Patterson's "pipes," while others passed the hours in card-playing, etc. Truro reached, the troops partook of a hot and substantial meal in the railway restaurant, marching in from the cars in detachments, as the dining room was too small to accommodate all at once. A few members of the battalion managed to get outside the station despite the vigilance of four sentries placed on duty, and several who were in search of liquor created a little trouble before being got on board the train again. One recruit of the 66th was placed in the Truro jail and is to be returned to the city. Two hours and a half passed before the men got away again, but at last all were safely inside the cars and the train sped on its way westward.

The reception at the stations along the line were very enthusiastic, the people turning out in large numbers to get a sight of the Halifax warriors as they were carried swiftly by. At Bedford and Shubenacadie there were quite large gatherings, which cheered the battalion lustily, while the crowd that greeted the volunteers at Truro numbered some hundreds, and made a perfect ovation on the arrival of the train. The town council had intended to make some formal demonstration on the Halifax contingent passing through, but the order for their departure so suddenly that no time was given for anything of that kind. A number of farmers turned out with their shotguns at different points along the road and as the train sped by fired volleys into the air, at the same time hurrahing in good lusty style.

The accommodation on the train is of a poor and not at all comfortable character for such a long journey, and is far from satisfactory to the men. Nearly every car is filled, each seat containing two, and some of the cars are without any water whatever. There are no cushions to the seats and the men will have to sit on the hard wood through the long dreary days and portions of the nights. Sleeping accommodations are placed in the corner of each car so that the occupants can enjoy repose in turns, one third at a time.

Along the road to Moncton
(From our own correspondent)

Military Train.
Saturday night

Soon after leaving Truro, the boys set to work "fixing up," getting ready for the journey, which they now had begun to think of as a reality. Hitherto most of us had hardly been able to persuade ourselves that we were really on the way to "the front," that we were soldiers en route for the North West. Baggage was distributed, brushes were produced and soon the traces of the march through the dirty streets of Halifax were removed. Shoes and trousers were rubbed up and made wear [sic] as military an appearance as possible. A hasty wash in a wayside stream served to increase very materially the comfort of those of us who had resolved not to be content with the very stinted allowance of the cleansing fluid at our disposal on the cars. The fruit of our thoughtful mayor's appeal for reading matter were distributed, belts and other accoutrements were disposed in such wise as to be as much as possible out of the way. Seats were padded with great coats. These somewhat serious performances over, the Scottish companies resolved themselves into a grand amusement committee. The gentle voice of the "kazoo," mingled with the strains of the flute and violin, alternated with vocal melody, such as only can be produced by a crowd of jolly young men and the skirl of Jock's pipes. Cards were produced, and here and there might be seen small groups absorbed with whist, euchre and "the game called poker." Everywhere good order and perfect harmony prevail, the few warlike individuals who had made themselves conspicuous in the earlier part of the day having subsided into something like peace and quietness. The regular routine of the march was established, and guard-mounting and relief and all the business contingent to the movement and government of troops began to make itself evident. The enthusiasm which greeted us at Truro was repeated at every station along the line. Cheering crowds occupied every platform to give us God-speed as we passed. At Spring Hill, which like most places we passed without stopping, a brass band was playing. We were very much pleased with this expression of goodwill, the more so when we learned that the men had come five miles to see us. Amherst, Dorchester and Moncton all turned out bands, and everywhere we saw the same closely packed crowd, the same smiling faces and waving hats and handkerchiefs, and everywhere heard the same hearty, good will cheers. Sackville added to the usual demonstration a new feature—a grand bonfire which lit up all the surrounding country. Sometime after midnight we finished supper at Moncton. If our experience is a fair guide to judge by, friend Hallet at Truro is a much better caterer than his fellow laborer at Moncton. Sandwiches, biscuits and cheese made up the bill of fare at supper. Such tea and coffee! Now we are off. How we shall put in the night is the living question.

At Spring Hill
(Special despatch to the *Chronicle*)

Spring Hill Junction, April 11.—The receipt of the intelligence that the Halifax contingent would pass through today caused intense excitement. This afternoon Mr. Leckie arranged for a special train to leave the mines at three o'clock, and about three hundred miners quickly availed themselves of the opportunity. After patiently sitting on flat cars for three hours a telegram was received stating that the volunteers would not reach the junction until seven o'clock. This did not dampen the enthusiasm of the miners and a greater number, with banners flying, were conveyed to the junction. The special with soldiers coaled at the shed and moved past the station slowly, the miners cheering vociferously.

The Moncton Reception
(Telegraphed by our own correspondent)

Moncton, April 11.—The train with the Halifax battalion arrived here in good order at 10.30 and after partaking of supper will proceed at once. The men have had a perfect ovation at all the principal stations and the country appears to be thoroughly aroused. Crowds assembled at the stations to cheer the Halifax lads as they passed through. At Londonderry and Amherst brass bands were stationed on the platforms, and the Moncton cornet band is now discoursing martial airs amid an immense gathering at the depot. Everywhere enthusiastic crowds cheer the battalion. Everything is being worked as smoothly as possible and the boys though considerably crowded in the cars, take it very good naturedly. There have been no casualties so far.

Sunday morning at Campbellton
(Telegraphed by our own correspondent)

Campbellton, N.B. April 12, 9 a.m.—The troops are breakfasting at this place, where they have just arrived. The weather is simply glorious. The doctors report all well this morning save a bugler suffering from a sore throat. The behaviour of the men from Moncton to this point has been admirable and they have evinced a thorough soldierlike spirit in the endurance of close confinement and irksome fatigue during the past night. The officers report that the troops were received all along the line from Truro to Moncton with the most extravagant demonstrations. Huge bonfires, blazing tar barrels and continual cheering from the stations passed testified to the sympathy of their countrymen with our citizen soldiers, and there is a universal wish expressed that the troops may fully deserve all the honours bestowed upon them. The scene is one of excitement all along the line and every one on the force is in capital spirits. The commissariat arrangements at this station are admirable.

At Trois Pistoles
(Telegraphed by our own correspondent)

Trois Pistoles, Que. April 12.—The battalion has just passed here, all in good health and spirits. The men are now enjoying a capital dinner, their second meal today. The district superintendents of the railway have been excessively attentive and kind, travelling with the force throughout the journey. Each company as they disembark from the train are sent route marching for twenty minutes to exercise. The result is beneficial to health and destructive to food.

At River DuLoup
(Telegraphed by our own correspondent)

River DuLoup, Que., April 12, 9.15 p.m.—The Halifax troops have just arrived here. They were received by a great crowd of people and a band of music. All continue in satisfactory health.

Notes

One of the recruits who enlisted on Friday was John Watt, an old captain in the 66th.

The contract for folding cap beds, mattresses and bedding for the contingent was filled by Messrs. A. Stephen & Son.

Some pious body had made preparation for the spiritual welfare of the troops by placing tracts on every seat in the train.

Just before the men left the drill shed Captain Curren gave out the number "66th" to those who had lost them off their caps.

The members of No. 3 company, 63rd have been photographed by Notman in a group and make a creditable appearance.

Some of the hilarious 66th men smashed a couple of panes of glass in one of the cars, just before leaving the depot. It is supposed to have been accidental, however.

The battalion on arriving at Truro was presented with twenty-eight dozen cases of condensed milk, of the Reindeer brand, by the directors of the Truro Condensed Milk company.

There was a good display of bunting on various public and private buildings on Saturday in honor of the departure of the first Halifax battalion ever ordered out for active service.

There were some narrow escapes from being run over at the station by the trains moving in and out of the depot, but fortunately no accidents were reported, although the track was alive with people all the time, who were almost touched by the cars as they moved to and fro.

In the city churches yesterday prayers for the absent ones were made at both the morning and evening services. Special mention was made of the hope that the rebellion might be speedily subdued, that there would be no more bloodshed and that the Halifax volunteers would soon return, safe and sound, to their homes and families.

The post office authorities have made arrangements so that any one wishing to send any mail matter to members of the detachment will only have to place the name of the party to whom the letter is to be delivered and "Halifax battalion." No further address will be required, as a special bag will be made up here for members of the corps.

An old employee of the *CHRONICLE*—E. O'Donnell, one of our mail clerks—answered to the call of duty, and went off with his brothers of the 63rd to meet the rebel foe. Hugh MacNab, a son of the well known job printer of the CHRONICLE building, and learning the trade with his father, is also with the 63rd, with other members of the Scottish company. Many of the city printers are in the ranks and will no doubt acquit themselves to their credit.

The deserters from the ranks are fewer than expected. In the garrison artillery a man named Richard Maryatt could not be found when wanted. A substitute, however, was obtained in the person of Stewart Genties of Dartmouth. A man of the 66th also funked, and as he is not in the habit of drinking, it is to be presumed that he deliberately deserted. If the threats of the militia authorities are carried out, the deserters will, if found, be dealt with in such a manner as not to forget the circumstances for some time. Some of the "poo-coms" were also absent when the roll was called. In No. 3 company the deserters were: Corporals Hurley and J. O'Connell (Purcell's Cove) R. Anderson and __ Purcell (stage driver). Sergeant. W. Brown of the 63rd is said to have gone to Boston.

Valedictory
Suggested by the departure of the
Volunteers Saturday morning

God bless you my brave countrymen
And protect you where you go,
And grant that you may never turn
Your backs toward the foe.
May He with His mighty arm
E'er shield you in the fight,
And give you strength and prowess
As you battle for the right!
God guard their wives and children
And draw them near to Thee,
As with streaming eyes and aching hearts
They lowly bend the knee.
And grant dear Lord, the battle won,
That they who sorrow now
May have their dear ones home again
With a chaplet on each brow!

P.L.

From the Halifax *Morning Chronicle*, April 14th 1885

OTTAWA REACHED
The Halifax Troops at the
Canadian Capital

ENTHUSIASTIC RECEPTION
Incidents of the Journey from Campbellton–
No Stoppage at Montreal

AT CHAUDIERE JUNCTION
(Special Despatch to the *Chronicle*)

Chaudiere Junction, Q., April 13.

It is now 4.30 your time. The actual running time from Riviere duLoupe to Chaudiere junction, 120 miles, was done in 4.18. Patriotic speeches at Riviere du Loup were responded to by Mr. Whitman. A dinner offered to the officers at Point Levi by Colonel Marquette is cancelled by the change to the Grand Trunk at Chaudiere instead of Point Levi. The action of the ICR has effected this saving of 14 miles. If the Grand Trunk exhibits the same activity in forwarding the troops the Haligonians will reach the scene of operations with such speed as to surprise themselves, and also let us hope the enemy. Just leaving. All well and cheerful.

Two Hours at Richmond, Que.
(Telegraphed by our own correspondent)

Richmond, Que. April 13, 11.30 a.m.—We have just arrived at Richmond, all well and hungry. We were delayed several hours at Chaudiere junction. Two meals have been served since 6.30 last evening. An invitation from the mayor of Montreal has just been received by Col. Bremner, inviting the officers and men to lunch at Montreal this afternoon. The battalion will wash and parade here before re-embarking. The behaviour of the men is excellent. The battalion leaves for Montreal at one o'clock. The men are now drawn up on the platform, the officers proving the companies. The artillery are universally admired, as they have been all along the line, and the volunteers' officers here have enquired if the battery belonged to the regular army.

We breakfasted yesterday morning at Campbellton, where all hands had a great wash and clean up, which, after the night's bunking on the cars, was very much needed. No Pullman was attached to the train, and the officers experienced considerable difficulty in disposing of themselves in their car, which was more crowded than any of the others. During the afternoon, the first and second companies of the 63rd quota organized a sort of choral service. Hymns were sung, accompanied by a violin, flutes, etc., there being quite a lot of musical talent among the boys. A word must be said about our indefatigable quarter-master, Capt. Corbin, who, up

---

to the present time, is one of the hardest working men in the whole force and is winning golden opinions from officers and men. The officers are reading up and instructing the non-coms and men in discipline. Company C and an enthusiastic portion of the 66th have started a temporary pledge to taste nothing till their return to Halifax, a sort of campaign keg, and is met with very gratifying results. We dined at Trois Pistoles at as fine a table as anyone would wish to set down to, a marked contrast to the mean fare furnished by the Moncton restaurant. Another brass band and an immense crowd were at River du Loup to welcome us. The 69th from the district, expect to follow in a day or two. It is composed mostly of lumbermen, all of whom are French. We were obliged to decline the invitation of Point Levis to the officers of the battalion.

Arrival at Montreal
(Telegraphed by our own correspondent)

Montreal, April 13.—The train with the Halifax battalion has just arrived here. By some unexplained action of the Ottawa military authorities and the Grand Trunk officials, the receipt of an order by the Grand Trunk to push the train through to Ottawa without stoppage was not wired to Col. Bremner. When the troops reached Montreal they were informed of the order, and then forwarded to Ottawa supperless. They had only one meal to-day and two yesterday. Although the men were prepared to bear hardships, if necessary, they deem such severe training impolitic, as the exhaustion and confinement is telling upon their general health. Renwick, of company H, has developed severe crysipelas from injury to an eye, and will be sent to hospital here. The mayor of Montreal, accompanied by officers of the Montreal militia, met the troops from Halifax at St. Henri depot. He expressed hearty regret at the misunderstanding and proposed the health of the battalion in a spirited and patriotic speech. The mayor also presented each company of the Halifax contingent with two boxes of choice cigars. A sergeant, corporal and two privates went shopping when at Richmond, were left behind there, owing to the sudden departure of the train. They will rejoin the battalion at Ottawa.

Grandly received at Ottawa
(Telegraphed by our own correspondent)

Ottawa, April 13.—The Halifax battalion arrived here at 10 o'clock tonight. There was an immense crowd at the depot, who cheered enthusiastically as the train drew up and again as it moved off. The men seemed to be in excellent spirits. Lieuts. Bremner and Cartwright, from the royal military college, joined the regiment here.

APPENDIX THREE
A Letter Home

Dear Mother: Somewhere in Quebec, Sunday,
October 22nd, 1916

It is some time since I really wrote you a letter. I've lived so much in the past few days that to write an account of it that would do it justice would take pages——perhaps reams.

Oct 23 . . . . I was interrupted last night by a bunch of the boys gathering around for a little sing-song which continued till "lights out". We are now into New Brunswick I think. Every little village we have passed through so far has been distinctly French in appearance. The first building in each village is the R.C. Church. They seem to go in strong for beautiful architecture in their churches even though their houses and buildings are not up to a very high standard—much like our own 25 years ago.

This morning we saw a man ploughing with a team . . . one horse and one ox.

Reg Topp is on this train as he got transferred with his pals of "D" company of the 170th. A week ago Sunday Mary Topp and another girl were up to Camp Borden and as eating accommodation was limited I took them to the Sergeant's mess for supper.— last Friday was the final farewell for the 170th and a great crowd of friends came up. It rained nearly all afternoon and spoiled the day for sight-seeing. However, my friends' friends seemed to have a good time. It is such a trial for them to see how the soldiers live under canvas. The heavy showers flooded a few of the tents in low-lying ground and in one of them I saw everything practically submerged and a pair of shoes floating in the middle of it. But the water soon disappeared in the sand over the wet surface. Friday night was the last night we spent in Camp Borden and on Sat. about 2 p.m. we entrained, mistakes were made in our arrangements for entraining and the men of the different platoons were not kept together in all cases. The result was that when we got to Union Station there was a great deal of confusion, and a few of the men did not meet their friends. One of the pathetic cases was Corporal Metcalfe of my platoon who missed his wife

---

and kids. He is such a fine fellow and so fond of his children that it spoiled the after-thoughts of our farewell for me.

I was on the platform directing traffic but was sent to a different coach from the one I occupy and so nearly missed Marjorie and Bailie. But I had lots of friends there and after the crowds that jammed together got moving it wasn't so bad. There was such a crush that several women fainted and the only way I could save a baby from injury was to take it from its mother and hold it shoulder height and being above the average height I managed to hold it till the crowd got restored to order. There must have been thousands there and the parcels handed to men would weigh tons, I think. As we pulled out of the station, for hundreds of yards people stood and waved to us holding out their hands to shake as we went by. We who stood on the plat-form had the advantage in the hand gripping act and we did full justice to it—

I did not see Mae, but Ellis had parcels of eats and smokes for us and handed them over but before he went back to get Mae the train pulled out.

The 170th surely went away knowing that they had thousands of friends behind them. It was a wonderful and touching send-off—something that we will never for-get and also which is worthwhile living to receive. I guess I won't see a Toronto paper for some time, and of course the reporters will be unable to do justice to such an incident in a newspaper account.

The train is bumping so much that I can hardly write. The scenery resembles that of Northern Ontario only is on a smaller scale. The rocks and mountains are not so bare and glaring as those along C.P.R. in Northern Ontario. We must detrain at Campbelltown [sic], N.B.

We have just been off the train for an hour's route march at Campbelltown, N.B. We got our limbs stretched and had a look at the place and the inhabitants and found everything good. The people on one street threw apples at us and caused a little disorganization of the ranks but the officers were the only ones to take excep-tion to any such disregard for military etiquette. There is a big river here and just beyond it a great hill lit up by the sun whereas where we are is under a cloud. The view is simply wonderful... and everybody is sitting up to take notice.

We should be in Halifax tomorrow morning about 3 or 4 o'clock. Our time is now one hour slower than the time here. We are now stopped at a pretty N.B. village and the bugles are giving a few calls for the general benefit. We do not see so many R.C. churches but other denominations have a representation in this province. I don't know whether we go right onto the boat at Halifax or not, but I will try to write you from there. It may be held for some time... perhaps until we get to England but you should get this o.k.

When you are through with this I wish you would send it to Rae.

With love, Cannon

APPENDIX FOUR
Military Travel 1914-1918

Militia & related passengers Year	Regular Train	Special Train	Total Passengers
Mobilization			
Aug. 1914-Dec. 1915	53,002	46,678	99,689
Jan. 1916-Dec. 1916	80,943	195,522	276,465
Jan. 1917-Dec. 1917	98,846	124,606	223,452
Jan. 1918-Nov. 1919	119,602	116,495	236,097
Totals	352,393	483,310	835,703
Demobilization			
Nov. 1918-Dec. 1919	11,175	15,702	26,877
Jan. 1919-Nov. 1919	118,927	219,639	338,566
Total Demobilization	130,102	235,341	365,443
Mobilization	352,393	483,310	835,703
Total	**482,495**	**718,651**	**1,201,146**
By Canadian Northern	314,536	145,948	460,484

(Source: *Canada's National Railways: Their part in the War*)

APPENDIX FIVE
Special Trains 1914-1918

Special Trains		Freight Trains	
No. of Special Trains	1,800	Tons carried	1,410,527
Engines used	10,882	(Includes provisions	
Baggage cars	1,972	& munitions)	
Colony cars & Coaches	12,527	Steel from Trenton &	426,604
Dining & commissary	2,407	Sydney, N.S.	
Sleepers & hospital	3,670		
Total equipment used	**31,458**	Total	**1,837,131**
Total No. train miles	**1,300,122**	Equivalent no.	
(not including empty cars)		of trains	**1,837**

(Source: *Canada's National Railways: Their part in the War*)

APPENDIX SIX

A Home-grown Hero

IT MAY BE IMPOSSIBLE TO DETERMINE HOW MANY OF THE seventy Canadians who received the Victoria Cross during the First World War travelled the Intercolonial to Halifax or Saint John. But the railway managed to produce a hero of its own in the person of a 28-year-old employee whose name is listed with about 5,500 employees of the Canadian National Railways in the 1923 book *Canada's National Railways: Their part in the War.*

This roll of honour includes employees of the Intercolonial, National Transcontinental, Prince Edward Island, Canadian Government, Canadian Northern, Grand Trunk and Grand Trunk Pacific Railways, several of whom were awarded the Military Medal, and one who won the French Croix de Guerre, for their valour in the war.

Only Jean B.A. Brillant of Bic, Quebec (he was named John in the Canadian Record,) was awarded the Empire's highest honour for valour.

Brillant was working at the Intercolonial station at Bic, Quebec when the war broke out, and during the winter of 1914-15 he joined the 22nd Battalion, the Quebec Regiment, and sailed for England in the Spring of 1915 as part of the second Canadian contingent.

The unit went to France as part of the Second Canadian Division, and by August of 1918 found itself engaged by the Germans near Meharicourt during the Battle of Amiens. The extract from the *London Gazette* of September 27th 1918 records Brillant's service, noting his "most conspicuous bravery and outstanding devotion to duty when in charge of a company which he led in attack during two days with absolute fearlessness and extraordinary ability and initiative, the extent of the advance being twelve miles...."

> "On the first day of operations shortly after the attack had begun, his company's left flank was held up by an enemy machine gun. Lt. Brillant rushed and captured the machine-gun, personally killing two of the

Lt. Jean Brillant, VC: an Intercolonial Railway employee serving at Bic, Quebec. Born at Assametquaghan in the Matapedia valley on Major Robinson's line, he distinguished himself during the Amiens offensive in 1918, and also won the Military Cross.

enemy crew. Whilst doing this, he was wounded but refused to leave his command. Later on the same day, his company was held up by heavy machine-gun fire. He reconnoitred the ground personally, organized a party of two platoons and rushed straight for the machine gun nest."

During that second action, Brillant and his men captured 150 prisoners and 15 guns. He was wounded for a second time, and again refused to leave his command. In the third action of the day, he led another rushing party toward a heavy field gun and was wounded again, falling unconscious.

Brillant also received the Military Cross, but died of his wounds on August 10th, the last day of the battle. The Victoria Cross was awarded posthumously on September 27th 1918. Brillant is buried at Villers-Brettonnex Military Cemetery, Fouilloy, France, ten kilometres from Amiens.

Ironically, the Amiens offensive, fought by Canadian and Australian troops, was the action that gave impetus to the end of the war. The Germans made one last stand, at Mons. Finally, by November 11th 1918, they were forced to capitulate.

APPENDIX SEVEN

Movement of Troops Over the Government Railways
Canadian Government Railways Employees Magazine
October 1915 Vol 1 No. 10

by L.B. Archibald, Superintendent,
Parlour, Sleeping & Dining Cars, Halifax

Between the fifteenth of January, 1915, and the tenth of June, 1915, in addition to troops moved by our regular trains, 545 Canadian officers and 6,932 Canadian soldiers have been moved over some portion of the Intercolonial Railway by special trains.

When a movement of troops is to be made. The Militia Department advises the Passenger Department of the Intercolonial giving the number and class of men, the stations between which the movement is to be made and the starting time. The Sleeping and Dining Car Department is then instructed to provide the necessary first-class sleeping cars for the use of the officers, and also to provide the necessary dining, commissary and table cars for use of both officers and men. The Superintendent of Car Service is called upon to furnish the necessary colonist cars for use of the men. All cars for this movement are then given a thorough cleansing.

The number of troops to be moved on one train varies but 40 to 50 officers and 500 to 550 men would be an average. For their transport, the following cars would be required, and the train made up in the following order behind the locomotive: 1 baggage car, 1 commissary car, 1 table car, 10 colonist cars, 1 first-class dining car and 2 first-class sleepers—16 cars, which is about all a first-class passenger locomotive can haul and make time.

As soon as the Dining Car Department is notified of the movement, an efficient Dining Car Conductor is assigned to this train. He is given the number of men to be taken care of and description of the meals (breakfasts, dinners and suppers) to be furnished. He then makes out his requisition on the Commissary Department for the stores required. These stores are promptly put up in packages and delivered to him, and placed on his dining and commissary cars by the dining car crew, after having

Troops aboard an Intercolonial Railway train enjoy the welcome from citizens of Truro, Nova Scotia, in this Valentine Co. postcard of the era. As evidenced by their headgear, and from the layout of the yard, these men were apparently sailors heading home to central Canada.

(Andrew Blackburn collection)

been checked off by him to see that the articles and amounts are correct. The dining and commissary cars are then iced and watered, but perishable goods such as meat, fish, eggs, bread, butter and milk, are not put on until just before the train leaves.

The baggage car contains the soldiers' equipment, and is generally full to the roof.

The commissary car, second on the train, is perhaps the most important one, as in it the cooking is done for 350 to 400 of the men. It was a baggage car originally, and temporarily fitted up for its present purpose with shelves to hold dishes, lockers for storage purposes, tables, large sinks for dish washing, and with four cauldrons, each capable of holding 30 to 40 gallons. From the ordinary steam pipe put in these baggage cars for car heating purposes, a pipe about three-quarters to one inch in diameter is led into each of these cauldrons in turn, and so arranged that steam can be let into any of them, or all of them at once, as occasion requires. These cauldrons are also fitted with drips to take care of the condensation. A full cauldron of water can be brought to a boil in 10 or 15 minutes and kept boiling thereafter by a very small pressure of steam through the above mentioned pipe. From this it can be understood that porridge can be made as quickly as when fire is used to boil the water. A cauldron full of coffee can be prepared in 10 minutes. Potatoes or other vegetables, hams or legs of mutton, corned beef or pork, can be boiled, and baked beans prepared as expeditiously as by the use of the large ranges. Carving, slicing of bread and other things of this kind are done in this commissary car, and the food carried in the table car next behind the commissary car, and can thus be very promptly served.

The "table car" above referred to, is simply a colonist car fitted up with tables at each of which four soldiers can sit and be comfortably served. There being eighteen sections in this car with a table in each section, 72 men can be fed at one sitting. Before the meal is announced the tables are all set up in the table car, with knives, forks, spoons, plates, cups, saucers, soup bowls, bread and butter, etc., already placed, all to save time. The dishes used are from those removed from our first-class service on account of being slightly chipped. The table-cloths are too much worn for first-class dining cars, but well adapted for this purpose, and give the car a very much better appearance than when only wood tables are used. A double outfit of crockery is also carried, so that while one set is being used, the other is being washed, thus saving time.

A menu card, showing the meals to be served to both officers and men, is prepared, and first submitted to the Militia Department for approval.

On one trip between Montreal and Halifax last winter, over 5,500 meals were served. On every trip, without exception, the officers in charge of the party have given a certificate that the service was most satisfactory, and not a single complaint was made from any quarter.

The ten colonist cars following the table car, are capable of seating 72 soldiers each, but the Government requires that only three men shall be assigned to a section instead of four so that ten colonist cars just accommodate 540 men.

Next in rear of these colonist cars is a first-class dining car, such as is run on our best trains. This is assigned for the use of the officers in charge of the party, and cars can also be used as an auxiliary for the commissary car at the forward end of the train, if required. The service furnished by this car is in all respects the same as furnished on our regular express train dining cars.

Following this dining car, we have two first-class sleeping cars for the exclusive use of the officers in charge of the soldiers.

During the period above mentioned, 2,370 meals were served to officers and 43,964 were served to the men.

For a train as above described, where three or four meals were served on the trip from Montreal to Halifax, about 1,000 lbs. of beef, 150 lbs. of sausage, 150 lbs. of bacon, 75 lbs. of lamb, 150 lbs. of fresh fish, 400 loaves of bread, 140 lbs. of butter, 40 doz. of eggs, 80 qts. of milk, 35 lbs. of oatmeal, 15 bus. of potatoes, 1 bus. of carrots, 1 bus. of turnips, 1 bus. of onions, 6 lbs. of tea, 150 lbs of sugar, 50 qts. of cond. coffee, 50 lbs. of rice and 80 lbs. of cheese would be required.

From this it can be seen that when the Canadian soldier travels, he brings his appetite along with the rest of his equipment. Nothing is too good for him.

APPENDIX EIGHT

The Explosion's Railway Toll

VINCE COLEMAN'S STORY HAS BEEN TOLD MOST RECENTLY —if imperfectly—in the Historica short profile seen frequently on CBC Television. In that clip, Coleman is depicted at his desk in a stone building (presumably North Street Station) quite removed from the blast site. In fact he was at Richmond, in the collection of wooden buildings that marked the original terminus of the railway, possibly less than one-thousand feet from the spot when the *Mont Blanc* struck a pier and came to rest with its cargo of burning explosives.

The list created by the Halifax Foundation, the Nova Scotia Archives and Record Management Service (NSARMS) and the Maritime Museum of the Atlantic includes more than 1,900 people who were killed instantly at 9:06 am on that fateful December 6th day, or who died later of the injuries suffered in the shower of broken glass and shrapnel that engulfed the north end of the city.

The foundation's list now provides clear evidence of the human impact of the explosion on the railway, allowing a roll call of railway employees to be created from the data gleaned from the records of the Halifax Relief Commission (set up in the aftermath of the explosion) and obituaries published immediately after the event, and in the ensuing years as victims passed on.

Intercolonial Railway

Most of the fatalities suffered by the Intercolonial Railway came at Richmond Yard, which was wiped out by the blast, and at North Street Station, which was damaged but not destroyed. Including Coleman, more than sixty employees lost their lives due to the explosion.

Nathaniel Aikenhead, 46, of Richmond, listed only as a Canadian Government Railways employee.

Wiley Canning, 25, of Douglas St., Truro. A brakeman, his body was found in Richmond Yard where he was waiting for his train to return to Truro.

John Casey, 37, of 51 Kaye St., Halifax. He was the yard manager at North Street Station, but his body was found at Pier 6 at Richmond.

William Chapman, 19, of 5 Duffus St., a trackman.

Vincent Coleman, 31, a dispatcher at Richmond. Coleman's story has been told quite graphically in Michael Bird's *The Town That Died* (McGraw Hill Ryerson, Toronto 1967).

Jabez Crowdis, 23, of 64 Veith St., listed only as a Canadian Government Railways employee.

Peter Day, Upper Water St., he was a fireman.

William Drake, 20, of 1557 Barrington St., a brakeman.

Vincent Dwyer, 21, of 1522 Barrington St., a fireman.

James Dwyer, no age or address, listed as a Canadian Government Railways employee.

James Elliott, 25, of 1287 Barrington St., a fireman.

John Elliott, 50, of 35 Veith St., an engineer.

Robert Ellis, 43, of 35 Hanover St., listed only as a Canadian Government Railways employee.

Jonas Farrell, 64, of 74 N. Creighton St., a sectionman.

George Fenerty, 16, of 214 Agricola St., listed only as a Canadian Government Railways employee.

George Ferguson, no age or address, listed only as a Canadian Government Railways employee.

Patrick Flemming, 59, of 1575 Barrington St., a labourer.

William Fougere, 49, of 201 N. Gottingen St., a trackman.

John Gaston, 70, of 13 Roome St., listed only as a Canadian Government Railways employee.

Victor Gomes, 23, of 97 Creighton St., a clerk.

Arthur Gough, 40, of 46 Longard Rd., a car repairer, died January 1918.

Herbert Greenough, of 29 E. Young St., a car inspector.

Francis Guess, 25, of 1341 Barrington St., also known as Frank Guest; he was a fireman.

John Guess, of 1336 Barrington St., listed only as a Canadian Government Railways employee.

William Guess, 30, of 1336 Barrington St., a car inspector.

Harry Hamm, 38, of 116 W. Young St., a car repairer.

Fred Hinch, 26, of 1345 Barrington St., a brakeman.

Francis Hope, of 134 Cunard St., a railway mail clerk.

Edward Horner, 19, of 95 Agricola St., a checker. His body was found in the ruins of Richmond Yard.

John Jackson, 34, of 1 Roome St., a brakeman. His body was found at Tuft's Cove, on the Dartmouth side of the harbour.

Lewis Jackson, 19, of 18 Duffus St., a clerk.

Joseph Langwith, 29, of 1345 Barrington St., a fireman.

Ralph Latter, 18, of 11 Kane St., listed only as a Canadian Government Railways employee.

William Lovett, 73, of 1291 Barrington St., an engineer.

John Malloy, 70, of 1337 Barrington St., listed only as a Canadian Government Railways employee.

Bartholomew McTiernan, 40, of 64 Roome St., an engineer. His body was found "completely consumed by fire in residence."

Charles Moore, 43, of 1496 Barrington St., a stevedore.

Samuel Moore, 31, of 76 Roome St., listed only as a Canadian Government Railways employee.

Robert Moore, 17, no address given. He was a "Calling Boy" for the railway, making it likely he died at North Street Station.

John Morash, 57, of 52 Veith St., a policeman.

James Mowatt, 35, of 7 Roome St., an engineer; his remains never recovered.

Martin Murphy, 57, of 35 Acadia St., a carpenter; he died January 18th 1918.

Patrick Murphy, 53, of 33 Duffus St., and Sheet Harbour, a car inspector.

Guy Neary, 27, of 1324 Barrington St., a yardman.

Robert Neary, 32, of Waverley, a brakeman.

Walter O'Brien, 29, of 18 June St. Listed as a "checker," he died at Pier 8.

Edmond O'Grady, 21, of 7 Rector St., a night clerk; his father Edmond was a brakeman with the railway.

Roy Pickrem, 17, of 66 Union St., listed only as a Canadian Government Railways employee, "killed on railway where working."

George Quirk, 42, of 45 Spring Garden Rd., a checker.

Thomas Scallion, 42, of 193 Creighton St., a car cleaner.

Joseph Shea, 27, of 1337 Barrington St., a trackman.

Maurice Shea, 47, of 1362 Barrington St., an engineer.

A. Shurman, no age or address. Listed as fireman, it is not certain if he died at the time of the explosion, but there are two such names on the list.

Ambrose Simmonds, 40, of 908 Barrington St., a brakeman; he died December 14th 1917.

James Stockall, 64, of 2 School St., listed only as a Canadian Government Railways employee.

John Stokes, 53, of 21 Acadia St., a carpenter; his body was found in Richmond Yard.

James Stratton, 34, of 1351 Barrington St., a fireman.

Benjamin Underwood, 27, of 1 Lowe St., Halifax, a fireman; he died in his home with his wife and two daughters.

Charles Upham, of 12 Rector St., a trainman.

George Wagstaff, 48, of 13 Roome St., a brakeman; he died in his home.

John Walsh, 61, of 6 Rector St., an engineer; he was the only survivor of an engine crew that left North Street Station a short time before the explosion. He died in hospital July 3rd 1918.

Roy Wamback, 19, of 1359 Barrington St., probably a general labourer.

Peter Waters, 37, of 20 Russell St., a freight handler; he died in his house with son, Peter.

Joseph White, 63, of Richmond, listed only as a Canadian Government Railways employee, he died in hospital, June 11th 1918.

James White, 63, of Maine Ave., listed only as a Canadian Government Railways employee, he died at home, June 11th 1918 "Injured in Explosion—direct cause of his demise."

Joseph Wier, 38, of 28 Atlantic St., an electrical foreman; his body was found near the Sugar Refinery.

Robert Wilson, 58, of 51 Duffus St., an engineer; he was found "in, or on train to Truro."

Two other railways sharing facilities on Halifax harbour with the Intercolonial also suffered fatalities from the explosion:

Canadian Pacific Railway

Peter Hughes, 39, of Black Point, stevedore.

William Johnston, 28, of 34 Veith St., walking boss. (A walking boss is a foreman with the responsibility and authority to supervise, place or discharge personnel and to direct the work of the longshoremen on the job in performance of all cargo handling and stevedoring activities.)

Albert Manuel, 39, of Black Point, stevedore. His body was not found.

Martin Marks, 55, of 107 Maynard St., stevedore; listed as working at Pier 9

Dominion Atlantic Railway

Alfred Frizzell, 51, of 64 Veith St., a conductor.

Frederick Hessian, 24, of 20 E Young St., a brakeman; died in his home.

John Matheson, 49, of 18 Richmond St., a car inspector.

Herman Weiss, 52, of 1372 Barrington St. Listed only as a Dominion Atlantic Railway employee.

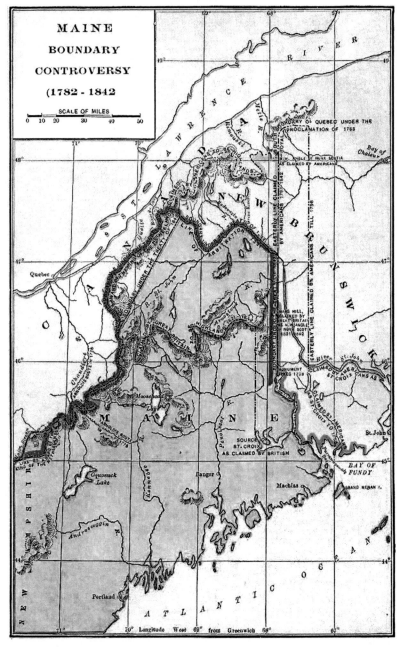

This map, from The American Nation: a History from Original Sources *(Albert Bushnell Hart, ed. New York: Harper & Brothers, 1906, Vol. 17) shows the detail of the Maine boundary problem that eliminated the Frontier route from consideration as the route of the Intercolonial Railway.*

(Library of Congress)

Bibliography

Antonucci, Michael—*"Code-Crackers"*, *Civil War Times Illustrated*, August 1995. Cowles Magazines.

Berton, Pierre—*The Last Spike: The Great Railway 1881-1885*. McClelland & Stewart, Toronto, 1971.

Bird, Michael J.—*The Town That Died*, McGraw Hill Ryerson, Toronto, 1967.

Bird, Will R.—*No Retreating Footsteps: The story of the North Novas*, Lancelot Press, Hantsport, NS, 1983.

Brooks, Richard—*The Italian Campaign of 1859*, *Military History*, June 1999.

Cameron, John—*A Legislative History of Nova Scotia Railways*, (Notes on the internet). See sources below.

Coleman, Terry—*The Railway Navvies*, Penguin Books, London, 1968.

Cooke, Brian—*The Grand Crimean Central Railway: the railway that won a war*. Second edition, Cavalier House, 1997.

Cumberland County Museum—*The Amherst Prisoner of War Internment Camp 1915-1919*, Undated, Amherst, NS.

Duhaime, Lloyd—*Hear! Hear! 125 Years of Debate in Canada's House of Commons*. Stoddart Publishers, Toronto.

Fleming, Sandford—*The Intercolonial Railway: A National Military Work*, Ottawa, 1867.

Fleming, Sandford—*The Intercolonial: A historical sketch of the inception, location, construction and completion of the line of railway uniting the inland and Atlantic provinces of the Dominion*. Dawson Brothers, Montreal, 1876.

Fleming, Sandford—*Memorial of the people of Red River: To the British and Canadian governments, with remarks on the colonization of central British North America, and the establishment of a great territorial road from Canada to British Columbia*. Quebec, 1863.

Glazebrook, G. P.—*A history of transportation in Canada Vol. 2.* Carlton Library, Toronto, 1964 (originally published in 1938).

Hanna, David B.—*Trains of Recollection*, MacMillan Co., Toronto, 1924.

Hatley, Paul B.—*"Traitor or Scapegoat?"*, *Military History* magazine, Cowles Group, February 2001.

Hedley, John—*Confederate Operations in Canada and New York.* Neane Publishing, 1906.

Hind, Henry Youle—*Eighty Years' Progress; or British North America; Showing that development of its natural resources, by the unbounded energy and enterprise of its inhabitants.* Sampson Low, Son & Marston, London, 1863.

Hopkins, J. Castell—*Canada at War: A Record of Heroism and Achievement 1914-1918.* The Canadian Annual Review Ltd., Toronto, 1919.

Hopper, A. B. & T. Kearney, with **John Andreasson**—*Canadian National Railways: Synoptical History of organization, capital stock, funded debt and other general information.* Canadian National Railways, Montreal, 1962, amended 1966.

Jervois, Sir William Francis Drummond—*Report on the defence of Canada.* G. E. Eyre, London, 1864.

Kitz, Janet F.—*Shattered City: The Halifax Explosion and the road to recovery.* Nimbus Publishing, Halifax, NS, 1989.

Klein, Aaron—*Encyclopedia of North American Railroads.* Bison Books, London, 1985.

Lardner, Dionysius—*Railway Economy.* Harper Brothers, New York, 1850.

MacKay, Donald—*The People's Railway: A history of Canadian National.* Douglas & MacIntyre, 1992.

Mackey, Frank—*"The winding road to Confederation"*, *Horizon Canada*, Vol. No. 54, March 1986.

Mika, Nick & Helma—*Railways of Canada: A Pictorial History.* McGraw–Hill Ryerson, Toronto, 1972.

Morgan, Henry J.—*Canadian Parliamentary Companion.* Montreal, 1873.

Morton, Desmond—*A Military History of Canada.* Hurtig Publishers Ltd., 1985.

Morton, Desmond—*A Short History of Canada.* Hurtig Publishers, 1987.

Pratt, Edwin A.—*The Raise of Rail Power in War and Conquest 1833-1914.* P. S. King & Son, Westminster, 1915.

Roberts, Earl W. & David P. Stremes—*Canadian Trackside Guide 2000.* Bytown Railway Society, Ottawa, 2000.

Rogge, Robert E.—*"Wrecking on the Railroad"*, *America's Civil War* magazine, September 1995, Cowles Media Co.

Rolt, L. T. C.—*Red For Danger*, (Fourth edition). Pan Books, London, 1986.

Rose, George MacLean—*A Cyclopedia of Canadian Biography*. Rose Publishing Co., Toronto, 1886.

Scott, Osborne—*Canada's National Railways; Their part in the War*. Canadian National Railways, Toronto, 1922.

Seton, Leonard A.—*"The Intercolonial 1832-1876"*, *Canadian Rail*, Canadian Railroad Historical Asssociation, Montreal, March 1958.

Scheips, Paul T.—*Darkness and Light: The Interwar Years 1865-1898*. American Military History, Army Historical Series, Office of the Chief of Military History, United States Army.

Stacey, Col. C. P.—*The Backbone of Canada*. Historical Section, Army Headquarters, Ottawa, and Canadian Historical Association, 1953.

Stevens, G. R.—*Canadian National Railways, Vols. 1 & 2*. Clarke, Irwin & Co. Toronto, 1960.

Taschereau, Pierre—*"South End Railway Cutting: Report No. 2 of the Area Studies Groups"*, *Halifax Field Naturalists News*, No. 27, Spring 1982.

Thompson, John—*Union Train*. Horizon Canada, Vol. 6 No. 69.

Trotsky, Leon—*My Life*. Scribner and Sons, New York, 1930.

Trout, J. M & Edw.—*The Railways of Canada*. Monetary Times, Toronto, 1871

Tuttle, Charles R.—*Tuttle's popular history of the Dominion of Canada*. Downie, Tuttle & Downie, 1877.

VIA Rail Corp.—*Rails Across Canada*, 1986.

Waugh, John C.—*"The Proving Ground"*, *Civil War Times*, April 1996, Cowles Magazines.

Wellard, Dr. Andrew—*Crossfire* magazine, No. 62, April 2000, American Civil War Round Table.

Westwood, John—*The Pictorial History of Railways*. Bison Books, London, 1988.

Internet Sources

Nova Scotia history	www.littletechshoppe.com/ns1625/nshist01.html
Canadian history	www.nlc-bnc.ca/confed/maps.htm
	www.canadiana.org
	www.canadaatwar.tripod.com
New Brunswick history	www.genweb.net/nb-hi/tidbits/bg.htm
The Rifleman Online	www.qor.com/history/northwest.html
Royal New Brunswick Regiment	www.personal.nbnet.nb.ca/bcasey/3037RCACC/2rnbr.htm
Railways	www.trainmweb.org/canadianrailways/
British railways	www.ukrailnet.co.uk/br1825/br1825.htm
Spanish-American War	www.spanamwar.com
Military railways	www.homepages.tesco.net/~martyn.witt/milrly/mil_rly_hist_a_4.htm
Military History	www.historynet.com
First World War	www.stothers.com
	www.millennium.ns.simpatico.ca/halifax10.html
Halifax Explosion	www.region.halifax.ns.ca/community/explode.html

INDEX

About Jay Underwood

Jay Underwood has had a life-long connection with the military and the railways. Born in Changi, Singapore in 1958, he spent the first 15 years of his life there, as the son of a Royal Air Force non-commissioned officer, before arriving in Canada in 1973.

As a child he recalls seeing the railways in operation in England and Malaysia and learned of his father's family involvement in railways: two uncles working for the London North Eastern Railway (LNER) and a great grandfather who was a navvy on the Nottingham-Grantham Line.

He finished high school in Pictou County, Nova Scotia and earned his diploma in journalism from Holland College of Applied Arts and Technology in Charlottetown, Prince Edward Island, where he also worked as a night-shift proofreader for the *Guardian-Patriot* newspaper. He then joined the staff of the hometown New Glasgow *Evening News* in 1978.

He was subsequently city editor of the Truro, Nova Scotia *Daily News*, and served for several years as the information officer for 1st battalion, the Nova Scotia Highlanders (North), Canada's largest militia infantry battalion.

He married Kathy Patriquin in 1981, only to find that her grandfather had been a conductor for Canadian National Railways, and later the station agent at Greenville in Nova Scotia's Cumberland County.

After serving briefly as city editor at the Timmins, Ontario *Daily Press*, Underwood returned to Nova Scotia to act as editor and publisher of the Springhill-Parrsboro *Record*, and the Enfield *Weekly Press*, before joining the Halifax *Daily News* as senior copy editor and a member of the editorial board.

Disabled from that position in 1992, he spent the ensuing years researching railway history, and his first book *Ketchum's Folly*, an history of the fabled Chignecto Ship Railway in Cumberland County (Lancelot Press 1995) was a best-seller.

He followed that with *Full Steam Ahead*, (Lancelot Press, 1996) a biography of Nova Scotia born Alexander Mitchell, the designer of the 2-8-0 Consolidation type steam locomotive that went on to become one of the leading designs of the Canadian railway steam era.

Underwood is currently president of the Nova Scotia Railway Heritage Society, and is a contributor to *Canadian Rail*, the journal of the Canadian Railroad Historical Association.

His article *Fruit of a Poisoned Tree*, an examination of the adoption of standard gauge on Canadian railways, won the association's award for best article in 2002.

Underwood lives in the community of Elmsdale, Nova Scotia, with his wife and two sons, and is leading a project to convert the old railway station into a provincial railway heritage centre.

*An Intercolonial Railway train crosses the Smith Brook fill in
the Cobequid Hills of Nova Scotia's Cumberland County in this
1910 Valentines Company postcard. Major William Robinson
warned this section of the line could become an obstacle
in winter to both civilian and military trains.*

(Jay Underwood collection)

Cover illustration

*The French-speaking 22nd Battalion leaving St. Jean, Quebec
in 1915, aboard an Intercolonial train. The regiment would
achieve an outstanding war record under its commander,
Colonel Georges Vanier.*

(National Archives of Canada C-14135)

824197

Made in the USA